REASON IN SOCIETY

University of Illinois Press, Urbana, 1962

REASON IN SOCIETY

Five Types of Decisions and Their Social Conditions

by Paul Diesing

To My Wife

ACKNOWLEDGMENTS

An interdisciplinary work like the present one is necessarily the product of many minds, even though only one name appears on the title page. Many of its basic ideas derive from discussions with friends and colleagues in various fields. More specific assistance has been provided by the following people, who read and commented on part or all of some preliminary draft: Royall Brandis, George DeVos, Robert E. Dewey, Murray Edelman, Max Fisch, Joseph Gusfield, Charles Hagan, H. S. Harris, Solomon Levine, Charner Perry, James M. Smith, and Bernard Suits. I have also benefited from the comments of students and colleagues in various departmental and interdepartmental seminars, colloquia, and discussion groups. I am grateful to Karl Ortwein for the solid support he provided during an important phase of the work. William MacPherson helped me find my way into the field of labor arbitration. The University of Illinois Research Board has provided typing assistance. Editors of the *Journal of Conflict Resolution* have given permission to use a portion of an article appearing in its pages.

CONTENTS

"Reason persuaded necessity"

Plato, *Timaeus*

Chapter 1

Technical Rationality

In many social theories rationality is defined as identical with efficiency. The efficient achievement of a single goal is technical rationality, the maximum achievement of a plurality of goals is economic rationality, and no other types of rationality are admitted. A typical example is provided by von Mises (1960:148) who writes, "The economic principle is the fundamental principle of all rational action, and not just a particular feature of a certain kind of rational action. . . . All rational action is therefore an act of economizing." Similarly, in organization theory the "rationalizing" of an organization is taken to mean the increase of its productive efficiency. A rational organization is an efficient one, and other principles or modes of organization are thought to be nonrational or irrational.

Such a conception of rationality limits its scope rather severely. The criterion of efficiency is applicable only to means and not to ends, unless these are in turn means to further ends. Thus ultimate ends, the basic aims of life, cannot be selected or evaluated by rational procedures; they must be dealt with by arbitrary preference, or intuition, or by cultural and biological determinism. And yet it seems unfortunate to have rational procedures available for the relatively less important decisions of life and to have none for dealing with the most important decisions. Nor is this all. Several rather common types of activity can only with great difficulty be assimilated to the category of efficient action and evaluated by standards of efficiency.

The various forms of psychotherapy, for instance, can hardly be conceived as techniques for the processing of some kind of human product. It seems odd to conceive of the therapist, or the patient, as a kind of technician whose work could be improved by time and motion studies. The mediation of labor disputes, of political disputes, and of international disputes is similarly resistant to a technical or economic treatment. In recent years game theory has been developed as an extension of economic rationality designed to deal with situations of conflict or competition; yet it too seems to have several limitations. The decisions of labor arbitrators apparently cannot be described or evaluated meaningfully in terms of game theory (Chandler, MS). Nor can game theory apparently be applied to the process of political discussion and decision (Wheeler, 1957). Thus, even apart from the ultimate ends of life, it seems necessary to get along without benefit of rational procedures in a number of highly important types of activity, according to those theories which define reason as efficiency.

The purpose of this book is to explore three other kinds of rationality which are basically analogous to technical and economic rationality without being reducible to them. These other kinds are applicable in areas of activity not presently open to technical or economic treatment. I shall consider, in addition to technical and economic rationality, the kinds of rationality appropriate in interpersonal relations, in law, and in governmental or control systems. The circumstances or conditions in which each of the five kinds of rationality are appropriate will be explored, and special attention will be given to certain more specific kinds of action, including psychotherapy, labor arbitration, leadership in goal-oriented organizations, and labor contract negotiations. Finally, in chapter 6 I shall discuss the nature of reason in general, and define it in such a way that efficiency is a special case.

My purpose is not to argue about terminology or to attack sacred symbols; consequently if anyone wishes to argue that social, legal, and political rationality are all ultimately special variants of technical or economic rationality I shall not object, so long as all the differences I point out are recognized and preserved. I do object to the proposition that technical or economic reasoning can be applied to social, legal, and political problems without very extensive modification. Nor do I think that the unique characteristics of social, legal, and political reasoning can be brought out by deriving or reducing them to economic reasoning; quite the contrary, they are brought out most clearly by contrast with economic reasoning.

The present chapter will deal with provisional definitions and with the method to be used in discovering and dealing with the four main kinds of rationality. The method will then be illustrated by brief application to technical rationality. I shall not treat technical rationality in any detail, partly because it is so well known already and partly because it is identical in most respects with economic rationality, constituting in a way a special case of the latter. Whatever differences exist can be taken up in the chapter on economic rationality.

It is necessary to take up questions of definition at the outset because for some people rationality is so closely identified with efficiency that it is impossible by definition for any other kind of rationality to exist. To avoid confusing the issues by injecting arguments about definitions, it is necessary to have some temporary initial definition in which reason includes but is not identical with efficiency. I shall take my initial definitions from Mannheim (1940:51–57), broadening them where necessary to avoid prejudging the issue. Mannheim's definitions are derived with slight modifications from Max Weber.

Mannheim distinguishes between substantial and functional rationality, the former applying to individual decisions and the latter to organizations. A decision or action is substantially rational when it takes account of the possibilities and limitations of a given situation and reorganizes it so as to produce, or increase, or preserve, some good. This definition includes two points: the decision must be an effective response to the situation in that it produces some possible good, and the effectiveness must be based on intelligent insight rather than on luck. Effectiveness I define as a wider concept than efficiency. It refers to the successful production of any kind of value, leaving open and problematic the question of what kinds of value there may be. The efficient achievement of predetermined goals is a special kind of effectiveness. If there are other kinds of value besides goal values then there are presumably also other kinds of effectiveness or rationality.

An organization is functionally rational, let us say, when it is so structured as to produce, or increase, or preserve, some good in a consistent, dependable fashion. The consistently good results must be based primarily on an internal structure which is able to continue effective operation through variations of personnel and through changes of environment. For instance, General Motors is able consistently to produce a variety of goods and services without regard to changes in management and other personnel and in spite of changes in market conditions.

Mannheim defines functional rationality somewhat more narrowly than is suggested above, so that it implies only technical rationality. He says, "We . . . understand . . . that a series of actions is organized in such a way that it leads to a previously defined goal, every element in this series of actions receiving a functional position and role. Such a functional organization of a series of actions will, moreover, be at its best when, in order to attain the given goal, it coordinates the means most efficiently" (1940:53). He then argues that functional rationalization results from the industrialization of society. If, however, we wish to open the question of whether there are modes of functional rationality other than the technical we must broaden the definition. Instead of requiring a previously defined goal and efficient means we can merely specify, as I have suggested, that the system be organized in such a way that it achieves some good consistently.

A third aspect of rationality can be conceived by abstraction from the other two. Decisions are made according to principles, and organized structures embody principles of order; accordingly principles can also be thought of as rational. An account of a type of substantial rationality will consist of a statement of the principles to be followed in decisions of this sort, together with subsidiary rules. Similarly, an account of a type of functional rationality will consist of a statement of the basic organizing principle to be found in a system, together with subsidiary principles. For instance, the technical principle "adapt means to ends" states what should be done in a technically rational decision; it defines a technical response to a situation. A technically rational organization, similarly, is one in which all means are efficiently co-ordinated to achieve the goal of the organization.

The various kinds of practical reason, in their three phases, can probably be discovered in several ways. One familiar way is to collect commonly accepted concepts about rationality, either those of social scientists and philosophers or those of ordinary people, and then analyze and systematize them. This way has considerable plausibility, because it is unlikely that everybody could be completely wrong in their conceptions of rationality. If many scientists are in agreement on some theory about rationality, there must be some truth in the theory. Further, it is rhetorically important to stay close to existing theories, since a completely unfamiliar theory would not readily be accepted. Nevertheless this method by itself is not suitable for present purposes, precisely because I wish to change existing conceptions of rationality. The ordinary conception identifies reason with efficiency in the pursuit of given ends, and this is the conception I wish to correct. Not everyone agrees with this conception — indeed, I think nearly every idea in the following pages can be found somewhere in existing theories — but it is by far the most common theory. In order to correct it, then, it is necessary to do more than merely gather a variety of scattered observations and opinions.

A more direct method is to define an ideal type of action and then, by *a priori* analysis, determine the logical conditions of effectiveness of that action. This method is plausible because it is the one always used to clarify the nature of economic rationality. Moreover, it cannot be avoided completely, since any theory about reason must somewhere exhibit the inner logic of rational thought. The weakness of this method lies in the fact that it is very difficult to subject pure speculation to any adequate internal checks of validity. The human mind has a boundless capacity for self-deception; as soon as empirical checks are left behind it is possible to convince oneself of almost anything, particularly if like-minded friends are available to cheer one on. It is desirable, therefore, to have some empirical referents on which to base one's analysis.

The simplest way to provide an empirical referent is to collect a sizable sample of some type of activity such as psychotherapy or arbitration, classify the procedures actually used, devise a rating scale of effectiveness, and then analyze the most effective procedures. Though this method has been used successfully in some areas such as that of chess playing, its weakness is that it depends eventually on the intuitive evaluations of experts in its selection of the most effective procedures. Moreover, it is likely that experts will disagree somewhat in their selections, and that their disagreement will be based partly on a difference of theoretical preconceptions.

Difficulties of subjectivity and bias are largely avoided by a second empirical method. Since this method is less familiar and since it will be important in the following chapters, I shall describe it in more detail. The method relies not on the conscious judgment of experts, but on the operation of what Pepper (1958) has called "natural selective systems." The ultimate agency of selection in a selective system is the human being; not the expert, however, but the unconscious choices of countless people. Choice is exercised on culture traits — techniques, rules, beliefs, values. Effective traits are selected, improved, and transmitted, while ineffective traits are rejected. The continued selection of effective traits is caused by automatic rewards and punishments which follow upon the use of a trait. The exact kind of reward varies with the selective system; it might be increase of power, or decrease of anxiety, or some other kind of successful achievement. However, in every case the reward is such as to automatically promote a continued and expanded use of the trait and to make possible its transmission to more people. Punishments are usually (with exceptions in the areas of interpersonal relations and law) such as to automatically obstruct the expanded use of the trait and to make its transmission more difficult. In other words, rewards and punishments do not primarily operate as conscious inducements to choose a certain trait, but work more like automatic reinforcements. Conscious choice of effective traits does occur, but only in a supplementary way.

It is important to notice that selective systems do not operate through the survival or nonsurvival of individuals or societies. What survives is a culture trait — technique, rule, and so forth — not an individual or a society. Survival or nonsurvival is a much too drastic effect to result from a single unconscious choice, and nonsurvival of societies hardly ever occurs. Even in extreme cases they simply merge with other societies. What we find in societies are small changes — increase of membership, increase of cultural or military or economic influence, increase of land area, increased life or health expectancies, or the reverse — but not simply survival or nonsurvival.

Selective systems, then, operate through the agency of individuals and on culture traits. They produce a gradual increase in number and quality of effective culture traits and a decrease of ineffective traits over a period of time.

The operation of a selective system reveals itself to observation as a trend of development. By a "trend of development" I mean a gradual process of change in which certain definite characteristics appear in a culture, a process which is cumulative in that these characteristics grow more and more pronounced, which continues steadily for a long period of time, and which is automatic in that it occurs apart from or even contrary to conscious human intentions. Technological progress is an example of such a trend. The main trends to be studied in the following chapters include economic progress, integration, stratification, and legalism. In addition, a few other subsidiary trends will be more briefly discussed.

Not all trends of development result from the operation of selective systems. Cumulative changes in a single culture lasting for two or three hundred years are not evidence for a selective system unless they can be interpreted as examples of something much more widespread. Such local changes as the trend from monarchy to representative democracy in Europe, the secularization of religion in Europe and in the Roman Empire, and the spread of Islam in Central Africa are not likely to provide evidence of natural selection. They are most likely the result of some unique combination of cultural factors, or a local by-product of some more universal trend, or sometimes part of a cyclical change in a fundamentally unchanged culture. Only those trends which appear in a wide variety of cultures for a very long time are likely to result from natural selection. Since the cumulative effectiveness which produces a rational trend is based on some constant in the nature of things and not on historical circumstances, its appearance cannot be limited to a few cultures or times. Just as a genuine rational principle must be cross-cultural, so the empirical evidence for it must also be cross-cultural.

It is not necessary that a rational trend be found in absolutely every culture through every year of its existence. Apart from the empirical impossibility of finding anything that universal, it is possible that rational trends can be checked for a time by some persistent opposing factors. Even such a widespread rational trend as technological progress is dormant in large areas of some cultures for long periods of time. In fact, I shall argue later that the various forms of rationality are partly opposed to one another, so that their corresponding trends could not all occur at the same time. Similarly, Mannheim (1940:51–57) argues that technical rationality is in some circumstances opposed to political rationality, and contends that today the increasing technical rationalization of society creates a serious threat to rational political thought. What we should expect of a rational trend, however, is that it appear in a wide variety of cultures and circumstances and times, and especially that it appear whenever opposing forces, whatever these may be, are dormant. All of the trends I shall consider, except perhaps legalism, are recognized to be near universal in this sense.

The near universality of a trend is by itself only presumptive evidence of the existence of a type of rationality. Further evidence must be obtained by examining the trend to see whether it really does reveal the operation of some selective system. If it does, this shows that the culture traits being accumulated and elaborated in the trend are effective in some way. The traits must then be analyzed to see what it is that makes them effective, that is, what about them is rewarding to their carriers. The objective of analysis should be to reveal the inherent logical conditions of effectiveness embodied in the trend, and to express this logical condition as a principle or principles. Only when both empirical evidence of near universality and analytical evidence of the existence of logical conditions of effectiveness coincide can one claim to have discovered a type of rationality.

The approach to rationality through the study of trends of development has weaknesses too. Rational trends do not come all wrapped up and labeled, so it may be possible to be deceived by some widespread nonrational trend, or to select local trends on the basis of some personal or cultural bias. And, once a trend is chosen, it is easy enough to read some nonexistent selective process into it and to find an imaginary self-evident logical principle in it. Or, even if one has discovered a genuine rational trend, it is possible to misstate the principle implicit in it, for instance by overemphasizing aspects which appear only in certain cultures.

Since no method is entirely adequate by itself, I shall use a combination of methods in the hope that each will supplement the shortcomings of the others somewhat. Where there is considerable agreement on the nature of a certain kind of rationality or on other relevant theoretical matters I shall mainly summarize existing theory. This will be possible in dealing with technical and economic rationality, legal rationality in part, and occasionally elsewhere. Where a well-known trend of development is available I shall examine it to find the selective system and rationality inherent in it. This will be possible in dealing with social and legal rationality, and will also provide supplementary information about economic rationality. Where neither theory nor well-known trend is available, namely in the case of political rationality, I shall depend mainly on *a priori* examination of a type of action and partly on the analysis of samples of effective action. Elements of each method will appear in every chapter, but the emphasis will vary.

Each chapter will take up the same points in the same order, as far as consistent with variations in method. First I shall describe briefly the part or aspect of society whose rationality is to be considered, relying as far as possible on generally accepted theories. Then the most prominent trend of development occurring in that aspect of society will be described and examined. On the basis of this examination the characteristics of a rational organization (functional rationality) will be worked out, and some comparisons and contrasts made. Next I shall discuss principles of decision making and specify the circumstances in which they are appropriate. Finally, I shall describe the kind of good produced. Practical reason has been defined here as a form of effectiveness in producing some good, so each kind of rationality must produce its own kind of good.

The best-known kind of practical reason is technical rationality, the efficient achievement of a given end. This kind of reason has been studied in detail from many standpoints; under the name of "the instinct of workmanship" it has played an important part in Veblen's social theory; and the historical trend associated with it has been regarded as a major cause of social change. Its existence is not doubted even by theorists who do not recognize the existence of any other kind of practical reason. Because its reality is unquestioned and because its characteristics are well known, I shall use it as an example of the kind of treatment to be given to each of the kinds of practical reason in this work.

Technical rationality appears in actions which are undertaken for the sake of achieving a given end. When such actions are repeated again and again they become standardized and turn into techniques, or ways of acting. Techniques also exemplify technical rationality, since they also are oriented to goal achievement.

The historical trend of development associated with technical rationality is technological progress, that is, increasing efficiency of productive techniques. This is frequently included in, or identified with, economic progress, since the two are identical in most respects;

their differences will be discussed in the next chapter. Food-producing techniques are the ones whose increasing efficiency is historically most important, since most of mankind's efforts throughout history have been devoted to subsistence; but the efficiency of all other techniques tends to increase also. For instance, violin playing has become gradually but steadily more efficient over a period of three centuries. Wherever a tradition of handicraft such as carving or pottery making develops, efficiency gradually increases without any apparent limit. Some forms of progress involve increase of human skill, others involve the increasing use of machinery and nonhuman energy, while still others involve specialization (division of labor) or a combination of all three.

The continuous and gradual nature of technological progress indicates that a selective process is at work. This process is at bottom simple: the person who uses efficient means succeeds, and the inefficient person fails. Greater efficiency means that more resources are left over to use in other undertakings, while lesser efficiency means contraction of resources and diminution of activities. So the more efficient person expands — he can employ more help, cultivate more fields, support more sons in business — while the less efficient person contracts. Moreover, both expansion and contraction are cumulative and automatic.

Natural selection is supported by conscious imitation and search. When people see someone succeed or expand, they wish to do the same, so they imitate his techniques. Nobody imitates a person who fails. So the use of a more efficient technique spreads by imitation, while the use of less efficient ones contracts. If a novel technique is still more efficient, it too spreads; if not, it disappears.

Efficiency does not increase if people are not interested in accumulating a surplus and expanding; if, for instance, a constant amount of resources is allotted to a certain activity, and results are satisfactory. It is only when resources are conceived to be scarce relative to a desired goal that questions of efficiency arise.

The natural selective process embodied in technological progress has occurred fitfully and sporadically in a wide variety of cultures and throughout human history. It has never permeated a whole culture until recently, but has occurred in different locations in different cultures. One culture exhibits a trend of increasing efficiency in canoe building and navigation, another in pottery making or weaving, another in religious ritual, another in agriculture, still another in dancing or music, and so on. Only in Western culture of the last few centuries has progress been continuous and widespread. Western culture accordingly provides us the clearest picture of the nature and conditions of technological progress.

In Western culture the natural selective process is supported by appropriate values and habits. First, efficiency itself, Veblen's "instinct of workmanship," becomes a positive value. People learn to strive for efficiency in their activities, and enjoy the sight of an efficient action or machine, even apart from any interest in the end it serves. Efficiency is the maximum achievement of a given end with given resources, so it includes within itself the values of maximization and achievement. Another value is that of impartiality or detachment in the evaluation of a given technique. When choosing techniques, the most efficient one ought to be selected no matter what other characteristics it may have, and when grading people, their skill at the given task ought to be the only consideration. These values will be discussed further in the next chapter. The most obvious associated habit is that of dividing a productive process into parts and tracing a causal sequence through the parts. This habit is important in technical decisions, since it enables one to discover the contribution of each part of a productive process and to invent improvements. For instance, a gymnastics trainer will learn the exact sequence of muscular movements involved in running so that he can eliminate waste movements and increase the skill of each separate muscle.

Since Western culture is the clearest and most complete example of a technologically progressive culture, other cultures can be expected to become similar in some ways if they experience an increasing rate of progress. However, they will not become identical; and the differences between Western culture and other technologically progressive cultures will enable us to see more clearly what cultural elements are essential to technological progress and what elements are accidentally associated with it in Western culture.

The occurrence of technological progress points to efficiency as a type of rationality. Organizations that achieve their ends efficiently are functionally rational; decisions leading to efficient goal achievement are substantially rational. A technically rational organization is one in which each expenditure of energy or other material makes *read "quantification"?*

a maximum contribution to a productive sequence, culminating in a given goal. A technically rational decision is one in which each step of a productive sequence is chosen because it is the best fitted to move the sequence along to a given goal. Technical decisions are not possible until after the economic questions of comparative costs have been answered. The best means is the one which makes the greatest contribution at least cost; but such a means cannot be discovered until comparative costs (prices) have been determined. Similarly, an organization can be technically rational only in the context of a system of prices.

Both technical decisions and technically rational organizations embody the same rational principle. The principle, stated in imperative terms, is "choose means adapted to ends" or, more generally when means are also modifiable, "adapt means to ends." A more exact version would be "maximize the output/input ratio." This principle is also embodied in technological progress, in the sense that progress consists of an increasing adaptation of a society's means to its ends.

In what circumstances should one be technically rational in one's decisions? The technical norm points to its own conditions of applicability: it applies whenever one is deciding about the means to be used in achieving an end. Anyone who entertains an end seriously has thereby committed himself to try to achieve it (this is what it means to have an end) and ends cannot be achieved without the use of effective means. Consequently whenever a person has an end, he ought to be technically rational in achieving it. The technical norm does not apply to decisions about ends, for instance, decisions made by organization leaders about shifts in the organization's goals (chap. 5). Nor does it apply to the comparison and ranking of goals (chap. 2). Nor does it apply to situations in which one is prevented from formulating a clear goal, for instance, in psychotherapy, where the definition of an operational goal by the therapist or the patient would restrict the patient's freedom to explore his own problems (chap. 3).

A distinction may be made between an *effective* means and the *most effective* means to a given end. If a person has an end, he is obliged to use a means that is effective toward it, but is not necessarily obliged to use the most effective means. All that is necessary is that his means be sufficient to achieve his end. If he knowingly uses an insufficient means when a sufficient one is available, either he is not in earnest about his end, or he is being unreasonable. But when several effective means are available, use of any one of them is technically reasonable.

Use of the most effective means becomes obligatory (reasonable) in special circumstances. When an end is not achievable in its entirety, either because means are scarce or because the end is unlimited, it ought to at least be achieved as far as possible. But it will be achieved to the maximum extent only if the most effective available means is used, and if all possible effort is used to increase the effectiveness of those means.

For example, if a person wishes to travel 100 yards he ought to use some means of transportation, though not necessarily the fastest or cheapest. But if his aim is to run 100 yards as fast as possible, an infinite end, the only reasonable thing is to use his body as effectively as possible and to devote all possible efforts to increasing his running skill indefinitely.

Thus the norm "choose means adapted to ends" applies to any decision about means, while the norm "maximize the output/input ratio" applies only when means are scarce relative to an end.

The kind of good achieved by technical rationality, both substantial and functional, may be called utility, or satisfaction of desire, or goal achievement. When a person effectively adapts means to an end, he achieves the end, and his desire is satisfied. When an organization is functionally rational, it achieves its goals as far as possible in the circumstances. Anything that anyone wants is a good that can be gotten by a technique — if the goal can be operationally specified and if the necessary means are available — so technical rationality applies to all goals.

In summary, I have used technical rationality as an example of the method to be used in discussing some of the forms of practical reason. The points to be covered in each case are: the historical trend of development and the type of organization produced by it; the method of making decisions; the conditions in which this method is appropriate; and the kind of good produced by rational action.

Chapter 2

Economic Rationality

My task in this chapter is not to establish the existence of economic rationality, since that is almost universally recognized. It is rather to treat it in so specific a way that it does not automatically become identical with all rationality, but can take its place as one kind of reason among others. When one wishes to extend the scope of economic rationality to the whole of life it is necessary to blur distinctions, to give terms their widest meanings, to use analogies and quotation marks freely, and above all to abstract from any specific institutional setting. But when one wishes to distinguish several kinds of rationality, each with its own scope and conditions, it is necessary to emphasize distinctions, to narrow and specify meanings, and to tie reasoning down to specific institutional and cultural contexts. Once this has been done, it is still possible to point out analogies and parallels without entirely eliminating the boundaries and distinctions that have been set up.

ECONOMIC ORGANIZATION

The institutional setting for economic rationality is obviously the economy, so we shall begin with this concept. An economy, as commonly understood, is that part of a society's institutions devoted to the production, exchange, and distribution of commodities. It takes in raw materials, transforms them into a variety of finished products, and distributes the products to the points of consumption. In other words, it is conceived as an open system, with both inputs and outputs.

The primary inputs are raw materials, energy, and motivation; as these enter the economy they are transformed into the factors of production — land, labor, capital, techniques, and organization. Further combinations of the factors of production result in finished products; most of these return to the economy as new factors of production, and the rest are consumed. Consumption is the ultimate goal of an economy; matter and energy its ultimate means. Neither goal nor means is itself part of an economy; rather they set the limits of economic activity.

Consuming should not be conceived simply in physical terms, as eating, wearing clothes, and the like. All such physical activities may easily be productive, in the sense that they serve to maintain a factor of production, namely labor. Similarly the enjoyment of leisure, hobbies, recreation, art, and so forth may also be a productive maintenance of labor power. Scientific activity may also be productive insofar as it leads to the discovery of new techniques, including new scientific techniques, and new modes of industrial organization.

The difference between production and consumption, economic and noneconomic activity, is not physical but valuational. It is a means-end distinction. Those activities whose occurrence needs to be justified by its results are economic, while those activities whose occurrence provides a justification for other activities but does not itself need justification are noneconomic. Eating, learning, and exercising are productive activities if they are justified by their effect on the productivity of labor; they constitute consumption if they are regarded as the maintenance of a standard of living. Production is the creation of an instrumental value, while consumption is the achievement of an intrinsic value.

The "output" boundary of an economy is thus the locus of a society's ultimate values, those for the sake of which the economy exists. Values such as standard of living, prestige, adventure and creative activity, ceremonial action, and knowledge are typical consumption values. Some values, such as standard of living, are located at the temporal end of a temporal process of production and exchange, while others, such as opportunity for adventure, are located throughout the economic process. In the latter case, economic activity is justified, not by a temporal and physical product, but by the opportunity to act in certain ways.

The internal structure of an economy is conceived as being neutral toward all ultimate ends. A good economy, it is said, can produce anything people want it to produce, and if people's values change, the productive process will also change. Economic activity in different cultures is in fact oriented to different ends — standard of living, prestige, eternal salvation, ceremonial activity, planned social change. Sometimes a single society will have two or more semi-independent economies, each oriented to different ultimate goals. The kind of goals to which an economy is tied will affect its internal structure in some ways; for instance, the valuation placed on entrepreneurial adventure will have some effect on the size and number of the business units. When adventure is highly valued there will be various pressures to maintain a large number of business units, while if security is highly valued such pressures will not occur. But the effects of various ultimate ends must all be called noneconomic since their sources are noneconomic.

Therefore, in describing an economy as the institutional setting for economic rationality we can abstract from noneconomic ultimate ends and their effects on internal structure. We can also abstract from the effects of the various specialized inputs available to different economies, since these are also noneconomic.

We conceive now of a pure economy, uninfluenced by the requirement of specific inputs or specific goals and operating only according to its own internal logic. This economy has a variety of generalized inputs and several generalized goals. The inputs are transformed into factors of production, which are transformed into commodities, which are distributed among the goals in some proportion.

So far I have been summarizing a standard conception of an economy. However, in this traditional conception the technical element of production is combined with the economic elements of exchange and distribution in a single system. Since I wish to distinguish technical and economic rationality it is necessary to separate the two kinds of elements into two separate systems.

Production considered as a separate process is simply a physical mixing of the factors of production and their transformation into a new product. The factors of production are necessary ingredients in any such transformation: men working (labor and skill) in a place (land) on materials (capital) with tools (fixed capital) according to some procedure (technology). All these factors are themselves products of some previous productive process, except for an occasional ultimate input, and all the products become factors of production in new processes, except for an occasional ultimate output. The ultimate purpose of production is to increase consumer satisfactions — the value of the output to consumers should be greater than the combined values of the inputs.

Distribution is also a productive or technical process, if it is conceived as the physical delivery of commodities to a new place. It mixes labor, vehicles, and roads as productive factors, and the value of the output is increased because of increased availability to the consumer. Distribution is an economic rather than a technical process only if it is conceived as a nonspatial allocation of values to alternative goals.

The two economic processes then are exchange and allocation. Exchange is a transfer of values between two economic units, while allocation is a transfer of values to alternative ends within an economic unit. An economy in the narrower nontraditional sense is a system within which exchange and allocation occur.

An economy in the narrower sense has several structural characteristics. First, it contains a plurality of alternative ends. These need not be ultimate ends, but may be intermediate ends of any degree of specificity. Indeed, a whole hierarchy of ends may exist, each with a set of subordinate ends attached to it. Ends are alternative when they have common means which are scarce, so that an increased achievement of one end necessitates decreased achievement of others.

Common means are thus a second characteristic of an economy. Means are common to several ends when they can equally well be allocated to any of the ends. For example, a simple kind of common means is time. Time is a common means whenever it is possible to do alternative things in the same time, that is, whenever there is no moral or legal bias for or against doing various different things. The problem of how to "spend" such time is an economic one, to be solved with an economic decision about allocation. When a moral bias does exist, as for instance on the Sabbath in an orthodox Jewish family, time is not a neutral commodity and hence not a common means, and there is no economic problem of how to allocate it.

A third characteristic of an economy, scarcity, has already been mentioned. Scarcity is a relational term, indicating that ends are not all fully achievable by available means. If means are held constant, the degree of scarcity varies directly with the number and intensity of ends. The degree of scarcity present in a society is culturally determined in part, since ends, that is, levels of desire or of aspiration, are culturally and psychologically determined. When levels of aspiration rise with changes in culture, scarcity increases even though resource levels may also be rising. Thus an affluent society, one with many resources, might well have a more serious scarcity problem than a poor society, if its goal demands had increased faster than its resources. In fact, a poor society could conceivably be almost untroubled by scarcity, in the sense that culturally determined ends were relatively satiable by available resources and modes of production. Such a society would have no well-developed economy, but only a series of separate productive techniques. Economists such as von Mises (1960:24) who have erroneously supposed that scarcity is a necessary prerequisite for any action have failed to understand the cultural aspect of scarcity.

A fourth characteristic of an economy is the availability of neutral media of value measurement (pricing) such as dollars and man-hours. These are not absolutely essential to the existence of an economy, but they are essential to the achievement of any considerable degree of exactness and accuracy in allocation. Allocation involves comparison of the values of various commodities; but comparisons cannot be at all exact unless values are expressed as prices in a single unit of measurement. For instance, the value of a coat cannot be compared with the value of a share of stock unless the two are expressed in the same terms. It will not help to price one in gold and the other in man-hours. Without common units of measurement and without prices, resources can only be compared directly with one another in "more or less" terms, and even this rapidly becomes impossible as the number of alternative resources increases.

The above four characteristics, alternative ends, scarcity, common means, and media of measurement, are all necessary as a basis for allocation. Two additional characteristics are necessary as a basis for exchange. They are the existence of a plurality of economic units, and a different ranking of values among the units. Without a plurality of units, exchange would be impossible; without differences in valuation, exchange would be of no advantage to anyone and so would not occur. All actual economies have a plurality of units, but it is possible to construct an imaginary economy with only one unit and with only allocation problems; such a study is called "Crusoe economics."

Economic units are the dynamic entities which do all the allocating and exchanging in an economy. They are of many different sizes — an individual or part of an individual, a family or part of a family, a firm, a formal or informal organization, and a government of any size. Any system which is able to hold together a set of goals, a "common good" for its members, can act as an economic unit. Internally, it can make allocation decisions if it is able to specify, compare, and choose among its own goals; externally, it can exchange if it is able to distinguish its own goals from those of other units. In other words, any integrative system (chap. 3) can act as an economic unit. One of the main characteristics of integrative systems is their holding together of diverse goals, and this is essential for allocation and exchange.

In many cases economic units also are legal persons (chap. 4) having property and contract rights. Whenever an economy has a legal basis, the procedures for exchange are specified in public rules, and the economic act of exchange becomes also a legal act of contracting. Consequently only legal persons, those having the right to make contracts, can exchange, and economic units must become legal persons.

Actual economies presumably have many other characteristics besides those I have mentioned — alternative ends, scarcity of common means, media of measurement, a plurality of economic units, and differences of valuation among the units. I have listed only characteristics which are essential conditions for allocation and exchange and therefore essential conditions for the very existence of an economy. The scope and complexity of a society's economy depends on the extent to which these six characteristics are present in the culture. In some cultures, particularly Western culture, economies are complex and extend throughout a society; in some preliterate cultures economies are simple, fragmentary, localized. A society has a simple economy when many of its resources or means are not neutral because they are morally prescribed to certain specific uses; when scarcity is relatively unimportant because cultural ends are limited and related to specific available means; when money is rarely used; when economic units are largely self-sufficient and so rarely engage in trade; and when the wants and resources of different economic units are all relatively similar, so that trade would benefit no one. Western economies are opposite in all these respects, and many preliterate economies are in various intermediate positions.

Consideration of the six essential characteristics of an economy, abstracted from unessential and noneconomic factors, also enables one to perceive the inner logic of economic processes more clearly. The logic of an economy is simply the logic of allocation and exchange. Goals demand achievement, but not all of them can be achieved because there is a scarcity of means. If some goals must be sacrificed, they should be the least important ones; or if partial achievement is possible, the most important parts of each goal should be achieved. This requires a detailed measurement of the comparative importance of each goal and each part of a goal. The available means should also be measured carefully so that just the right amount can be assigned to each end — not too much and not too little. When means are being assigned, the most important goal or part of a goal should receive the first assignment, then other goals in order of decreasing importance, until the means are used up. The use to which the last means is assigned should not be less important than any remaining disallowed use; this is the marginal utility principle.

Whenever there are other economic units with differing valuations, the value of one's resources can be increased by exchanging resources of lesser value to oneself for those of greater value to oneself. Exchange should continue until the demand for resources is approximately equalized throughout the economy. At this point resources will have been distributed to the units where they are most highly valued, and so allocated within those units as to effect a maximum goal achievement.

From this consideration of the logic of an economy it is plain that we are dealing with rationality. An economy which operates in the way I have indicated is a functionally rational one, because it effects a maximum goal achievement, and this is the commonly accepted mark of economic rationality. At least some of the six characteristics which are necessary to the existence of an economy are also conditions of its rationality. Maximum goal achievement is possible to the extent that (1) the ends of economic units are comparable and measurable on a single scale, (2) there are no limits on the assignability and use of means, (3) economic units are integrated enough to engage in rational allocation and exchange, and (4) information about the supply and demand prices of other economic units is available. In other words, a rational economy simply has the characteristics essential to any economy, and has them to an extreme degree.

The rationality of an economy is sometimes expressed in the language of perfect competition. A perfectly competitive economy is the most rational one, it is argued, because in such an economy all factors will be allocated to their most economical use through the continual occurrence of allocation and exchange. Anything which reduces the extent of competition in an economy reduces its functional rationality. Therefore social policy should be devoted to the aim of increasing competition as far as possible, since in this way the economy will be made as rational as possible.

The idea of competition, as used in this argument, is a corollary of the idea of alternativeness or substitutability of ends. Ends which are alternative are inevitably in competition with each other for common means. Each mean that is allocated to one end is lost to all the others, and ends must therefore bid against each other to get means allocated to themselves. Whichever end can promise the highest return from use of a given mean should be assigned that mean, to achieve the goal of maximum utility.

For example, when a person is in a position of being able to either read, or take a walk, or listen to the radio (supposing each activity is morally neutral at the time), all three activities are in competition with each other for his time. Each promises a certain return to him for the use of his time, and he chooses whichever activity (or combination of activities) promises the greatest return.

In the same way, means can be thought of as competing against each other for employment, whenever alternative means exist for a given end. Competition among means may be called technological competition, while that occurring among ends is economic, since it results in an allocation of means to ends.

Economic-technological competition is completely impersonal, and occurs whenever common means exist for alternative ends. It occurs among alternative uses for a person's time, money, and energy; among alternative products of a firm for the firm's resources; among alternative goods and services for customers' money; among alternative customers for scarce goods and services; and among alternative applicants for scarce jobs.

Competition among ends, in turn, implies as a further corollary mobility among means. When ends are competitive, the means to them must be held in readiness to be shifted from one use to another. Provisions for shifting means must be readily available — provisions such as transportation facilities, information services, educational and re-educational services. Sometimes mobility consists of a readiness physically to move to some other locality, as in the case of labor and products; sometimes it involves only a readiness to shift to new uses in the same location, as in the case of land.

Competition and mobility can occur in a variety of legal settings. It may occur in a setting of small firms producing similar products for a free market; but it also occurs within a monopoly or a public corporation, as well as in an economy controlled by public planning. Which type of legal setting is easiest to achieve and most conducive to competition and mobility at a given time depends on a variety of noneconomic circumstances. It depends on the level of technology, since types of management possible at one level are not possible at another level; it depends on the distribution of wealth and power, since small firms are easier to maintain when power is widely distributed; it depends on the nature of the value system, the strength and extent of the kinship system, the nature of the self-concept, patterns of authority and status, and so forth.

The argument as to the relative desirability of free markets, planning, or monopolies at a given time is therefore not a purely economic argument, and its answer cannot be deduced from the idea of a pure, rational economy. Instead, it is basically a political argument about decision-making structures (cf. chap. 5). It is an argument as to what type of management structure is most likely to yield rational economic decisions. For instance, one recent version of the free-market argument attempts to show that officials of a large centralized state or corporation cannot possibly make the rational decisions that are constantly being made by myriads of small firms. Proponents of planning, on the other hand, argue that channels of information and communication are such that resource allocation patterns can be most directly and intelligently controlled by centralized decisions. Both sides agree on the desirability of competition among ends and mobility of means, but disagree on how it may best be achieved.

It is important, therefore, not to confuse the idea of competition in a pure economy with the narrower idea of perfect competition among small independent firms in a free market. A pure economy is an organization of alternative ends and common means, while a free market economy is an organization of small firms having legal personality and cultural selfhood. A pure economy exhibits functional economic rationality, while a free-market economy is a mixture of economic, political, and legal rationality. Any increase of economic rationality in a society necessarily, by definition, involves an increase of competition in the sense of substitutability of ends, neutrality, and commonness of means, but does not necessarily involve a movement toward small-firm free-market conditions.

ECONOMIC TREND

The universally recognized economic trend is economic progress. It is ordinarily thought of as a rising standard of living, or more precisely as an increase of productivity per man-hour. Increased productivity, however, results from a combination of economic and technical changes, and cannot be taken as simply equivalent to economic progress unless this idea is conceived to include technological progress as well. If one wishes to distinguish the two trends, the technological components must be removed to achieve a clear idea of economic progress in the narrower sense.

Technological progress consists of an increase of efficiency of specific productive processes, together with the social conditions making possible increased efficiency. The transition from increased efficiency of specific techniques to a general increase in total product involves the addition of an economic factor, increased alternativeness of ends. The economic factor makes it possible to compare productive processes with each other and determine the amount of resources to allocate to each in order to achieve a maximum product with given resources. Without a fair degree of substitutability among ends a society might achieve technical virtuosity in specific activities without necessarily increasing total productivity. Increased total productivity, therefore, is dependent on an increased alternativeness of ends, and this is economic progress in the narrower sense.

Economic progress in this sense is simply an increased extension and purification of a society's economy. A pure economy is a system of common scarce means and alternative ends, so an increased alternativeness of ends in a society is equivalent to an increased extension of its economy.

We are all familiar with the detailed changes occurring during economic progress. Most of the sociocultural changes occurring in the Western world in recent centuries are either a part of, or a result of, economic and technological progress. One cultural element after another has been absorbed into the ever-widening economy, subjected to the test of economic rationality, rationalized, and turned into a commodity or factor of production. So pervasive has this process been that it now seems that anything can be thought of as a commodity and its value measured by a price, and that all values can be thought of as utilities. The same process of economic rationalization is now beginning to occur at an increasing rate in the underdeveloped countries, this time as the result of conscious design, and provides a cross-cultural picture of the characteristics of economic progress.

The elements that become commodities during economic progress include time, land, capital, labor; also personality itself, as well as all the artifacts produced by man: art objects, ideas, experiences, enjoyment itself, and even social relations. As these become commodities they are all subject to a process of moral neutralization and increase of mobility and competitiveness.

Another phase of economic progress is the development of a set of values and decision techniques appropriate to the valuation of commodities and measurement of utilities. The value system that tends to appear is the universalist-achievement ethic, including fairness, impartiality, equal opportunity (Parsons, 1951, chap. 3). It is accompanied by techniques such as that of looking for clear alternatives, finding common denominators for alternatives, and extending especially the use of money as a common denominator of different goods.

Let us consider the changes produced during economic progress in more detail. Time, in economically advanced cultures, has become a commodity to be bought, sold, and produced like other commodities. People do not merely live through time; they "spend" time. That is, they are conscious of a scarcity of time, and try to use their supply of it as wisely (economically) as possible. Time is scarce because alternative things can be done in it, and doing a certain thing prevents one from doing other things during the same time.

The economically reasonable thing, then, is to use one's time to do the things that are most important, so that one may "make the most" of one's time, that is, maximize the returns from the use of this commodity. People who do less important things in preference to more important ones are said to "waste" time; that is, they fail to maximize the returns from the use of their time. Similarly, one can "save" time by using a smaller amount of it for some standard task, thus releasing the remainder for other uses; one can "buy" time by offering some other commodity in place of it; and both saving and buying are ways of "gaining" time. That these and similar terms no longer seem metaphorical when applied to time indicates how thoroughly time has been made into a commodity and brought into the economy.

Like any other commodity, time has to be measured in order to be used most economically. It has to be broken down into small units, each of them equal and interchangeable, and each equally valuable. And this is just how time is treated in economically advanced cultures. Apart from the ever-present clock or watch, which measures time impartially and with any desired degree of accuracy, people are conscious of time passing steadily by and being evenly used up, minute after minute, hour after hour, day after day. They measure their time precisely in small units and are able to estimate with high accuracy the amount of time spent on a task. They budget their time well into the future, allocating exact amounts of it to each alternative use, and changing activities when the allocated time has been used up.

Time becomes a scarce commodity by being neutralized. That is, people gradually lose the conception that it is right to do certain things at certain times, and substitute the conception that time should be spent at doing whatever is most important. In traditional economic theory, this is called a shift from custom to reason in the use of time. When time is governed by "custom," each part of the day and the year has its right or proper task assigned to it, and life is a succession of activities. The time of one activity cannot be used in a different activity; that would be improper. Hence alternative uses for time do not, in general, exist; there is little or no competition among alternative uses of time, and no scarcity of time.

This noneconomic conception of time is so foreign to our economic-oriented minds that some people may wonder whether people ever have to make decisions in such a culture. The question is plausible because a large percentage of the ordinary decisions in our culture do deal with alternative uses of time, so that "making a decision" is connected in people's minds with "what to do" in a given time. When time is not a commodity such decisions are rare, and the decisions that concern people are of a different sort.

Time that is not conceived as an expendable commodity does not have to be measured and broken up into small units. Instead, it is divided according to the cycle of activities — the seasons, day and night, work and ceremony. The seasons are not thought of in terms of a large solar clock or calendar, but are seen as a sequence of activities, such as planting time and harvest time. The years are not thought of as stretching evenly and endlessly on to infinity, but are clustered around important events such as battles, droughts, and accessions to office. Days are not divided evenly into hours and minutes, but into activity spans: the cool of the day, evening, and so on. Activities themselves are not controlled by an impartial, external, measuring instrument, but develop according to their own internal rhythm. They begin when things are ready, develop to a climax, and end when they are completed. The sense of timing that individuals develop is not an ability to estimate the number of minutes that has passed, but rather an ability to feel the inner rhythm of an activity and to maintain its movement. Thus clocks and watches are unnecessary; or if they are introduced into the culture, they are used as ornaments or sources of idle information (for example, cf. M. Mead, 1954:70–72).

Remnants of this noneconomic conception of time still exist in our own culture, just as rudiments of an economic approach to time appear in economically nonprogressive cultures. The extent to which time is a commodity varies from one culture to another, depending on the extent of economic progress; but in no case has economic progress reached such a point that all time has become part of the economy and completely subject to calculation.

In our culture there are still times which are not entirely neutral — Sunday is a day of rest, night is for sleeping, and holidays are for celebrating. It is not right to work during these special times. Yet even these moral scruples have been partly taken into the economy, measured, and assigned a price. People are prepared to sell these special times at a special price: double pay for Sundays and holidays,

10 per cent extra pay for night work. In some occupations even this distinction has disappeared, and all units of time receive equal pay.

Another remnant of the noneconomic conception of time is the idea of "leisure time." The day is divided into work and leisure time, with weekends and vacations belonging to the latter. Working time is accurately measured and carefully allocated, but leisure tends to run along more freely and is measured less accurately. A person may know exactly how much his working time is worth per hour, but will not put the same exact valuation on his leisure or vacation time. In leisure time a person may feel some of the inner rhythm of his activities which disappears in working time.

It may seem that this division into work and leisure time is irrational, since the exact calculation occurring during working hours is not extended into leisure hours. Without a more impartial valuation of leisure and work time it is impossible to determine whether one is making the most economical use of one's time—it may be that some leisure hours are wasted and could be more profitably devoted to overtime work; or perhaps leisure time is too scarce and should be increased at the expense of work time.

Actually, however, the division serves a definite economic purpose. The two kinds of time correspond to two phases of the economy. Some productive activities are rather fully incorporated in the economy; they have been carefully measured and priced, and their use is ordinarily subject to rather exact calculation. Other productive activities have as yet been only partly rationalized; their exact money worth is not known, and their use is based on only the vaguest estimate of comparative utility. Activities such as entertainment, hobbies, sleeping, or just chatting are certainly economically valuable, since they bring returns to their consumer, but their degree of value is ordinarily known in only a vague fashion. The fully rationalized activities are engaged in during working hours where they can be subject to exact valuation and calculation, while the partly rationalized activities are saved for leisure time and evaluated much less exactly.

Now it ordinarily happens that when people first begin to set a money value on something they set the value far lower than it actually should be. This error of valuation is frequently observed in primitive cultures into which a money economy has recently been introduced. People will neglect their usual activity to work for money wages under the impression that they are getting rich, and are surprised to find themselves getting constantly poorer. The customary activities they neglect actually brought them a much higher income than wage labor, but they do not realize this because of their overvaluation of money. The same thing sometimes happens in our society when a person is able to extend his working hours indefinitely, or finds it possible to sell something not formerly considered a commodity. He imagines that he is getting richer by cutting down on his "waste" leisure time, while actually his life is getting more impoverished and his time becoming extremely scarce and valuable.

A fixed division between work and leisure time prevents such errors of valuation and thus actually contributes to maximization in use of time. Semirationalized activities that would otherwise be unduly avoided are preserved through inexactness of calculation.

At the same time this division is bound to be a temporary one. With further economic progress leisure time activities become more completely rationalized in terms of cost-price accounting and are taken up more fully into the economy. For example, the development of a do-it-yourself equipment market makes it possible to estimate more exactly the cost of craft hobbies as compared with professional work, so that the two can be conceived as real alternatives. As this happens people's leisure time becomes subject to more exact calculation, and the distinction between work and leisure gradually disappears.

Thus the distinction between various kinds of times is characteristic of a certain intermediate stage of economic progress. It does not exist at an early level of economic development and tends to disappear again at a later stage of development. Primitive peoples do not "go on vacation," not because their work is so interesting that they never tire of it, nor because they have to work constantly to keep alive, but because the distinction between two kinds of time is foreign to them. Also in a pure, ideal economy there would be only one kind of time and one kind of calculation to apply to all activities.

Like time, land and labor gradually turn into commodities during economic progress, and the intermediate stages of this process are marked by distinctions between different kinds of land and labor. In primitive agricultural societies land is typically conceived, not as a factor of production, but as an essential part of one's society. It symbolizes the infinite continuity of generations, past, present, and future. Working the land is a ceremonial and ritual act which relates the living members of a society to their own ancestors and their descendants. It gives them a place in the order of things; it is a basis for identification with parents; and it also enables them to participate in the immortality of future generations. Agriculture is not one job among many, to be pursued because it promises maximum returns, but rather a moral obligation and a privilege, since it gives a person his place in society and his self-respect. The questions of whether or not to raise a crop, what kind of crop to raise (sometimes), whether to buy or sell land, are not economic questions but moral ones, if indeed they can be conceived as questions at all. Even when economic progress brings a diversification of occupations, the nonagricultural specialists try to continue working a small plot of land on the side, because it is right. The other occupations are not conceived as real alternatives to agriculture, but rather as supplements and offshoots of it.

In nonagrarian cultures land frequently has the same social function as in agrarian cultures. One's land is the home of the ancestors, a heritage to be passed on to one's descendants. The unity of place symbolizes the infinite unity of the society. The present generation does not "own" the land as one owns a share of stock, but merely inhabits it and holds it in trust for future generations.

With economic progress these moral attitudes toward land are forced out of existence and land becomes a neutral commodity. Peasants who continue to farm — or live — in the traditional way become poorer than their economically advanced urban counterparts. Market pressures force them to become more productive, to diversify crops and introduce new industrial crops, to use new techniques which force-feed the soil and extract bigger crops from it. Machines come between the farmer and his land, so he need never feel earth between his fingers. With machinery comes the necessity of increasing the acreage of the farming unit, so that in some cases it can no longer be run most economically by a single family. The factory farm, with managers, foremen, and seasonal workers, emerges as the most economical type of farm production. Farming becomes a business, with land as a morally neutral factor of production.

The same process of rationalization occurs with cattle, buildings, and other natural adjuncts to society. In many African cultures cattle are a semi-economic prestige symbol and in India they are a sacred social symbol; but in economically advanced cultures they have become an impersonal factor of production.

In our culture an echo of the noneconomic attitude toward land remains in the distinction between different kinds of land. Agricultural land, which is almost completely a commodity, is distinguished from land for one's house and yard, which retains some noneconomic character. One's house still remains in some cases as the ancestral home, a link with the past which the present generation holds in trust for the future. It is also the place in which leisure-time craft activities occur, including a noneconomic type of farming which retains some of the moral values once characteristic of agriculture. The style of houses, furnishings, and landscaping are in many cases governed more by tradition and social prestige considerations than by strict economic calculation, indicating that these things are still regarded primarily as social symbols rather than commodities.

As economic progress continues this semi-economic category of land is brought more and more completely into the economy. The house and yard becomes "living space," designed and standardized by the housing industry to suit all tastes with maximum efficiency. People develop the habit of buying a house as one buys a car; they shop around for a bargain in their favorite style, or they hire a landscape architect and interior decorator to get the most for their money. They expect to trade their present model in on a new one in a few years when income increases, living needs change, or further technical improvements make their present model obsolete. The house becomes a kind of apartment in the suburbs, inspiring little or no personal pride of achievement and providing no attachment to past or future, no permanent community membership based on place.

Like land, labor has long been conceived as a commodity by economists, but its actual transformation into a commodity is still incomplete. In economically unprogressive cultures one does not choose an occupation from several alternatives; instead, an occupation is usually inherited as a part of one's position in society. The inherited occupation defines one's social position and needs, and becomes an important part of one's self-concept. Change of techniques is possible within the inherited occupation, but change of occupation usually occurs only as part of a radical break with society.

Some of this attitude toward occupation still persists in modern society. It still frequently happens that a son will follow his father's occupation, and that identification with the father's occupation provides a basis for one's self-concept. More usually, however, the growing boy comes in contact with a large set of different occupations in his daily experience, and the frequent question, "What will you be when you grow up?" tells him that a choice is expected of him. So even if he does continue in his father's line, the continuation appears as a choice among several socially acceptable alternatives. In addition, it frequently happens that the father's work takes place away from home and away from his son's experience, so that identification with the father does not extend to the father's occupation. When this happens, occupation loses its symbolic connection with inherited social position and with masculinity, and the occupations within the boy's experience become real alternatives. It then becomes possible to perceive choice of occupation as an economic problem involving a search for the job that will yield maximum returns from a person's skills. When occupation is chosen in this fashion, there is no psychological reason against change of occupation as soon as a more productive opening appears, and the chief barrier to occupational mobility is the accumulation of skills which would be wasted in a new job. An occupation chosen for economic reasons is not expected to affect one's personality to any significant extent. A person does not feel any particular attachment to his present job or identification with his colleagues; instead, his interest is directed to new openings that promise greater returns. He perceives himself as selling his time, skill, and labor in a particular fashion, and is ready to change his job when the labor market changes. Some types of labor have almost completely become commodities in this fashion, while other types retain a considerable noneconomic character. In general, traditional women's occupations have been included in the economy to a much smaller extent than have men's occupations. Until recently there was no morally acceptable alternative for a woman other than home and children, so that choice of occupation was not possible. And even where other occupations are morally available, they may not be acceptable emotionally. Usually the growing girl sees her mother performing housework and identifies with her on that basis. Housework and raising children becomes part of the complex of womanhood which defines the girl's ideal self, so that other occupations are perceived as supplements and offshoots of homemaking rather than as real alternatives.

With increasing economic progress these moral and emotional barriers gradually disappear, and homemaking becomes one of several valid alternative careers. When this happens, it is necessary to choose homemaking as a career rather than simply inherit it. It is necessary to compare the alternative careers and select the one that promises greatest returns. The existence of a market for domestic help makes this possible; it enables a woman to estimate her productivity per hour as a housekeeper and compare it with the income she would receive as a secretary or teacher. The estimates of comparative productivity will probably not be very exact or accurate, because many of the returns from homemaking are still of an intangible sort, but it is possible to make a rough calculation.

Probably the last sort of labor to become a commodity through economic progress will be childbearing. There is certainly no sign at present that childbearing is regarded as one of several equally acceptable ways of expending energy and time. Nor is there any market that would enable a woman to calculate the money productivity of her childbirth labor per hour, so that it could be compared with other types of labor. Instead, childbearing is still regarded as a biologically inherited task, a part of one's social role and a basis of one's self-respect. Thus it is the best example in our culture of the noneconomic approach to labor that characterizes economically unprogressive cultures.

One phase of economic progress, then, is the continual inclusion in the economy of more and more of human life, including times, places, labor, and leisure activities. As each of these is taken into the economy it is freed from the influence of "custom and tradition," that is, from psychological, moral, and legal restrictions on its use, and becomes mobile, available for many uses. It comes to be treated as a neutral means to alternative ends, and as an alternative to a variety of other neutral means. It is allocated to its various uses on the basis of more or less exact calculation of its productiveness in each use, and of the productiveness of alternative means. To facilitate such calculation and comparison it is standardized and broken into small equal units, each treated as a separate entity as far as possible.

Another phase of economic progress is the development of media of value measurement, comparison, and exchange. Such media are necessary because they extend the range of possible comparison between alternative commodities or alternative courses of action. Two commodities or other alternatives can be compared directly with each other in an intuitive judgment of profitability; but as the number of alternatives increases, a direct intuitive comparison of one with another rapidly becomes impossible. Indirect comparison through some common medium of measurement becomes necessary if comparison is to be made at all.

At least three lines of development in media of measurement can be distinguished, though the details of development are not necessarily identical in each culture. First, there is a development from several media to a single medium. In some economically unprogressive cultures commodities are classified in three or four groups; a commodity can be compared with others in its group but not with one belonging to another group (Firth, 1939). Each group of commodities has its own medium of comparison and exchange, and the differences of media reflect and contribute to the limitations on the alternativeness of commodities. As the range of alternativeness of commodities increases, the different media give way to a single universal medium of comparison and exchange.

In our culture remnants of nonmonetary media of comparison survive around the fringes of the economy. For example, when friends and neighbors help each other on some leisure-time task such as painting, moving, or baby-sitting the value of their labor is measured in terms of man-hours or days. People regard themselves as being some number of hours in debt to a neighbor, and try to repay the debt by other labor, baked goods, garden produce, or other semicommodities worth a roughly equivalent number of hours of work. It would not be right to repay with money or with goods brought from the store; nor are the debts and payments valued in terms of dollars and cents. In this case the distinction between two media of comparison, man-hours and money, reflects the distinction between two kinds of times, work time and leisure time, and two corresponding kinds of labor.

A second line of development is from media which have their own intrinsic value to a medium which is itself valueless and has only symbolic value. For example, the standard medium of value measurement in a culture might shift from wheat and cattle to gold and precious stones to paper money and checks to numbers in an account book. In this development the medium of measurement is purified of irrelevant intrinsic values and thereby becomes better adapted to its special task of measuring and comparing other values.

It may be that this development is not a purely economic one. It may depend also on noneconomic factors such as the development of national states which guarantee the value of paper money, checks, liens, and such. In this case details of monetary development in a given culture would depend partly on how power is distributed. On the other hand, the demand for a valueless medium of exchange may be one of the factors contributing to the centralization of state power, as a guarantee of the stability of money.

A third, closely related line of development is from a tangible, physical medium to an intangible, symbolic one. The previously mentioned sequence from wheat to accounting numbers is an example of this development. The decrease of physical bulk of the medium simplifies transactions and thus increases the mobility of commodities; and increased mobility of commodities and speed of transactions is essential as economic progress continues. (It also clarifies the essentially symbolic nature of the medium of measurement and exchange; as Hegel would say, it enables man to realize that economic transactions and economic values lie wholly in the mind and are controlled by the mind.)

The development of money and extension of its use is accompanied by the development of financial institutions (banking, accounting, insurance) including institutions devoted to measuring values in money terms. This is to be expected, since any technique, and especially an important one such as the measurement and comparison of value, tends to become institutionalized and develops its own specialists, its own research, and its own theory. However, it is possible that the line of development of financial institutions in any given culture is not determined solely by economic forces, but by a combination of economic and other factors. In this case the financial institutions which develop with economic progress would be expected to take on different shapes in different cultures. In parts of Melanesia and Indonesia, for example, the developing financial institutions are closely tied to the social relations within which trade occurs. It may be, on the other hand, that socially influenced developments characterize only a rudimentary stage of economic progress, and that in an advanced stage financial institutions tend to become independent of noneconomic forces and develop in their own characteristic way in any culture. Further investigation is necessary on this point.

A third phase of economic progress is the development of habits and techniques of economic calculation, and of values that facilitate calculation. These habits and values are developed by people as they adapt themselves to a world of commodities, markets, money, competition, and mobility. People develop the habit of evaluating courses of action, expenditures, and so forth by comparing them with alternatives, so that the most profitable alternative can be selected. They learn to look for alternatives where none seem to exist, and to clarify confused situations by distinguishing alternative courses of action; they learn to estimate and evaluate the effects of a course of action with some exactness; and they learn to compare alternatives by finding common units of measurement such as money and time. In addition people learn to regard their day as a series of expenditures and receipts — expenditure of time, effort, information, money, friendliness, and so on, and receipt of other people's similar expenditures. They feel that they ought to try to get the most out of their day, and that this will be accomplished by calculation and by planning daily expenditure. Hence they learn to pay attention to budgets and schedules, to keep exact account of expenditures and receipts, and to change activities that prove unprofitable. These habits are so familiar to us, so much a part of common sense, that we sometimes take them for granted or suppose them to be part of human nature; yet they are of minor importance in parts of the world not strongly influenced by economic progress.

The values developed by economic progress are also familiar to us. The root value is maximization: people ought to try to get the most out of life. Good is conceived as essentially quantitative, as something that can be increased or decreased without limit. Happiness is something to be pursued like an occupation; but the pursuit is endless, because a greater happiness beyond any present one is always conceivable.

This economic conception of the good life contrasts sharply with Plato's account of the good in the *Philebus*. He puts goodness in the class of the finite or structured, along with harmony, equality, and the like, and declares that pleasure is an extremely inferior kind of good because it belongs to the class of the infinite, the class of unorganized aggregates. Economic welfare clearly belongs to the class of the infinite, and one gets it by maximizing without limit.

Aristotle's conception of the good life also contrasts with the economic approach. He regarded the endless pursuit of profit as a corruption of a household art. External goods such as money ought not be maximized, but should be amassed only in moderate quantity; and all other goods, those of body and soul, are not even capable of maximization. Both of these ethical theories seem strange to a culture dominated by economic progress, and are in danger of being reinterpreted to make them more plausible.

The value of maximization is developed by economic progress because people are continually being put into situations in which maximization is reasonable. Living in a world of commodities, markets, and mobility, they are continually faced with alternatives: alternative commodities to buy, things to do, prices to charge; and when one is faced with alternatives, it is reasonable to select the more profitable over the less profitable one. So people learn to look for the most profitable alternative, and when this habit is generalized and made explicit, the value of maximization is the result.

A second element of the value system developed by economic progress is the means-end schema. Commodities are neutral, intrinsically valueless; they are useful as means. As the number of commodities increases with economic progress, the number of means increases, and people's daily life is more and more concerned with the wise use of means. The increasing scope of the economy forces people to make an increasing number of allocation decisions, in which means are allocated to alternative ends. Hence people come to think of decisions in terms of means and ends; they come to believe, with Weber, that all practical questions are questions of means and ends (cf. Parsons, 1937:xiii).

A third element of an economic value system is impartiality of a certain sort. It is the sort that has been called "neutrality" in this chapter, and it applies to means that are common to alternative ends. When several means are available for one's ends, it is reasonable to give them all an equal consideration if one is to find the most profitable means or combination of means. If one shows a partiality to some particular means, this may hinder the discovery of some other more effective means; and this is irrational because it prevents maximization. Thus the value of impartiality is dependent on the value of maximization.

People are taught the value of impartiality by their participation in economic life. Such participation continually confronts them with decision situations involving alternative means, which because of their very alternativeness demand equal consideration. When faced with the possibility of buying the same article in two different stores, for instance, it would be economically irrational to refuse to compare the two to see which was the better buy.

The value of impartiality thus applies primarily to pure commodities, and is learned through dealing with them. Once the value is established in a culture, however, it spreads to semicommodities and even noncommodities. An important variant of this value, for instance, is the equality of opportunity value, which applies to human beings in occupational contexts. Equality of opportunity means that, in competition for honors, jobs, and so forth, each contender has an equal chance to prove himself worthy of selection. It is supposed that each contender is in competition with all the rest, just as alternative ends compete with each other for the scarce means in economic calculation; and it is supposed that the selection from the contenders will be made on the basis of maximum profitability, as in economizing. Thus human beings are conceived as alternative ends competing for scarce means, and when they are so conceived, the value of impartiality applies.

Impartiality is also applied to time, so that each moment of present and future is entitled to equal consideration; to land, as when sites are being selected for new enterprises; to labor, and so on. The value judgment that all these things ought to be treated impartially is the value correlate of the way they are actually treated during economic progress, as other moral influences are neutralized.

When the three value elements of maximization, impartiality, and the end-means distinction are combined and systematized, the result is utilitarianism, which in its various forms has dominated Western ethical thought for two centuries. The main ideas of this theory appear in a number of schools of thought which disagree in details. Disagreements persist as to the definition of the good, the way of verifying a definition, and the status of subordinate moral rules; but there is widespread agreement that the good is something that is maximizable, that it is an end to be achieved by the wise use of means, that it is scarce in the sense that possession by one individual prevents possession by others, and that people are impartially entitled to a chance to pursue it. Theories such as modern hedonism, the interest theory, the basic needs theory, and ideal utilitarianism agree on the above points, though disagreeing on details. Utilitarian ethical theory was first systematized in England, the country of most rapid economic progress at the time, and is widely accepted in one form or another in our culture; but it is not prominent in ancient and medieval philosophy, and does not appear to my knowledge in the value systems of preliterate cultures. Hedonism appears in earlier philosophies such as Epicureanism, but the idea that happiness should be pursued without limit through careful calculation is new. Nor is the element of universality and impartiality important in ancient hedonist theories.

A fourth value element appearing during economic progress is the value of competition. By this I mean not the abstract, impersonal idea of competition among ends which was discussed earlier in the chapter, but the idea of personal rivalry. The idea of rivalry is not, as Veblen (1934) and Ayres (1944) supposed, a barbaric survival from hunting economies, but simply an extension to human beings of the abstract idea of alternativeness among ends and means. The extension is made plausible by experiences in which people, in the form of labor, actually do compete as alternatives to each other. Frequent experiences of this sort teach people that human beings can be separate and in competition with one another.

Competition is thus appreciated as a factual possibility; it is also accepted as a value, since when people are alternative to one another, it is reasonable to compare them to see which has the most to offer. Just as a comparison among ends is reasonable because it leads to maximization, so comparison of competing human beings and selection of the best one is reasonable because it supposedly will maximize returns from the use of labor.

The values of maximization, impartiality, competition, and the means-end distinction are probably the main elements of the value system produced by economic progress. It is fairly clear that these value elements are strengthened by economic progress, because they are prominent in economically progressive cultures and rare in underdeveloped cultures, and because they are logically related to the economic norm underlying economic progress.

It is more difficult to say in the case of some other values whether and to what extent they are strengthened by economic progress. The empirical way to answer the question is to find out what values are regularly produced in a variety of different cultures during economic progress. However, this sort of evidence is difficult to interpret. Some changes in values occurring during economic progress might result from a combination of economic and noneconomic influences, and others may result from the adaptation of social and cultural elements to economic changes rather than from direct economic influences. We are at the borderline of the cultural organization produced by economic progress, where it is difficult to separate economic influences from other determinants. Even the four value elements mentioned above may be reinforced or modified by noneconomic influences in any particular culture.

For example, it may be supposed that the personal achievement value is also produced or strengthened during economic progress. Empirically, this value is prominent in the countries which are farthest advanced economically; it is part of the "universalist-achievement" ethic associated with advanced parts of Western culture. Logically, the value of achievement seems closely related to the value of competition; a person placed in a competitive situation is supposed to make the most of himself and make the best possible showing, and is supposed to be judged on his achievement. And when the competition value is generalized to the whole of life, it becomes a belief that a person is worthy of esteem only insofar as he has personally achieved something; and this is the achievement value.

On the other hand, the achievement value appears in some economically unprogressive cultures, particularly in hunting cultures, in an even more pronounced form than in Western culture. Thus it cannot be solely or directly related to economic progress.

A second example is the Protestant ethic, long thought to be associated with capitalism in some way. On the one hand, it seems likely that such a complex of values is the unique result of a variety of influences, converging in a single culture. On the other hand, value complexes similar to the Protestant ethic appear in the economically progressive strata of some non-Western societies, such as the business class in small town Java (Geertz, 1956:134–158). Further evidence and thought are needed on this question.

Another rather difficult question is whether the value elements mentioned above are the result or the cause of economic progress. This question has especially been asked with regard to the Protestant ethic. The simple preliminary answer is that they are both cause and result. Logically, it is clear how, for example, the value of impartiality would contribute to economic progress by speeding up the moral neutralization of formerly noneconomic factors which were in the process of becoming commodities. But it is also clear that continual dealing with a variety of commodities including labor would strengthen the value of impartiality. The detailed interrelations between values and economic institutions are more difficult to trace, and are not as yet well understood.

The social organization and value system produced during economic progress has now been indicated in some detail. The selective process on which economic progress is based will be considered next. This subject is discussed in detail in a number of books of economic theory, so it is perhaps not necessary to go into detail here. Marx and Engels sum the subject up neatly in the *Communist Manifesto*: "the cheap prices of its [the *bourgeoisie's*] commodities are the heavy artillery with which it batters down all Chinese walls" (1932:325). In other words, an economically advanced person, country, or phase of life produces more from a given amount of resources than one less advanced; it becomes more prosperous and powerful, and consequently expands its influence in various ways. Economically less advanced persons, countries, or areas of life either voluntarily imitate the more advanced ways in order to get commodities more cheaply, or they are forced into economic development to preserve their independence against the power of the more advanced. Many other factors, such as the availability of capital and raw materials, influence the particular responses to the demand for development, but these are not relevant here.

The same selective process is involved in technological progress, but it is more limited in scope. Technical improvements, like economic advances, are rewarded by increased product and increased power; therefore they tend to spread and to produce further improvements, but only in limited areas. For example, an improvement in violin technique or in running technique, once developed by a single person, tends to be imitated by others through choice or necessity, and to stimulate further improvements, but only in a narrow area. The violin techniques will spread to other phases of violin playing, to other stringed instruments, perhaps to wind instruments a little, but hardly any further. Running techniques may stimulate similar technical improvements in other sports, and perhaps in military training as well, but will hardly extend their influence beyond that.

The reason for the limited influence of technical improvement is that they deal only with more efficient means to a single end; but if ends are morally and psychologically isolated from one another, an improvement in the fortunes of one does not affect the other. If violin playing and running are separate areas of life, technical improvements in violin playing do not affect runners adversely, so there is no necessity for them to improve their techniques. Nor are they likely to admire the increased effectiveness of violin playing enough to voluntarily imitate the violinists' attention to technique. Thus it is possible to combine great technical skill in one area of activity with disinterest in techniques in other areas. Preliterate cultures often combine tremendous technical virtuosity in some activities—kinship organization, wood carving, pottery making—with extremely crude techniques in other areas—digging sticks, lack of written records. There are even cases (Nash, 1958) in which industrialization—certainly a form of technological progress—has come to a peasant society and remained for many decades without particularly inducing technical improvements in other areas of life. The goal of cloth production is pursued efficiently in the factory, but since this goal is morally and psychologically isolated from other goals, the mechanization, mass production, and specialization of the factory does not spread to other areas of life.

In contrast, economic progress must spread throughout a culture, because it consists precisely of the process of making more and more ends alternative to each other. It is continually absorbing new ends, assigning them a money value, and making new means available to them. In so doing it removes the moral and psychological barriers which isolate ends and protect them against the pressure of technical advances in other areas. When one part of a culture is well advanced economically and another part is still protected against economic calculation, there is continual pressure on the protected area to become economically rationalized. Today we experience this pressure all around the fringes of the economy—in leisure-time activities, in housework and women's activities, in use of house and yard space. Home economists, recreationists, architects, community boosters, and charity workers are continually trying to rationalize the fringe areas so as to increase productivity in them and make new resources available to them.

As the economy spreads throughout a culture it also stimulates generalized technological progress by relating isolated ends to each other. The violinist and the athlete are related by being put into competition for the public's entertainment dollar. Technical improvements by one affect the other adversely by attracting more entertainment money, and force corresponding technical improvements in the other. For this reason it is only economically advanced cultures which exhibit generalized technological progress; primitive cultures develop great technical refinements in some areas, but remain backward in other areas. Technological progress is thus partly dependent on economic progress. Veblen's failure to realize this is a serious defect in his theory of technological progress.

One can make the same distinction between the values accompanying technological progress and those accompanying economic progress. In terms of content the two sets of values are very similar and perhaps identical. Both include the value of maximization, though in the case of technical processes a single end is to be maximized and in the case of economic processes a plurality of ends is maximized. The value of impartiality, neutrality, detachment, which Veblen calls "an habitual recognition and apprehension of causal sequence . . . without a sense of dependence on any preternatural intervention in the course of events" (Veblen, 1934:154) is also common to both systems, though the technician feels he ought to be impartial toward means, and the economizer, toward ends. However, means frequently are ends and ends are means, depending on one's point of view, so that the difference of emphasis is slight. The means-end distinction itself is also central to both systems, as is the related decision habit of dividing means into small parts and measuring the effectiveness of each part.

The main difference between the two is not in their content but in the range of activities to which they apply. As economic progress spreads throughout a culture its accompanying values also come to apply to more and more areas of life, and the opposite values such as particularism and ascription (cf. chap. 3, p. 90f.) gradually disappear. If, however, there is technical improvement in specific areas without generalized economic progress, those specific areas may be characterized by universalist values without affecting the particularist-ascriptive values of the rest of the culture. Thus in industrialized Cantel (Nash, 1958) activities outside the factory are governed to a considerable extent by particularist-ascriptive values; in industrialized Japan (Levine, 1958, chap. 2; Ishino and Bennett, 1952) particularist values are said to govern large areas of activity outside industry and even some areas of industrial life. The distinction between technological and economic progress is theoretically useful because it provides a way of describing these cases in which there is technological improvement in specific activities without an extension of the calculating, marketing orientation to the whole of life.

ECONOMIC DECISIONS AND THEIR SCOPE

In the discussion of economic organization I stated that the two basic economic processes were allocation and exchange. Allocation is a distribution of values among the alternative ends of an economic unit, while exchange is a transfer of values between economic units. Each of these two processes is based on its own kind of decision procedure; allocation is based on economizing and exchange is based on bargaining (except when prices are fixed in a market). Economizing is an impersonal procedure dealing with means and ends, while bargaining is a social procedure involving two socially related economic units.

Economizing

Economizing is an evaluation and selection of ends, and it occurs when two or more ends are in competition with each other. It occurs, for example, when one is in a position to ask, "Should I do this or that today?" or, "How much of this should I give up to get some of that?" or, "What order of priority shall we assign these tasks, in case we are unable to do all of them?" The competing ends are evaluated by comparing the returns possible for each of them in the situation, and that end or combination of ends is chosen which promises to yield the greatest total return from the available resources. A single end may be chosen over all the others, or several chosen in some proportion, or a priority scale of ends set up, or several ends arranged in a time sequence, or several different resources assigned to several different ends or groups of ends.

Economizing is a rational process, because when one must choose among ends that are genuinely alternative, it is reasonable to choose in such a way as to get the most out of them. This is, in a way, an extension of technical rationality — when ends are alternative, they are all parts of a larger end, and it is this larger end which is to be maximized. It is reasonable to achieve the larger end as far as possible, in turn, because that is what it means to have an end. This point can be expressed as an economic norm, "allocate means to alternative ends in such a way as to maximize the ends."

Economizing and bargaining are the standard and almost the only decision processes treated in modern decision theories. They have been dealt with in exhaustive detail, and their many variants, principles, and subprinciples have been worked out in economic theory, game theory, statistical decision theory, and the theory of satisficing. Consequently there is no need for a detailed treatment of economizing here, since many volumes on the subject are readily available. Instead, I shall deal with the less explored subject of the conditions in which economizing is appropriate.

Any form of decision making is appropriate only when (1) objective conditions call for its use by presenting the kind of problem which it can resolve; and (2) conditions are present which make its successful use possible. I shall consider both of these. First, economizing is *necessary* when an economic problem exists, that is when ends are alternative in the sense that achievement of one end implies a sacrifice of another end. If no sacrifice is necessary no choice of ends need be made and no problem exists, since all can be realized together. Sacrifice of one end is necessary to achieve another only when both are dependent on common means which are scarce; or, in other words, when both are unlimited relative to the jointly available means.

Thus alternativeness of ends is dependent on two other conditions, namely the existence of unlimited ends and the existence of common means. Ends become unlimited in a variety of ways, but chiefly through the removal of cultural limits on them, or by the development of value systems containing unlimited ends. Means are common when they are morally and psychologically neutral, that is when there are no legal, moral, or psychological conditions which tie the means to one particular end or ban their use for some other end. Means tied to or banned from particular uses are normative means in Parsons' terminology (Parsons, 1937:74ff.). For example, it is not possible for a manager to ask whether he would get the most out of his men by using them at the plant or by telling them to paint his house for him, because private uses of one's employees are distinguished from business use and are banned. In industries with considerable job grading and seniority rules, a foreman cannot even calculate the most economical use of his manpower within the plant, because of the limits set on the reassignment of labor. These questions could be asked only if the legal limits on the use of labor could be removed or evaded. The legal rules limit the extent to which labor can be treated as a commodity, a neutral means subject to economizing.

Second, economizing is *possible* only insofar as the problematic, alternative ends are comparable on some scale. When this condition is not met, there is no way of finding out which end or combination of ends will bring the greatest return, and so there is no economic way of choosing among them. For example, it is difficult to compare the value of going to church on Sunday with the value of conversation with a friend, in terms of which would bring the greatest return, supposing that the two were somehow alternative. The two are hardly comparable since there is no unit of measurement common to both of them. The two values are, indeed, hardly measurable at all; both of them are, traditionally at least, absolute values, not susceptible to division into parts or change of degree. A choice could be made between them if necessary, but it would be a difficult choice to make and to justify in economic terms. A person faced with the two ends as real alternatives would most likely make the decision in some noneconomic fashion, for instance, by trying to change them around until they were compatible and no longer alternative, perhaps by taking the friend to church (social rationality), or by determining priorities of commitment or obligation to one or the other (legal rationality).

It is a little easier, but still difficult, to compare the rate of return from a do-it-yourself home construction task with the returns from hiring a professional to do the job. In this case the two costs can be compared if the value of one's time per hour is known, but the "psychic returns" from the craftsmanship activity cannot be compared with the returns from the professional job to the same degree of exactness. Here again there is no common unit of measurement; and in fact no one has yet devised an objective unit of measurement for psychic returns.

The fact that not all ends are comparable with one another was recognized by John Stuart Mill, who expressed the point in his doctrine that pleasures differ in quality. He failed, however, to solve the problem that this posed for utilitarian theory, as Bradley pointed out (1951:57ff.). When one is faced with two pleasures differing in quality, one still has to decide which is preferable; but in order to do this, it is necessary to find some common scale of measurement, and this reduces quality to quantity. Some decision can probably always be reached between two alternatives if necessary, but it will be difficult to explain the decision in economic terms unless the alternatives are somehow comparable. If they are not comparable or only slightly comparable people will try to reach a decision on some noneconomic basis.

Both conditions which together make economizing necessary and possible are cultural conditions. It is the value system of a culture which determines the extent to which ends can be alternative, which makes some means normative and others neutral, and which allows media of value comparison to develop. Individual and subcultural variations occur within the general limits of the cultural value system and allow one person to economize in situations where another person cannot. For example, in our culture many people feel it would be wrong to calculate whether it is worthwhile to work for regular wages on Sunday, or on Saturday in some cases. The Sabbath to them is a sacred time in which one ought not work — it is a normative means, prescribed for religious and family uses only. For other people Sunday or Saturday is a semineutral day of rest, and they are prepared to estimate the wage rate at which they would be willing to forego that rest. For others the day is a completely neutral means, a time just like any other time, to be used in any way that promises the greatest return. With regard to comparability of values, in at least one culture (the Trobriands) it is possible for a husband to estimate the value of his wife's sexual favors to him and to compare it with the value of other gifts; but in our culture an economic valuation of such things is impossible. Subjectively, of course, the cultural limitations on economizing are not recognized as cultural, but appear as absolute moral obligations, dictates of justice, decency, and the like.

Both kinds of cultural limitations on economizing are gradually removed during economic progress. The main characteristic of economic progress is the increasing alternativeness of ends, which involves removal of moral limitations on ends and on the use of means, as they are turned into commodities. A secondary characteristic is the development of media of measurement and comparison, culminating in the universal extension of money measurement, which enables one to compare the values of alternative ends.

The extent to which economizing is possible in any given culture, therefore, depends on the degree of economic progress that has occurred in the culture. The more economically advanced a culture is, in general, the wider the scope for substantial economic rationality. If this view is correct, it is no accident that the first systematic formulation of utilitarianism occurred in the economically most progressive Western country. The orthodox theory as developed by Bentham and others correctly pointed out the direction of development of British institutions at that time — a development in which ends were becoming increasingly comparable on a money scale, and means were becoming increasingly neutral and mobile. The variations introduced by Mill and later by G. E. Moore, Ross, and others expressed the present and perennial incompleteness of this development.

Mill's recognition of different qualities in pleasure was empirically sound because a single medium of value measurement had not yet been extended to all ends, while Bentham's denial of differences in quality expressed the economic demand to reduce all media of measurement to a single medium as far as possible. Moore's principle of organic unities was empirically sound because markets and accounting systems had not developed sufficiently to permit measurement of the value of the marginal product of all factors of production; Bentham's rules of measurement, though impossible to apply, express the economic demand to isolate each factor of production and measure its contribution to the product. Ross's emphasis on absolute obligations appeals to present-day common sense because many normative means still exist today; the orthodox insistence on the supremacy of the principle of utility expresses the economic demand that all means be freed from moral restrictions so that they can be used to best advantage.

It is not to be supposed that the development toward money measurement of all ends and neutrality of all means will ever be completed. It is extremely doubtful that a pure economy devoid of all noneconomic restrictions could ever exist; and the trend toward such an economy is in some respects even being reversed today, through the operation of noneconomic trends. For example, labor is in some respects becoming less of a commodity, through the development of legal barriers against labor mobility. In this respect the qualifications provided for utilitarian theory by Mill, Moore, Ross, and others do not merely express the temporary incompleteness of an economic trend, but rather state permanent social and legal limitations on the scope of economic rationality. There will always be some ends that are not reducible to money measurement, some organic unities the contribution of whose parts is not measurable, and some normative means. The number and importance of these noneconomic factors may diminish with continued economic progress, but they cannot be expected to disappear altogether.

The extent to which any particular end or means is subject to economic treatment depends not on its intrinsic nature, but on the extent to which it has been included in the economy. Factors which have become pure commodities are subject to fairly exact measurement and calculation, while semicommodities and semi-alternative ends can be measured and compared with other values to a lesser degree.[1]

At least three degrees of exactness can be distinguished in economic calculations and judgments, corresponding to the different degrees of inclusion of ends in the economy. The three may be called judgments of comparative utility, of marginal utility, and of objective marginal utility.

Judgments of comparative utility are possible with respect to ends that are at the fringes of the economy, ends such as leisure-time activities, hobbies, social activities. This lowest degree of economizing consists of simply comparing the ends and choosing the one that

---

[1] Fromm's argument on this point (1955:148) is based on a misunderstanding. He argues that concerts, lectures, trips, and parties are never subject to economic calculation because their value is incommensurable with the value of money. The error here is in supposing that money — or time — itself has a value which is compared with other values in rational calculation. Actually money and time should only be media through which other values are compared when they become alternative to each other. Thus money and the market, by providing prices, enable one to compare the value of a trip with the value of a series of concerts; and time measurement enables one to compare the values of a concert and of a party that occupy the same amount of time. Trips, concerts, lectures, and such remain incomparable with each other only so long as they are unique, special occurrences and there is no regular market for them, no expectation of a regular, standardized supply of them.

intuitively seems most desirable. A judgment of this sort is still economic, since ends are being compared and an attempt made to select the end that promises maximum returns. It is the kind of judgment that Mill proposed for pleasures of differing quality, and that Lewis (1946, chap. XVI) proposed for choosing among alternative organic unities. In each of these cases it was supposed that the values could not be measured and compared in quantitative terms, and therefore had to be compared as a whole with their alternatives.

Semi-economic activities cannot be subject to any more exact judgment than this because neither the activities themselves nor their enabling means (costs) can be measured in money terms. Leisure-time activities are not performed for a market, but for one's own enjoyment. They are never bought and sold; hence no price has been assigned them, and their money value is not definitely known. Nor are the costs of such activities usually known. The means used by them are semicommodities — leisure time, living space, hobby skills — whose present price is not ordinarily known because there is no regular market for them. There is, indeed, a sporadic kind of market for leisure time, and the money price of some materials such as transportation, tools, and furniture can be estimated; but total costs are difficult to estimate and are rarely known.

For example, a person faced with the alternative of spending an evening at home reading or going to visit friends can hardly do more, from an economic standpoint, than make a blunt comparison of the two activities and their consequences to see which he prefers. He is spending something, but cannot estimate its money value; and the activities themselves are regarded as subjective experiences which have no price and cannot be quantified.

Though judgments of comparative utility are necessarily vague, it is possible to increase their exactness to some extent. This is done by eliminating differences in cost as far as possible before comparing values. Instead of simply asking, "Does A seem preferable to B?" one asks first, "How much of A and how much of B can be done in a given time and with a given expenditure of money and effort?" Then those amounts of A and B can be compared to see which is preferable. In this way one discovers which end promises the greatest return from a given expenditure; and this is more exact than a direct comparison of ends involving differing levels of expenditure.

Unfortunately, the cost incurred in leisure-time activities cannot usually be held constant for different activities, so that this additional exactness is not often possible. But if differences of cost are ignored in comparative judgments there is no direct comparison of the profitability of the alternatives. Comparisons of this sort are almost completely arbitrary, and constitute the lowest level of economic rationality.

Mill's proposed comparisons of pleasures which differ in quality are on this lowest level of exactness. The judgment he suggests, which ignores questions of cost and questions of diminishing returns due to one's previous experiences, can hardly be more than arbitrary from an economic standpoint. In such a situation some type of noneconomic judgment would be much more appropriate than a judgment of utility. There is indeed no reason to suppose that the "moral experience of mankind" has assigned values their comparative position on a utilitarian basis, as Mill assumes.

When costs are known and measurable in money terms, a second degree of exactness is possible in economizing. This higher degree is commonly possible for consumers buying goods in a market, where the goods have definite costs. The effect of setting a money price on means is to quantify them, so that they can be used in varying amounts instead of as indivisible units. One can spend any amount one wishes when buying peas, or housing, or concerts, because there is a regular market which quantifies these commodities. This increases the consumer's range of choice enormously, and with it the possible accuracy of his judgments. Instead of asking merely "Do I prefer A or B?" he can ask, "How much A and how much B, combined, do I prefer to any other AB combination?" Because both A and B have common means, measured in money, he can transfer means freely between A and B and obtain any desired combination of them. This is a marginal utility judgment.

It is sometimes argued that consumers' judgments cannot approach the exactness of marginal utility analysis and are limited instead to the lesser exactness of indifference curve analysis (Hicks, 1939). Actually the two methods are not absolutely different; marginalism is the ideal limit which indifference curve analysis approaches as it gets more exact. Its exactness depends, in turn, on how well developed the market for a given commodity is.

For example, a consumer's preference for quality in canned tomatoes is appropriately described in indifference curve terms. He can

ordinarily discriminate two or three degrees of quality at most, because the market differentiates quality to that extent. He prefers the
better quality, but cannot ordinarily measure the strength of his
preference to the exact penny; and when faced with standard price
differentials, usually settles on one brand and sticks to it (Katona,
1951). On the other hand, the market in cloth and clothing is highly
developed with regard to quality, and the experienced clothing buyer
can discriminate extremely small differences in quality and assign
exact money values to these differences. His behavior approaches
more closely to the ideal of marginal analysis.

Thus the second degree of economizing is also, like the first, subject to varying shades of exactness, depending on the state of the
market for any particular commodity.

Note that a well-developed market system dissolves the barriers
between Mill's pleasures of different quality. In any large music
center, for example, a budgeting family can make a fairly exact comparison between the value of food and the value of musical concerts.
They can decide how many dollars are to be allocated to each per
year, and with some experience can reach a maximizing combination
to within a few dollars. To be sure, this would be impossible if they
asked Mill's question, "Is the intrinsic value of music higher than
that of food, entirely apart from quantity?" Such a question is silly;
it is not a practical question and has no answer. Given a week of
constant music and no food, anyone would prefer food to music. The
question to ask is, "How many dollars should we spend on food and
how many on music?" This question is rational and practical, is actually asked, and can be answered.

Even with a well-developed market system, however, there is an
inevitable element of subjectivity in consumers' choices. The market
enables a consumer to be exact in comparing the cost of alternative
goods and services but tells him little about the value he will get by
consuming them. The consumer must make this estimate himself,
on the basis of past experience in consuming those commodities.
Since his own experience is necessarily limited compared with the
wide range of experiences that go into the formation of a system of
market prices, his judgments are likely to be relatively inaccurate.

This inaccuracy is diminished greatly when both means and ends,
costs and products, have a money price. The businessman who buys
commodities in a market, transforms them, and sells the finished

product does not have to be subjective in any of his judgments, apart from market fluctuations. He knows both the cost of the means he uses and the value of the ends to which he can allocate them. As a result he can estimate the proper proportion of means to allocate to his various products with a high degree of both accuracy and exactness. Indeed, given sufficient market information the necessary economizing judgments can even be made by an electronic computer, thus nearly eliminating human subjectivity and error. For example, estimates of the proper proportion of resources to allocate to varying crops at several different commodity price ratios have been made on the Illiac computer. Judgments of this sort may be called objective marginal utility judgments, and represent the third and highest degree of exactness of economizing.

Note that the problems of measuring contributory values in organic unities, which was emphasized by Moore and Lewis, is solved by market development and by cost-accounting techniques. Lewis' example of a small boy working for circus tickets is taken from a semi-economic area where no real market exists; but in a well-developed market the problem of measurement is routinely solved. Any industrial product could be thought of as an organic unity, in the sense that the value of the product is greater than the sum of its costs, and that the organization of its parts is important to the total value. A good manager can, however, decompose such unities, measure the contributory values included in them, and recompose them in such a way as to maximize value. Cost accounting produces information on the cost of each contributory part of the product, and the market provides information on the value of the marginal product of each contributory part. It does this by indicating the price of an alternative product in which the contributory part is missing or diminished in volume. For example, the price of a well-known brand of aspirin minus the price of an equivalent aspirin without a brand name equals the contributory value of a brand name. By combining this information, the manager can compare the marginal cost of each contributory part with its marginal value. Where marginal cost exceeds marginal value, he can reduce the proportion of that part in the total product, and where marginal cost is lower than marginal value he can increase the proportion. For example, where labor costs are high relative to marginal value, he can decrease the proportion of labor in a product and increase the proportion of labor-saving machinery. Thus he not only measures contributory values at the margin, but also maximizes them, and all without any use of "intuition."

It may be objected that industry and markets deal with instrumental values only, while Moore and Lewis were discussing intrinsic values. This distinction is, however, irrelevant. Intrinsic, consumption values can be measured as accurately as instrumental values if a market can be developed for them. For example, the satisfaction of sitting in a well-planned back yard is presumably an intrinsic value and an organic unity as well. The housing and landscape market enables the would-be sitter to measure all the contributory values involved as well as their cost, and even enables him to recompose a new back yard that will maximize his satisfaction. The market does this by providing examples of back yards of all sorts, each with some contributory value missing or in different proportion. By imagining himself sitting in each of these yards, the would-be sitter can estimate the total intrinsic value of each combination, and by subtraction he can estimate the contributory value of each part. For example by subtracting a yard-sitting experience in a poor neighborhood from the same yard-sitting experience in a good neighborhood the contributory value of the neighborhood is obtained. The market price of each yard gives information about the cost of each factor, in a similar fashion. The future sitter can then compose an optimum yard combination by comparing the cost and the contributory value of each factor and each proportion of factors.

The back-yard problem cannot be solved with the same degree of exactness and accuracy as the industrial problem, but only because the market for yards is not so well developed. For example, the contributory value of one's own work in planning and fixing the yard cannot be more than vaguely estimated, because this is a leisure-time activity on the fringe of the economy. The contributory value of a professional landscape architect can, however, be measured. Also the inevitable subjectivity of a consumer's prediction of his own future satisfaction reduces the accuracy of the calculation. As a result some phases of the economic judgment involved in back-yard buying can reach only the first level of exactness, while other phases reach the second and third levels. The industrial economic judgment will be primarily on the third level.

Even in business, however, it is not often possible to achieve complete exactness and accuracy. The value of the finished products which a business man produces is measured not by present but by future prices — the prices that will exist when production is completed. The farmer, for instance, must know next fall's prices in order to make his spring-planting judgments. This introduces a new element of uncertainty into economic calculation; perhaps not as great an element as the subjectivity which a consumer is faced with, but considerable nevertheless. In addition, the financial transactions occurring in the center of the economy involve extremely complex combinations of resources which are often difficult to chart accurately.

In spite of these barriers to accuracy, a high degree of both accuracy and exactness is necessary in the business judgments occurring in a well-developed economy, since even small errors of information or of judgment often lead to large losses.

The necessary accuracy is made possible partly by further development of the market, and partly by the development of statistical techniques, cost accounting, and other accounting techniques. A market in future transactions produces the future prices that the businessman needs. This future market is originally based on the subjective judgments of professional speculators; but with the development of statistical and predictive techniques, the subjective element is gradually reduced. Cost accounting increases the accuracy of information about the cost of the various means that must be allocated by the economizing manager. Other accounting techniques increase his control over the many lesser allocation transactions which he must take into account in his decisions. The development of accounting, business statistics, and even information theory must be regarded as a phase of economic progress, since it makes possible the extreme accuracy and exactness of economizing at the third level.

In some cases cost and price uncertainties which are irreducible by further market development can be reduced or transferred by accounting conventions and by political decisions. Depreciation costs, for example, cannot be exactly estimated because of objective uncertainty. An oil company cannot know the exact depletion rate of its underground oil resources, and the depreciation rate of much industrial machinery depends on future inventions which cannot be predicted. In these cases an accounting convention assigns some arbitrary depreciation rate. It is also possible to fix the rate by political decision; and similarly, objective future price uncertainties can be reduced by political price guarantees. In this way the remaining irrationalities in economic decisions can be reduced, and in addition the direction of economic development can to some extent be brought under political control.

However, it is impossible to eliminate uncertainty in any complicated problem, and even in everyday situations the degree of uncertainty is frequently significant. When uncertainty is great enough to have a significant effect on the outcome of activity, it should be explicitly dealt with in the decision procedure. There are several ways to do this, depending on the kind of uncertainty that exists.

First, if the uncertainty can be reduced to a limited series of possibilities, a strategy can be prepared in advance for each possibility. For example, a shopper ignorant of prices can construct in advance a demand curve covering the range of possible prices; a manager can work out alternate production strategies pending the completion of a labor contract. The concept of alternative strategies has been developed in game theory.

Second, if there is a definite range of possibilities, a probability calculus can be applied to it to locate the most desirable alternative. This alternative is the one that will result in minimum loss if things go badly, but maximum gain if they turn out well. Probability procedure of this sort has been highly developed in statistical decision theory.

Third, if the uncertainty is completely indefinite but promises to be reduced within a definite time span, it can be dealt with by increasing liquidity of assets. The effect of this is to make possible rapid changes of strategy as the uncertainty is reduced. The greater the uncertainty, the greater the degree of liquidity should be, and as uncertainty is reduced, liquidity is also reduced. For instance, a person expecting to move to an uncertain destination within three years can respond by maintaining high liquidity — renting instead of buying, cultivating only superficial friendships, maintaining broad interests, and so forth. Here the degree of uncertainty is also subject to a probability calculus to determine the proper degree of liquidity.

Fourth, if the uncertainty is to begin at a definite future time (as in the previous example) a preference can be shown for short-run ends, achievable before the beginning of the uncertainty period. Conversely, if the period of uncertainty has a definite end, a preference for long-run ends and short-run liquidity is advisable, for example in wartime. The proper responses to uncertainty have been developed in great detail in game theory and decision theory, and need not be further treated here.

In summary, economizing is the allocation of scarce common means to alternative ends in such a way that the ends are maximized. It is reasonable to maximize ends when they are unlimited, that is when means are scarce, because that is what it means to have an unlimited end. Economizing is made necessary and possible by cultural conditions which make ends alternative and which provide media of comparison for them. The cumulative production of these conditions is economic progress, so that the spread of economizing is a result of economic progress.

The exactness and accuracy of economic judgments are also increased by economic progress. Three degrees of exactness and accuracy can be distinguished, depending on whether neither ends nor means have an established market price, or means only have a price, or both ends and means are priced. Variations of exactness are also possible within each degree, so that the three degrees are actually parts of a continuum ranging from nearly arbitrary judgments to judgments of machinelike precision. The vaguest and most inaccurate judgments occur in dealings with semi-economic factors at the fringes of the economy, while the most exact and accurate judgments occur at the heart of the economy where markets and subsidiary techniques are well developed.

Bargaining

Bargaining is a process of fixing terms of exchange between two economic units. One engages in it in order to get as favorable terms as possible for oneself or one's cause, as part of the general attempt to maximize utility. During bargaining each side tries to control or influence the perceptions and beliefs of the other so as to induce acceptance of favorable terms. In other words, bargaining is a game, and concepts and methods of game theory apply to it. There are always two players, there are always rules, the players devise strategies and counter-strategies according to their resources, and winning depends on a combination of strategy and resources, or skill and chance. Most bargaining games are zero-sum in that one player's gain equals the other's loss, but non–zero-sum games are also possible, as I shall indicate later.

The strategies and rules of bargaining vary according to the types of control or influence available. But since the ways of controlling people are endless, there is no limit to the possible kinds of bargaining strategy. In any particular cultural and social context only a few types of strategy are possible and only a few types of rules are applicable, but out of context both rules and strategy are indeterminate. Consequently a thorough treatment of bargaining would be impossible here, and even the considerable literature on the subject represents only a beginning. To avoid getting lost in detail I shall limit myself to discussing three of the main types of control, and the types of strategy and rules related to each.

First, one can control and countercontrol through use of power. The threat to punish one's opponent changes the relative value of his action alternatives and makes it advantageous to him to accept terms he would otherwise refuse. On the other hand, counterpunishment plus the cost of using power reduce the advantage to be gained. In general, when power is the primary bargaining tool, bargaining terms tend to reflect, very approximately, the relative power of the two players; but there are many qualifications.

The first qualification is that not real power but known or imagined power is important in bargaining. If a player does not know he has power, he cannot use it; and if his opponent does not know or believe it exists, it cannot be used to influence him. Conversely, an imaginary power in whose existence one's opponent can be persuaded to believe is just as effective as a real power. This fact is one basis for the importance of bluffing, the most common and most basic ingredient in power bargaining strategy. Bluffing is especially important when power is vague and hard to measure, and in temporary short-run bargaining contacts. In long-term bargaining relations it is difficult to maintain deceptions or illusions about relative power.

A second qualification is that neither real nor imagined power but only committed power is effective in bargaining. A player must actually commit himself to the use of power before it becomes a threat to his opponent. And where there are good reasons to limit commitment, effective power relations may be quite different from actual power relations. Two rules are relevant in determining the proper amount of power to commit: (1) the more important the issue, the more power should be committed; (2) the more expensive the use of power, the less it should be committed. These rules sometimes operate to reduce power differentials. An issue may be of extreme importance to a weak power and of minor importance to a strong power, and the weak power, taking a "we have nothing to lose but our chains" attitude, may commit itself heavily enough to offset the diffident commitments of the stronger power. Deception as to the amount of power one has committed is another important form of bluffing.

A closely related qualification concerns the use of power one has committed. If the actual use of power is costly, the cost may largely offset the advantages gained, and it may be desirable to avoid actually using power. This point can be expressed in the rule that one should limit demands to those which can be obtained without having to carry out one's threat. (All these rules can be formulated in more exact mathematical terms.)

A fourth qualification is that it is often advisable to spare one's opponent for future exploitation by avoiding extreme demands that would cripple him. Thus a powerful union may limit its wage demands in order to avoid bankrupting an employer, though it could easily do so, and a strong country may spare a weaker one to keep it available for possible future coalitions.

Finally, the most important qualification is that power is never constant. It is always possible to increase one's power, for instance by coalitions, and to reduce the power of one's opponent. Consequently when power is important in bargaining, the strategies of bargaining are always intermixed with the techniques of power accumulation. Estimates of future changes in power become crucial, since each player wishes to conclude the bargain at the moment when his relative power is greatest.

However, in spite of all these and other qualifications, it still is the case that bargains cannot diverge too much from relative power positions. Since the sanction of a power bargain is power, a bargain that departs too far from power realities is always in danger of being overthrown by the losing side. This fact sets limits to the amount that can be won by even the most clever strategy.

A second type of control or influence important in bargaining is the application of norms to one's opponent. Norms are applied by reminding an opponent of his obligations, clarifying his obligations for him, or putting him under obligation. Since all social relations are built in part out of norms and since cultures provide other more general norms, this type of control is always available. Norms cannot be reduced to power, by saying that the operational force of a norm is the power of the potential group that would go into action if the norm were violated (Truman, 1951). This kind of explanation is significant in some political contexts, but fails in the characteristic cases in which a person himself believes in the norm that controls him. Here one must say that the most important and perhaps the only important member of the group giving meaning to a norm is the person controlled by it; but this is merely a roundabout way of saying that he believes he has an obligation.

Although the variety of usable norms is unlimited, several characteristic types recur frequently in bargaining situations. Most commonly one finds procedural norms which put the two players in a procedurally equal position and give them an equal chance to outwit one another. For instance, an offer ought not simply be rejected but ought to be matched by a counteroffer; a concession ought to be matched by a counterconcession; a player should be given sufficient time to explain and justify his demands and concessions. Some norms of this sort are probably a necessary part of the bargaining relationship, since without them bargaining could hardly be successful. Substantive norms which define value equivalences and priorities for exchange purposes are also common, but these must be specialized to the particular bargaining relationship and developed or adapted by the players themselves. These norms determine whether a concession is genuine, whether it matches an opponent's concession in value, whether it justifies a demand in a different area, and so on. Strategies based on these procedural and substantive norms always involve the magnifying of one's own offers and the deprecating of the opponent's concessions. They are designed to show that the opponent is unfair and they thus put moral pressure on him to yield advantages.

Another common group of norms relates to gift giving, the basic norm being that a gift ought to be repaid with a return gift. When gift norms are operative a good strategic rule is to keep one's opponent in debt, but not too far in debt. This enables one to put selective pressure on him for repayment, and also reduces his right to make further demands. In some cases the creditor has the right to suggest a return gift and the debtor is obliged to provide it; such a norm makes generosity an even more effective strategy. Bargaining then moves by gifts and countergifts rather than by demands, and the most generous donor wins.

Particularistic norms are also very common in bargaining. Such norms define obligations deriving from the particular characteristics of a bargainer or a particular relationship between bargainers. Thus in a gift exchange a rich person, or an adult, or a father or uncle are often obligated to much more than a merely equal return gift in relations with their opposites. As in all social relations, the terms of exchange are symbolic of the relationships, and exchanges between people of different status must be different, nonequal. Strategies based on these norms involve the making of subtle reminders about the special status of one's opponent, and also the exaggeration of that status (boot licking). One can also attempt to invent or simulate special relationships; thus an employer may feign extreme poverty due to hard luck, and a distant relative may exaggerate a tenuous in-law relationship. Such strategies appeal to pseudo norms and imaginary obligations, but may nevertheless be successful in short-run contacts.

Underlying all genuine norms are the basic norms of fairness and of reciprocity (chap. 4, pp. 164–166). The more particular norms are specifications of what constitutes fairness or reciprocity in a specific relationship or situation. Consequently a bargain reached through the use of norms will be relatively fair, and the players will carry it out because they think it is fair. Fairness is the sanction of a primarily normative bargain just as power is the sanction of a primarily power bargain. This fact sets limits to the amount of deception possible in strategies based on norms — if the bargain is too obviously unfair (or unreciprocal) the cheated side will try to get even.

A third type of control used in bargaining, though less frequently, is information and discussion. Such controls are made possible, among other ways, by shared goals, or at least respect for one another's goals as valid. When the goals of both sides are respected by each, bargaining takes the form of a joint inquiry into how both sets of goals can be achieved at least cost. Each player can control the other by pointing out errors in his conception of how to do this, and by providing information which redirects inquiry. The basic rule is to look for those concessions that are of least value to oneself and of most value to one's opponent, and to make those demands that are of most value to oneself and of least value to one's opponent. Since the rule applies to both players, both together search for the maximizing solution. This type of game is non–zero-sum, since A's loss need not equal B's gain, and therefore the total gains of each will exceed the total losses of each. Bargaining strategy consists (1) of providing as much information as possible about one's real feelings, preferences, frustrations, so that the opponent can better estimate the value of his concessions, and (2) of going beyond the opponent's immediate demands to his basic goals to test one's own concessions. Initial demands are treated as first approximations, to be corrected by more information and more careful comparison and prediction. There are also strategies based on pseudo respect for the goals of one's opponent and misinformation about one's own goals; these are likely to be successful only in brief contacts, since in a long-term relationship extensive deceptions can hardly be maintained.

Bargaining is always a mixture of several kinds of control in varying proportions. For instance, when discussion is used, gift-return norms and substantive norms of fairness and equity must also be present, to insure that the concessions of both sides balance out in the long run. The variety of kinds of power, of norms, and of goals, as well as the variety of possible combinations, make for endless variety in bargaining games.

Though bargaining and economizing are both economic processes in that they aim at maximizing utility, there are important contrasts between them. Economizing occurs in a market setting; bargaining, in a setting of social relations and cultural norms. Economizing is impersonal, dealing with subject matter made impersonal by a market; bargaining is personal, on subject matter given personality and character by cultural institutions. The forms of economizing depend on the condition of the market and the commodities created by it; the forms of bargaining depend on the types of control made available by a culture.

ECONOMIC VALUE

The good produced by economic progress, economic organization, and economizing is utility. This is the same good as that produced by technical rationality, which indicates again the close relationship between the two kinds of rationality. Utility is a generic term which refers to "anything you want," any end whatsoever. All ends are parts of utility, and an economic organization produces any end impartially.

Strictly speaking, utility or economic value is not identical with any end in all its particularity, but only with the goodness of an end, that which all ends have in common. Economic value is the value aspect or the value essence of any end, the aspect which is measured by price.

There is a slight difference of emphasis between the technical and the economic usage of "utility" which sometimes leads to confusion. In a technical context, utility is a means to some end or to any end; for instance, "public utilities" are means to a variety of public and private ends. In an economic context, "utility" refers to the ends themselves, or more precisely to the comparative value, the price, of the ends. The distinction is similar to that between use value and exchange value. When a person asks "What is the utility of this thing?" or more simply "What good is it?" he might be asking the technical question, "What use is it?" or the economic question, "How much is it worth?" Mill was using the term in its economic usage when he wrote "Those who know anything about the matter are aware that every writer, from Epicurus to Bentham, who maintained the theory of utility, meant by it, not something to be contradistinguished from pleasure, but pleasure itself, together with exemption from pain . . ." (1910:5). Since pleasure and the absence of pain are the only intrinsic values Mill recognizes, he uses "utility" as a generic term for all intrinsic value.[1]

Economic value or utility can also be called "pleasure" in a certain sense of the term. "Pleasure" here refers not to something psychological, but to choice; it means, "whatever you want." The term is used in this sense in the phrases "I'll do as I please," "remain in office at the Queen's pleasure," "a report will be made at the pleasure of the board." The opposite of pleasure is not pain, but duty. If the utilitarians had confined themselves to this meaning of pleasure, they would have been on sounder ground and would have avoided many fruitless psychological arguments about motivation, such as the argument whether we are motivated by a desire for pleasure or desires for specific objects.

The subjectivity of this conception of value is objected to by some (Ayres, 1942; Jordan, 1952) who think all value ought to be treated as objective. If we wish to define economic value in objective terms, it would consist not of want satisfaction but of need satisfaction. The

---

[1] Cf. Lamont, 1955:88–90, for the same distinction.

utility of an object would be not its desiredness, but its contribution to the continued activity of the consuming organization. An organization is then conceived as a productive system which takes in necessary resources and transforms them into products, which it exchanges for more resources. Surplus value is used for expansion of activities, creation of new organizations (children), control of future resources, or is wasted. The choice between these two alternate conceptions of economic value is not of direct concern here, since both can be so formulated as to fit the observed facts of economic and technological progress. That is, progress can either be described as producing a greater quantity of satisfactions of desire, or as enabling a greater number of organizations, including organisms, to continue activity in a more secure fashion.

Since utility in the economic sense is a comparative value, it appears only in ends that are alternative to other ends. Insofar as an end is unique, it cannot be part of an economy and be subject to economizing. A unique end might be said to have infinite utility, except that this concept makes no sense, since calculation cannot deal with infinites.

For example, freedom is sometimes thought of as a unique value, a priceless good. Silone expresses this conception in his account of a conversation with a Russian publisher. The Russian says, " 'We're glad we haven't got your liberty, but we've got the sanatoria in exchange.' . . . I observed that the expression 'in exchange' had no meaning, 'liberty not being merchandise that could be exchanged' " (1950:102–103).

Salvation is another example of a supposedly noneconomic good. Salvation is a definite end, so it can have means and a technique of achievement; but it is not alternative to any other end. It is priceless. The technical question, "What must I do to be saved?" makes sense and can be answered; but the economic question, "How much is salvation worth to you?" does not.

The limits of economic value are the same as the limitations on the applicability of economic calculation. Both are limited to comparable ends, that is, ends which have been made comparable by economic progress. Whether any particular end is a utility or not depends, therefore, not so much on its intrinsic nature as on the extent of economic progress at any given time. To be sure, values are sometimes changed considerably by becoming utilities. Thus a freedom which had a price put on it would not be the same as a freedom valued as the precondition for all other values; and a friendship preserved only because of its high dollar value would not be the same friendship any more. Some values can never be treated as utilities without losing their essential characteristics as values. Three of these will be discussed in the following chapters.

Chapter 3

Social Rationality

The theory of social relations has undergone a great development in the present century, which is still continuing. One part of the theory, however, that is concerned with the rationality of social relations, has remained undeveloped. In fact, quite often social relations and social action are thought of as irrational or nonrational, in contrast with economic action. I shall be concerned in this chapter with the way in which social relations can be rational, and with the type of decisions appropriate to them. I shall retain the contrast between social and economic action, but argue that it is a contrast between two opposed forms of rationality, rather than between rational and nonrational action.

One reason for the lack of understanding of social rationality is that it is almost entirely unconscious in its working, whereas economic, technical, and legal rationality are all in large part conscious. Since the study of unconscious processes is of recent origin, traditional theories of practical reason could not deal adequately with unconscious rationality, and have had to give undue prominence to the conscious types of reasoning.

SOCIAL RELATIONS, ROLES, AND SOCIAL SYSTEMS

A social relation (interpersonal relation) is a pattern of shared experience. It develops whenever two people interact in more than a momentary way. Each relation includes an action component, namely the things people do together, and a feeling component or "cathexis," namely the feelings they express and share with each other. For example, in the neighbor relation the action component includes saying hello, talking briefly about certain subjects, borrowing and helping each other to a certain extent. The feeling component is a mild degree of friendliness, from which dependent and paternal feelings are excluded. Action and feeling components cannot normally be separated to any extent. Action is the vehicle through which feeling is expressed; action is the form and feeling is the content of a relationship. Action can occur without corresponding feeling, but then it is not the same action any more. The same is true for feeling apart from action.

Any relation that endures for even a short time develops in addition a conceptual component, which is how the two people involved think of their relationship. This includes beliefs, namely how each person thinks he and his partner are acting and feeling; obligations, consisting of how each thinks he ought to act and feel or is expected to act and feel; expectations, consisting of how *others* expect him to act and feel; and ideals, conceptions of what behavior is ideally desirable though not normally to be expected. Obligations and expectations serve to direct behavior and make it predictable. A well-developed relation includes a variety of different expectations and obligations, which provide a basis for action in a variety of foreseeable circumstances. Ideals, on the other hand, are a basis for changing obligations in new, unforeseeable circumstances.

The total conception of what each person is and ought to be doing and feeling is called his role. Thus from a conceptual standpoint every social relation is composed of a complementary pair of roles. Often these pairs are opposites, as with husband-wife, teacher-student, buyer-seller relations; sometimes they are equal and symmetrical, as with neighbors.

Roles are by no means always clear and internally consistent, nor do they necessarily correspond to real feelings and actions. Instead, all role components may be more or less different or opposed both to each other and to the real relation. For example, a husband might actually have a dependent and hostile relation to his wife, think of himself as lazy, amiable, and humorous, feel he ought to be more responsible and serious, and entertain several vague, semiconscious, and unconscious ideals of the super-capable, dependable, witty, aggressive, easy-going husband. If there is considerable opposition between a person's role and his feelings, or if the feelings themselves are in conflict, it may be difficult or even impossible for him to express his feelings toward his partner. In this case we say that he is unable to relate in a given area, even though he may go through all the prescribed actions. When a person is unable to relate his feelings to real people, he will turn toward substitute or symbolic objects or toward imaginary objects.

Ordinarily, however, the various components of a relation maintain some degree of internal consistency. Each component interacts with all the others and shapes them to some degree, with a resulting gradual increase of consistency. Action is shaped to a considerable extent by feeling since it expresses feeling, but feeling is also changed to some extent by changes of action. Beliefs, obligations, expectations, and even ideals shape action readily and feeling with more difficulty, and are in turn modified to conform to feelings and actions.

The conceptual or role component of a relation is usually institutionalized, that is, shared by all members of a society and reinforced by a group identification, sanctions, ceremonies, education, and other devices. An institutionalized role is called a cultural role, and is exemplified, with variations, in a number of particular social relations. When an anthropologist gets information about some culture from an informant, he will hear about cultural roles rather than about particular social relations. He will hear about what husbands ought to do, what they can usually be expected to do, and sometimes, if the informant wishes to make a good impression, what they ideally would do. Accounts of what particular husbands actually did might then be added as examples, but only by way of clarifying the cultural role.

All the roles in a culture, taken together, constitute its system of social relations, or more simply its social system. A social system, then, is an organization of cultural roles, including expectations, obligations, and ideals. Like a drama, it provides actors with complementary roles and enables them to act together. Unlike a drama, social systems provide only generalized cues and suggestions, leaving the actors the task of creating their roles and relations in detail. As individuals get older they shift from one set of roles to another, each time gaining a new perspective on the common life, the social system, that all share.

To the outside observer, a social system may seem like a static abstraction from the particular living, changing social relations he observes, and he may even think that it is a mere construct of his own imagination. Yet for the participants themselves it is more than an abstraction or a construct; it is the precondition of their forming social relations at all. It is only by sharing a common social system that they can understand one another's behavior and can form relations with one another. Without it they would not know how to act, or how to interpret one another's actions so as to respond adequately. Once two people have established a real relation they can go beyond the general hints and meanings supplied by the social system and create their own unique variations; but without the initial common understanding supplied by a common culture they could not even make a start.

Some people suppose that human beings have an innate knowledge of how to respond to one another; but this is largely false. Apart from a few gestures, cries, and facial expressions the meaning of human behavior is culturally learned. When an anthropologist visits an unfamiliar culture he tries to get beyond his stock of innate responses as rapidly as possible. He immediately takes a role in the new culture, the role of stranger or newcomer, learns the proper responses, establishes relations, and then goes on to learn new and more specialized roles.

Since social systems are the only basis for forming social relations, it is necessary for them to be complete. They must have some role available for everybody so that no one is permanently left out. All conceivable human behavior must fit into some role so that it can be assigned some meaning and be responded to. Completeness is insured by the existence of residual roles, which are available for people who do not fit more specific roles. Residual roles include, for outsiders, such roles as stranger, enemy, newcomer, potential convert or customer or ally; for insiders, roles such as eccentric, criminal, insane, saint, subversive, idealist.

The totality of roles that a person has learned to take during his life, together with the system of cathexes developed in these roles, constitute his personality (cf. H. S. Sullivan, 1949; G. H. Mead, 1934). Some of these roles are recognized and accepted, and these constitute the self. Others, usually more numerous, are not recognized and are rejected, and these are the not-self, the "it" which comes out in strange and regrettable behavior.

Since personality is composed of roles and cathexes, all personality change consists of either a change in existing social relations or the taking on of a new role. This does not mean that personality is a fickle, easily changeable thing; quite the contrary. Once a role and its accompanying cathexis is learned, it is never entirely eliminated from the personality, although it may change considerably. When a new role is learned old roles and feelings flow into it and condition it, or if this is not possible they become submerged or otherwise modified to accommodate the new role. Sometimes a personality cannot accommodate itself to a proposed new role at all, and it remains an alien, unattainable type of behavior or an obviously external sort of play acting.[1]

The first roles and cathexes that one learns in life are the most important ones. They are the foundation and core of the personality. They enter into and condition all later roles, and set permanent limits to the changes possible in the personality. All learning is a perpetual return to the task of changing, reworking, readapting them, and this task is each person's biggest lifelong problem. All changes of personality are variations and reaffirmations of the roles and feelings learned in the first years of life. Even in times of rapid social change, when social systems are in flux and people are determined to break with the past, changes in personality stay within limits set by early cathexes. The more personality changes, the more it stays the same.

The self, on the other hand, can sometimes undergo radical transformation. A new role or some crisis may upset the balance of a personality so that dominant roles become submerged and formerly submerged roles become dominant as a new self. Subjectively this feels like the birth of a new man, though the personality as a whole still remains essentially the same.

Since personality is composed entirely of social roles and cathexes, all action, thought, and feeling has a basic social aspect. There is no purely individual area of action; individuality is to be sought for in the unique development of social relations and roles, not apart

---

[1] Sometimes the term "role" is used to refer to external play acting which conceals the real self and its feelings (for example, Goffman, 1956). In this usage roles are parts only of superficial, polite social relations and are excluded from the deep relations which constitute the core of the self. This usage should not be confused with the broader one I am following.

from them. Conduct that appears to be individual in the sense of being nonsocial is actually social in some disguised form; for example, "selfishness" is often a disguised form of dependency and/or rebellion, "impersonal" behavior may express feelings of alienation, rejection, or rivalry, "poetic fantasy" and communion with nature are usually a symbolic repetition of earlier relations to one's mother. The object of the social behavior need not be actually present, but may be represented by some symbol.

The assertion that all sustained feelings, actions, and ideas are social does not imply that one ought to neglect one's inner life. It does not imply that one ought to forsake contemplation, fantasy, and privacy for a life of talk and group activity. Philosophers such as Dewey who assert the ubiquity of the social are sometimes misunderstood in this fashion. On the contrary, the assertion implies that even one's inner life is social, since it develops from cathexes learned in social relations. How far one should cultivate a private life, and whether cultivation or neglect are even possible, is an entirely different question.

To be sure, conduct also has a biological, instinctual base and to that extent is not social. But the biological element, taken by itself, would consist only of reflex and random actions, unorganized bursts of feeling, and general temperamental tendencies (impulses, in Dewey's sense). Sustained, developed emotions and organized action have to be learned, and are learned only by participating in a system of social relations.

Since personality is formed only in the matrix of a social system, all people sharing a common social system can be expected to have broadly similar personalities. They are all assigned the same childhood roles, and although these admit of a wide range of individual interpretation, the variations can be expected to cluster around some modal or typical pattern. A similarity of roles can be expected to produce a similarity of emotional response and thus a similarity of cathectic patterns. The variety of adult relations are in turn a development of the possibilities implicit in the common childhood roles, so that the same clustering of individual interpretations will continue. Thus for any social system a typical personality can be constructed. This construct has been called "Basic Personality" (Kardiner, 1945), "Modal Personality," "Status Personality" (Linton, 1949), and "Social Character" (Fromm, 1949). Unlike social systems, personalities, and social relations, a basic personality does not exist in its own right as a dynamic entity; it is an abstraction created by the observer of a culture. It is neither a norm, nor an ideal, nor a person, nor an event or transaction, but a statistical mode. It is, however, useful in understanding the dynamics of social systems, since it represents the most frequent personal reaction to, and action on, social systems. Just as individual personalities and particular social relations are continually interacting, so the typical basic personality and the universal social system are continually acting on one another. Only it is not the basic personality which interacts, but rather individual personalities; and the basic personality construct is the modal generalization of individual actions.

So far we have considered social relations, social systems, and social action only insofar as they involve human beings. The world of social relations, however, extends beyond human beings to include animals, inanimate objects, and indeed the whole of nature.

Human beings establish social relations to nonhuman objects by extending and transferring feelings learned in human relations. Pets, for instance, take the place of humans when they are assigned roles as children or companions. Sometimes relations with animals serve as substitute outlets for feelings that cannot be expressed in human relations; thus a person in a subservient social position may take a dominating role with animals, or a person who has difficulty expressing deep love toward humans may find it possible to love animals instead. Nature may come to be the object of feelings originally developed in relations with one's mother, a fact which has been expressed in myths about the earth mother and mother nature. Finally, one's relation to God, or to the universe in general, is a transfer and extension of earlier relations with parents.

A much more important use of nonhuman objects, however, is as symbols of human relations. Symbols evoke the feelings one has for other people when they are absent, and strengthen them when they are present. The use of pictures and mementos for this purpose is worldwide; and places, such as houses, churches, and towns, have an even stronger effect in calling up past relationships. Students often find themselves displaying unaccountably childish behavior when they return home, even when parents are not present, and their more mature self does not reappear until they are back in school buildings. Adults sometimes experience the same uncomfortable regressive feelings on re-entering schools.

Group relationships are also symbolized by nonhuman objects — flags, totemic objects, places, heirlooms, and like objects. These symbols evoke the individual's group role, his loyalty, rebellion, obligations, ideals, and the group's expectations toward him.

Frequently the power of symbols to call up old relations is not consciously noticed or understood. Milk, and food in general, is a universal maternal symbol in our culture; but people frequently do not recognize the direct connection between their conscious attitude toward milk and their unconscious attitude toward a maternal relation. Cigars and cigarettes often have a similar symbolic function, and an enormous variety of objects — jewels, shoes, feet, trees, cars, horses, gardens, flowers, water, high places, and such — are standard unconscious symbols. The language of dreams employs these symbols to express hidden feelings belonging to unrecognized roles, and mythology is rich in the same symbolism.

Unless the continuous symbolic significance of nonhuman objects is recognized much human behavior and feeling is inexplicable or misunderstood, and its degree of irrationality is exaggerated. Most, and perhaps all, human attitudes toward nonhuman objects are conditioned by social relations and roles which they symbolize. The symbols either stand for the other person in the relation, in which case they call forth role-playing behavior and feelings; or they stand for the relationship itself, in which case they evoke their unconscious attitude toward that relation. Thus people's feelings of desire, dislike, avoidance, longing, and so forth toward inanimate objects and places express unrecognized relations and constitute cases of social action in disguise.

Human beings also frequently stand as symbols of social relations. An individual may stand directly for another person, and call up the feelings and actions originally directed toward the other person. In psychology this is called transference. Transference is a special, extreme case of the universal tendency of old roles and relations to flow into and condition new ones; in this case the new role is basically a repetition of the old one in disguise. Or another person may stand for one's self or a part of one's personality, in which case attitudes toward self (or not-self) are projected on to the symbolic person. Children are frequently used as symbols, both of other people and of one's self in former relationships. Transference or projection to children is especially easy because they repeat the relational patterns of one's own childhood, in which the basic roles constituting one's personality have been learned. Thus an oldest son can readily symbolize oneself as oldest son, and a younger son stand for one's younger brother.

Frequently a whole race will stand for some part of one's personality, usually a rejected part. This is race prejudice. Attitudes toward the alien part of one's personality are projected on to the alien race, accompanied by elaborate rationalizations. Shakespeare gives a striking illustration of this process in the last scene of *Othello*, when Othello identifies himself-as-guilty with the despised Turkish race. In this example the attitude toward the alien race is redirected to its original object, and the circle is completed.

Human beings and actions also symbolize groups and group relations. Of all the functions of kings, their symbolic function has best stood the test of time; and most smaller groups have a similar "figure-head" who evokes and focuses group attitudes toward himself (cf. Hegel, 1942, sec. 275ff.). Ceremonial and ritual actions are used by all groups to symbolize the group to its members and to strengthen group relations. In ceremonies every conceivable sort of object, animal, person, and action can be used as vivid symbols of the group. The classical study of ceremony as group symbol is Durkheim's *Elementary Forms of the Religious Life* (1947).

One more use of nonhuman objects in social relations remains to be mentioned, and this is perhaps the most important use of all. It is the use of objects as cues for role playing. Cues are used to send information about the role one is playing and the roles one expects others to play in response. They are vital in establishing rapport, that is, in activating a relation; and even after relations have been activated, cues must be used to indicate detailed developments in roles and role expectations. When cue confusion (Bennett and McKnight, 1956) occurs, social relations fail to get established, and the result is misunderstanding, anxiety, and anger for all concerned. Cues occur in all social communication, and especially at the beginning and early stages of a relation. In the language of information theory, cues are instructions on how to interpret information.

Some standard cue objects are clothes, hairdo, houses and furnishings, cars, office furnishings, location in the office, business location, and the like. These are used to indicate the general social position one is assuming and how he expects to be treated. Clothes in particular can be varied in subtle conventional ways to indicate the exact degree of formality one expects, to express various kinds and degrees of feeling and indicate what emotional responses are appropriate, and to call attention to specific relationships and group memberships (uniforms). More detailed cues are provided by the style of one's language, by bearing, gestures, and inflection. People learn to perceive and interpret all these cues subconsciously, and to respond in equally subconscious ways with cues of their own. Frequently a person intent on deception unknowingly gives himself away through cues he cannot help sending.

In most formal group meetings the roles of group members are indicated by cue objects. The group leader is always placed in a special position, and the degree of his authority is indicated by the height of his seat and its distance from the other members. Thus in most classrooms the teacher's role is cued by his raised platform, extra-large desk, and privilege of walking freely about the room. Leaders can indicate a personal deviation from their ordinary or official role by other cues which show disrespect or some other deviational attitude toward the official cue objects.

Gifts are another standard kind of cue, used to indicate kind and intensity of relationship. Reciprocal and equal gifts indicate a peer relation, while giving less than one receives indicates a dependent relation, as between children and parents.

Thus the nonhuman world is a vital part of any system of social relations, in the form of cues and symbols. Social relations live and develop by means of nonhuman objects, and indeed could hardly occur at all without them.

In summary, social relations are patterns of shared action and feeling. Each participant in a relation has a cathexis, that is, a feeling which is attached to the other person and which is expressed in action. Social actions are given pattern by cultural roles, which include expectations, obligations, and ideals. A system of cultural roles is a social system. Personality is the whole set of cathexes and roles which a person has learned during his life. The concept of basic personality is a construct indicating the typical personality produced by and in response to a social system. Nonhuman objects are used both as direct objects of relations and more usually as symbols and cues.

The world of social relations is very nearly the whole of life. All human actions have a primary social aspect as role-playing behavior, and all nonhuman objects can be used as symbols and cues of roles and relations. An account of a culture which described only its social system and basic personality structure, without explicit reference to economic, political, and legal institutions, would be very nearly a complete account. It is only when one looks at the diachronic development of a culture that nonsocial aspects begin to attract attention. Technological progress and economic progress become noticeable very readily when they are present, and other developmental trends appear on closer observation. But to an ordinary member of a society even these trends are noticeable primarily in the way they affect his social relations, rather than as developments in their own right. Technological and economic progress attract attention because of their constructive or disruptive effect on social relations, rather than for the increased utility they provide. Social relations and social systems are the very core of life, and all other aspects are peripheral in comparison.

SOCIAL TRENDS

The characteristics of economic and technological progress appear most clearly in Western culture, and especially in those features differentiating it from preliterate cultures. Trends in social systems, on the other hand, are most clearly observable in certain primitive cultures. Since primitive cultures have been relatively undisturbed by the disruptive effects of rapid economic progress, their social systems have been left free to develop in their own intrinsic fashion. The social system of Western culture, in contrast, has been continually forced to accommodate itself to economic, technological, legal, and other changes, and thus could not develop independently. It has been to a large extent a dependent variable, and has indeed often appeared more as a hindrance to economic and other changes (under the title "custom" or "tradition") than as a source of change in its own right.

Not all preliterate cultures are equally suitable for observation of trends in social systems. Many of them have been subject to important noneconomic disruptive influences, particularly to culture contact and its resulting wars, migrations, revolutions, and imperialisms. Only where culture contact has been minimal for a long period of time, that is, in small isolated cultures, have social systems been able to exhibit their own inherent trends of development fully. It is in these isolated cultures that social trends and social rationality can best be studied.

Social trends can also be studied fruitfully in small groups, especially those that are artificially isolated for a time. Small groups exhibit the same developmental trends as larger societies and cultures, but in a much more particularized way, so that the smallest details of change can be observed. On the other hand, small groups can be isolated and studied for only a short period of time, during which only the barest beginnings of structural development can occur. For instance, compare Homans' study of the development of a small group in the bank wiring room with his study of the fully developed Tikopia family system (Homans, 1950, chaps. 3, 9).

The basic trend of social systems, when isolated, is toward greater integration. A system is integrated when the activity of each part fits into and completes the activity of other parts, and when in addition each part supports, confirms, and reinforces other parts by its activity. A social system is integrated when the roles of which it is composed are internally consistent and fit together. More specifically, it is integrated when all the obligations belonging to a single role are consistent with one another, when the obligations of each role agree with the expectations other people have for that role, when both obligations and expectations are as consistent with ideals as external circumstances permit, and when the sequence of roles a person is expected to take are so similar and graduated that it is psychologically possible to grow into each successive role.

A social relation is integrated when the obligations, expectations, beliefs, and ideals of each role are consistent with one another and with the feelings and desires of the person taking the role, and when both roles and both sets of feelings fit together and support one another. A personality is integrated when all the cathexes and roles of which it is composed blend together into a single dominant feeling complex and a single self-concept, and when the self and the not-self shade into one another without any sharp division or opposition.

Integration is something more than both mechanical efficiency and logical consistency. The parts of a smoothly running machine or an efficient business organization fit into each other, but offer no mutual support. Each part remains the same whether it is working in the machine or separated from it. The reason each part remains unchanged by its interaction is that the parts do not really act on one another, as in a social relation, but merely transmit energy through one another. The distinction between a machine and a social system is that between an impersonal set of relations and a personal set, between a system of interactions and a system of transactions, in Dewey and Bentley's sense (Dewey and Bentley, 1949). Similarly, a set of logically consistent propositions may fit together in the sense that each adds some new affirmation to the total set, and none affirms what any other denies; but still each proposition remains a distinct entity and is not changed by its association with other propositions. If on the other hand each proposition were to illuminate the others, add meaning to them, provide supporting reasons for them, and make them more plausible, the set would be integrated or coherent. It would be similar to the belief system of an integrated culture, in which each separate belief supports, confirms, and enriches the meaning of other beliefs.

Integration, like technological progress, develops through a selective process in which both individuals and social systems participate. Individuals in social relations try to reduce conflicts and tensions within roles and between roles. They try to live up to their obligations a little more and to find some accommodation between conflicting obligations; or, if obligations are too severe and are unattainable, they substitute more realistic obligations and turn the unattainable ones into ideals. They learn to temper their role expectations, and to conform in some degree with the expectations of others toward them.

However, individual integrative activity is often feeble and ineffective, and is also accompanied by nonintegrative tendencies; tendencies to balk at others' expectations, to reject obligations, to make conflicting demands, and to serve conflicting ideals. But social systems select the successful products of individual activity and eliminate the failures, so that the total result is a gradual increase of integration of the whole system.

Systems which exhibit this double process, of individual effort and social selection, are called integrative systems. Social systems are the primary examples of integrative systems, but also any relatively independent part of a social system, as well as personalities and individual social relations, may be called integrative systems.

The basis of selection in integrative systems is the fact that integration brings with it stability and resistance to change. The more tightly interconnected a system of roles, cathexes, or beliefs is, the greater will be the support of each role for every other one, and the greater the resistance of the whole system to change. The presence of conflict, on the other hand, brings weakness and instability with it, and the greater the conflict, the greater the instability. Because of this instability, systems that are in conflict tend to develop a variety of random changes in conflict areas, and to keep changing until the conflicts are reduced. Thus the total amount of conflict in a system tends very gradually to reduce and the degree of integration to increase, as long as new conflicts are not induced from outside the system.

Well-integrated systems resist change because of the mutual support of their parts for each other. For example, suppose that in a certain social system mothers and daughters typically have personalities of such a sort that they get along together with a minimum of conflict. Suppose also that it is right for mothers and daughters to live close together and share their daily lives with each other. In this situation, several things will happen: living together will strengthen the mother-daughter relationship; this will strengthen the feminine, mother-daughter identification and stabilize the feminine personality structure through successive generations; and the role obligation to live together will be accepted more firmly because of its agreement with what people like to do. The longer this situation persists, the more resistance to change it will develop.

Conflict removes the mutual support of roles, cathexes, and beliefs for each other and thus exposes them to forces of change. This can be observed in single roles and relations as well as in systems of relations. Conflicts of obligation and expectation within a single role, for instance, expose individuals who take the role to constant doubt and anxiety about their actions. Whatever they do seems to be wrong or to have bad results. Some of this doubt will be turned toward the norms of the role, leading to a devaluation of the norms and a search for different norms. Some doubt and anxiety will be turned inward to other parts of the personality or outward to other roles, bringing instability wherever it is turned. The doubts and the search for different norms will continue, generation after generation, until more consistent sets of expectations and obligations are developed and institutionalized. The instability of the feminine role in our culture is an example of this; conflicts of expectations toward women, along with conflicts of identification and other conflicts, produce a widespread dissatisfaction with the feminine role and a search for new role content. A great variety of solutions are invented and tried out, and most of them disappear within a generation. The solutions that last will be those that provide some place for most of the different kinds of feelings developed in women, and most of the actions and feelings expected of women. These solutions would in turn be subject to further selection, apart from external interference, with the more conflicting, anxiety-provoking combinations gradually dropping out.

The same thing is true for individual relations in a social system. If the husband-wife relation is full of conflict in a given culture, for instance, that relation and the whole area around it will be marked by instability. A great many particular marriages will break up, and there will be a search both for new and different partners and for new living arrangements. Depending on the culture, various substitute arrangements will begin to appear; clan relations might become stronger and more important, with marriage a casual and temporary affair, or lovers and mistresses might become more prominent as substitute relations, or new family living arrangements and even new forms of marriage might develop. Which of these arrangements survives depends on which fits best into the other social relations of the system and also provides a place for the cathexes developed by husbands and wives.

The stability of an individual role or relation depends not only on its internal consistency but also on how it fits with all other parts of its social system. For example, if an internally consistent feminine role could develop in our culture, it would not necessarily survive just through its own consistency. It would in addition have to make possible a good, conflict-free mother-daughter relation, so that the role could be passed on through identification to succeeding generations; also the role must fit sufficiently well into existing husband-wife relations to permit holders of the role to marry successfully, raise children, and transmit the role to them; and finally, the role must permit good mother-son relations because these are part of the foundations of the husband-wife relation. Conversely, conflicts in any of these relations will produce echoing conflicts and uncertainties in the feminine role, as well as in other roles.

Thus a high degree of conflict in any part of a social system will produce instability in large areas of the system, and the experimental development of new roles and relations will be intensified until a higher degree of over-all integration is developed.

The effect of conflict in producing readiness to change has frequently been observed in studies of acculturation. One of the principles of acculturation is that the less integrated fringe areas of a social system are most receptive (*ceteris paribus*) to new cultural influences and most likely to be acculturated, while the more integrated roles and relations will resist acculturation the longest. Thus in cultures such as the Navaho, where feminine roles are relatively well integrated and supported by good mother-daughter and clan relations, while masculine roles contain more conflict and are weakened by relatively poorer father-son and husband-wife relations, women and women's roles have been much more resistant to acculturation than men and men's roles. Conversely, in Japanese-Americans a far more rapid rate of acculturation has been observed to occur in women than in men, and this is probably associated with the existence of severe strain in traditional Japanese feminine roles. The same is true of cultures as a whole: relatively well-integrated cultures such as the Hopi have resisted acculturation much more thoroughly than have looser, less integrated cultures such as the Navaho. The principle that integration means resistance to acculturation is only one of a number of principles necessary for explaining acculturation, and in the examples cited other factors have contributed to the results cited; but still the degree of integration is one of the factors affecting acculturation and culture change.

The integrative trend rarely develops to any great extent in most cultures, because of both external and internal interference; but if left undisturbed, it could theoretically go on indefinitely. External interference is provided by geographical changes and by culture contact, both of which necessitate extensive and rapid culture change; also by economic and technological progress, which also produce rapid culture change. Rapid change almost inevitably produces considerable individual conflict and cultural disorganization, thus undoing the results of past integration and setting new integrative problems.

Apart from external interferences, there is also an internal check on the integrative trend. This is produced by a secondary social trend, the trend toward equilibrium. Equilibrium results from a different mode of social selection out of the same individual efforts that also result in integration.

A system is in equilibrium when opposing forces within it balance each other and hold in check the actions and changes which each one by itself would produce. For example, a single social relation is in equilibrium when two opposing cathexes, such as love and hate for the same person, balance each other and prevent both a strengthening and a deepening of the relation or a weakening of it. A personality might be in equilibrium between opposed cathexes and roles — a feeling of dependency toward a father figure being opposed to a set of obligations and expectations demanding independent, decisive action. In this case the establishment and consolidation of dependent relations would be prevented by the sense of obligation to be independent, and the taking of an independent role would be hindered by the dependency feelings.

An equilibrium does not as a rule involve a complete paralysis of action, but rather reveals itself in behavior that oscillates between the two sets of forces. Thus the relationship marked by love-hate or other ambivalence would oscillate between periods of closeness and affection and periods of quarreling and separation. The person who combined dependent feelings with a duty to be responsible and decisive might succeed in being decisive part of the day and helpless the rest, or decisive toward some people or in some situations and dependent toward other people; or his relation to a single person might go through a regular cycle of independence-dependence-independence. In this way both forces are expressed in action, but each is checked in its further development by the other.

A social system is in equilibrium when it contains two integrated sets of roles which are in conflict with each other. For example in pre-acculturated Navaho society, and in many other matrilineal societies, there is a conflict between the clan system and the family. The clan roles demand loyalty and frequent visits to relatives or even living with them; they demand of men that they take care of their sisters and show preference for their sisters' children over their wives' children; they demand that relatives work together, share property, and help each other. Clan roles are reinforced by strong emotional ties between relatives, especially mothers and daughters. Family roles demand fidelity to one's spouse, mutual affection, and independence from relatives. These roles are reinforced by attachments between fathers and children, though in some matrilineal societies fathers and children are not officially related at all. Each system, clan and family, is a consistent, self-contained set of roles, and each opposes the other.

An equilibrium differs from a simple conflict in that it involves additional forces which freeze the conflict and prevent it from being resolved. A simple conflict tends to weaken both conflicting factors and produce a series of changes aimed at reducing the conflict; but in an equilibrium this is prevented. For example, the clan-family equilibrium mentioned above expresses itself for men in the necessity of having to travel back and forth between their wife and their mother(s), neither of whom are allowed to see the other. If this were a simple conflict or an individual problem it would be inherently unstable and would soon change or disappear. The man would decide either that it was silly to visit his mother so much, or that he should not have taken on the additional burden of supporting a wife in view of his obligations toward his mother, or he would move his wife and his mother closer together. If this were a simple social conflict, all these variations and more would soon appear, and the more integrative solutions would gradually begin to predominate and become stabilized. In other words, the integrative trend would appear.

But in an equilibrium none of these variations is possible. Manifold clan ties prevent a man from discarding his duties toward mothers and sisters, or from desiring to do so in most cases. The same clan obligations prevent him from moving mother and wife together, since this would remove the wife from her clan and prevent her relatives from fulfilling clan obligations. Family ties, supported by hostilities within the clan and other factors, more or less prevent the family system from breaking up. Thus there is no way out; the good family man must continue to divide his actions and affections between family and clan, and the conflict persists.

The above example also illustrates why there is always a trend toward equilibrium in social systems and indeed in all integrative systems. An equilibrium is resistant to change, in a way that simple conflicts are not. Although simple conflicts tend to change and be resolved as part of the integrative process, a conflict in which each side is supported by an integrated system of forces resists change.

Thus a selective process takes place, in which simple conflicts tend to disappear nearly as fast as they occur, while those conflicts involved in an equilibrium of forces tend to persist. Among equilibria as well, the large, complex ones tend to outlast the simple ones. The large equilibria tend to draw more and more of the social system into a great polarization of forces, as each side absorbs and integrates more roles into itself. Thus the Navaho family-clan equilibrium tends to divide the legal system between loyal partiality to clan and impartiality for all; it tends to divide occupation and property holding into two types, to polarize attitudes toward Western culture, and so forth.

Integration and equilibrium are the two rival forms of social selection. Each is a source of stability in roles, cathexes, and relations, and each selects from the same basic human attempts to resolve conflicts, adjust roles, mediate differences.

The tendency to equilibrium is the primary internal check on the integrative trend. As soon as an equilibrium develops between two parts of a social system or two directions of change, further integration is halted or severely slowed down. And because of the great length of time required for a whole social system to become well integrated, one or more equilibria are almost certain to develop. Thus even a social system completely isolated from external disturbances is unlikely to increase its degree of integration indefinitely.

Of the two processes, integration can be regarded as primary for two reasons. First, all cultures must maintain some degree of integration to exist at all, while equilibrium is unnecessary except in special circumstances. Second, even an equilibrium is dependent for its stability on some degree of over-all integration of its parts. If the two sides of an equilibrium were not held together by some common elements or some mutual support, they would simply separate or destroy each other. Also each side of an equilibrium is dependent on internal integration for the power to resist the forces opposing it.

Besides integration and equilibrium, two other developmental trends have been thought to occur in all social systems. They are stratification, that is, a hierarchical distribution of status and prestige leading to the development of a class structure, and also the distribution of authority in some more or less consistent pattern. However, these are better classified as legal trends, since they are basically similar to generally recognized legal trends and dissimilar to the integrative trend, and since they develop in legal rather than in social systems, as will be indicated in chapter 4.

One might also ask whether disorganization is a trend, since it is a cumulative process that occurs in many social systems. It is not a trend because it does not establish any describable pattern, but moves rather toward the absence of pattern, that is toward chaos. Disorganization cannot be described positively, but only negatively as the removal of some established pattern. It consists either of a loss of integration or of the disturbance of an equilibrium. Chaos in turn cannot be discussed positively, but only negatively as the absence of some type of order. To paraphrase a saying of Plato, chaos is the "other" of order. There are as many types of chaos as there are types of order, and the various types do not necessarily occur together. A social chaos would be a situation in which there were no generally accepted roles and consequently no social relations; an economic chaos would be a situation in which there was no unit of value measurement common to any two things, and consequently no way of determining the comparative value of anything. Although a complete social or economic chaos could not possibly exist, a considerable degree of social chaos could exist together with a considerable degree of economic organization, and vice versa.

RATIONAL SOCIAL ORGANIZATION

The universality of the integrative trend indicates that some principle of effectiveness is present. Social relations and social systems would not tend so persistently to become more integrated unless the result was somehow effective. What kind of effectiveness is involved here?

Integration occurs in social systems, in actual social relations, and in personalities conceived as systems of roles. Consequently the effectiveness would be in doing whatever it is that all of these systems do. But all of them are action systems; they make action of all sorts possible. Consequently if integration increases the effectiveness of action systems, the effectiveness in question is that of promoting action.

Integration is a logical precondition for the successful completion of any social action. It makes action possible by (1) channeling the necessary emotional energy and preventing it from being diffused and lost; (2) eliminating conflicts, which would block action; (3) providing supporting factors which strengthen action and carry it to completion. Also, (4) it makes action meaningful (Dewey, 1930, part IV, sec. 1) by relating it to past actions which it fulfills and to future actions which preserve and continue its achievement. An isolated action, with no history and no consequences, is insignificant; it disappears and is forgotten. An action integrated into a continuing system of action lives on in its effects, and gives one the consciousness of participating in a larger venture.

An integrated social system is therefore a rational one, since it is effective in making action possible and meaningful, and the integrative trend in social systems is a trend toward rational social organization. The case is exactly parallel to that of economic organization and economic progress.

The same conclusion follows if we reconsider the selective process which produces the integrative trend. An integrative system resists change because action is continually being carried to successful completion in it. The energy available to the system is channeled, used up, and regenerated continually. In an unintegrated system energy is blocked, and exerts pressure for random substitute outlets; this pressure makes the system receptive to change in that new outlets for blocked energy will be promptly used. In other words, an integrative system is resistant to change because it is effective in making action possible; and an unintegrated system is open to change because it is ineffective.

When I say that an integrated system makes action successful I mean only that action proceeds to its own internal completion, whatever that may be. A successfully completed action need not be efficient, though it may be. Nor do I mean to imply that a highly integrated social system or social relation, because it resists change, is also effective in promoting the survival of the society that has it. That proposition is probably false, as Gouldner (1959) has shown. Survival of a whole society is a more ultimate criterion of effectiveness which is not in question here. Integration promotes the survival of the social system rather than the survival of the people in a society. What happens in extreme cases is that a highly integrated social system remains unchanged but people desert it and take on a new social system.

Let us consider the rational social organization produced by the integrative process in more detail. It has five primary characteristics. First, roles are internally consistent. That is, the various obligations and expectations comprising a role are consistent both with one another and with the ideals for that role. A consistent role enables the person taking the role to act in a straightforward fashion so that other people attempting to relate to him can understand, predict, and respond to his behavior successfully. Behavior of this sort might be said to have integrity.

Consistency is an elusive sort of thing, difficult to define and to measure. A set of obligations, expectations, and ideals is consistent if a person finds it possible to carry out all of them without great strain; but whether or not this is possible depends as much on the person taking the role as it does on the role itself. A role that is consistent for one person may seem impossibly contradictory to another. For instance, a judge's role is, ideally, to dispense both justice and mercy; but where one judge will find this possible on the whole, another judge may succeed only in being sometimes just and sometimes merciful. The difference will lie in the two judges' conceptions of these ideals, in their imaginativeness and perceptiveness, and in their sympathy, firmness, and character in general. A student is expected to be both original and sound in his thinking; but the extent to which this is possible depends on how originality and soundness are defined by individual teachers and students. Ideas that seem both original and sound to one teacher may seem sound but unoriginal to a second, and original but unsound to a third. And where one student may succeed in steering a safe course through his teachers' expectations, another may find it impossible to do so. A candidate for office ought to conduct a vigorous, time-consuming campaign, but ought also to attend to his present job, and ought also to raise campaign expenses only in certain prescribed ways. Whether these obligations are consistent depends on the character and ingenuity of the candidate and on a large variety of other circumstances. Thus the degree of consistency of a role cannot be determined apart from reference to the type of personality available to take the role, and the circumstances in which the role is taken. In general, a role can be called consistent in a given society if it can be carried out by the basic personality of that society without great strain.

Consistency among the whole set of roles to be taken by a person at a given time is also important. As in the case of internal role conflict, conflict among simultaneously held roles produces psychological strains and a pressure to modify the roles in some fashion.

The second characteristic of a rational social organization is that pairs of roles fit together without conflict. For example, if a leader role exists in a given social system there must also be a follower role which is its complement in every detail. For every prescribed action of a leader qua leader there must be a corresponding reaction prescribed for followers, and vice versa. The existence of pairs of roles enables individuals to establish social relations by taking them on.

Actually complementarity of roles is not a problem in any social system except a very rapidly changing one. It occurs almost automatically, because roles are always defined in terms of their opposites. A leader's role consists of actions to be taken toward followers, and vice versa; a teacher's role, of actions expected or obligated toward students, and so on. The problems that beset social systems are not problems of complementarism, but rather problems of role consistency and problems of producing the right personalities for each role. The role conflicts that seem to occur in all social systems are actually either conflicts within roles or conflicts between role and personality.

For example, what looks like student-teacher conflict is likely to consist of conflicts of expectation toward teachers by students and corresponding conflicts of obligation among teachers, and vice versa. Several teacher roles usually are available for students to react to — a dictating role, a prison-guard role, a kindly father role, a stupid father role, a big brother role, an actor role, and so on — and conflicts occur when a teacher believes he is taking one role while students see him in a different role or roles. Or the conflicts grow out of the divergent feelings that individuals bring to their roles. If a person's feelings diverge sharply from those proper to the role, his behavior will not conform to expectations, and responses become difficult to make. These two types of conflict are the commonest types to occur in social systems, and both are frequently mistaken for role conflicts.

The third characteristic of a rational social organization is that the sequence of roles which a person is expected to take throughout his life contains no sharp discontinuities. For example a well-known case of discontinuity is that between the Comanche warrior role and the old man's role. The warrior was expected to be fierce, aggressive, and instantly ready to defend his honor, while the old man was expected to be gentle, tolerant, and skilled at peacemaking. The difference in personality requirements for the two roles made it difficult for many men to make the transition and perform both roles adequately. A somewhat similar discontinuity exists between the job-holder and the retired or unemployed person in our society.

Continuity of successive roles is what makes adequate socialization possible. Every role and accompanying cathexis that a person learns becomes a permanent part of his personality, and conditions all his future roles. It may change considerably as it combines or conflicts with new roles, but it is never completely replaced by them. Each new role that a person learns becomes a blend of old cathexes and new obligations, and if a blending is not possible the new role will not be learned adequately. Only those roles that continue and develop earlier roles in the life cycle will be learned and carried out adequately.

When a discontinuity exists between earlier and later roles, the later roles will not be adequately carried out, and a pressure toward change will result. Either the new role will be changed in a variety of ways to make it compatible with the personalities of those taking the role, or the incompatible personality traits will be repressed and will then be a constant source of tension and instability. Such tension will express itself subjectively as a conflict between desire and obligation, desire representing the partly repressed personality traits and obligation representing the role, seen as more or less alien to the personality. Discontinuities of role are probably the main source of instability and change in social systems, as well as being the main source of traditional ethical pseudo problems such as the relation of duty and pleasure, internal *vs.* external origin of duty, and society *vs.* the individual. Continuity of roles, on the other hand, is one of the most important sources of stability in relatively well-integrated societies.

The fourth characteristic of a rational social system is its compatibility with the nonsocial environment. Every social system exists in and makes use of a varied environment, to which it must be adapted if it is to continue in existence. The environment includes both geographic-technological-economic conditions and physiological conditions. Geographic-technological conditions demand a certain spatial distribution of population and a certain temporal distribution of energy expenditure; social relations must be such that they can be maintained within these limits. For example, an extensive kinship system demanding close and continuous contacts between relatives cannot survive in conditions demanding sparse settlement or considerable mobility. Physiological conditions include physiological needs, maturation rate, levels of ability, thresholds of excitability, and so forth. The social roles demanded of a person must stay within limits set by maturation levels, and must allow for a sufficient gratification of needs.

All social systems achieve and maintain a minimum adaptation to environmental conditions, simply because they must. If distances are too great to maintain extensive kinship contacts, the contacts are dropped or reserved for annual ceremonial occasions. If children are raised under unhealthful conditions they either die or acquire immunity, and the social system must adapt to a high infant mortality rate. These physical necessities are so unavoidable that they set absolute limits for social systems. Consequently knowledge of geographic-technological conditions enables one to predict the general outlines of a social system, though of course environmental conditions are only one of several classes of determinants of social systems.

Though a minimum adaptation to environment is necessary and universal, higher degrees of adaptation are neither as necessary nor as universal, and all social systems retain some degree of maladaptation. All such maladaptation imposes a strain on individuals which in turn leads to instability and a variety of changes. For example, the Moslem ideal of making pilgrimages to Mecca is well adapted to distances and modes of travel in Arabia, but becomes more and more unrealistic as the distance to Mecca increases. For Indonesian Moslems the pilgrimage is extremely difficult, though not impossible; and the strain resulting from this maladaptation has been cited as a source of culture change in Indonesia (Geertz, 1956). With regard to physiological conditions, there are no cultures in which infants are successfully toilet-trained at one month, because that is impossible; but there are cultures in which attempts are made at that early age, with resultant strains and repercussions throughout the culture.

Maladaptation is induced by technological change, which removes the technological-environmental conditions to which a social system has adapted and forces it to readapt. If the rate of technological change is greater than the rate of social adaptation, the result is "cultural lag," that is, maladaptation. Another source of maladaptation is diffusion, in which beliefs and practices adapted to one environment are transmitted to a different environment.

Just as maladaptation to environment is a source of social change, so adaptation reinforces and stabilizes social systems. During the integrative process, then, points of greater adaptation are preserved and the total degree of maladaptation is gradually lessened.

All four characteristics mentioned, role consistency, fitness of pairs of roles, continuity of role sequences, and adaptation to environment, are sources of stability in social systems, and their opposites are sources of conflict, instability, and culture change. Since the integrative trend is the result of a selective process in which sources of change tend to be eliminated, these four characteristics gradually become more pronounced as integration increases. All four are characteristic of a rational social organization because they are all necessary conditions for the successful completion of social action.

Besides these structural characteristics, a social system tends, as it grows more integrated, to develop a certain type of value system which further reinforces the structure of roles. Some of the components of this value system are particularism, ascription (Parsons and Shils, 1951:76ff.), and loyalty.

Particularism is another name for a morality of special obligation; it is the belief that one's obligations to people are always based on their particular relation to oneself. Obligations are strongest when relations are closest, namely toward relatives and toward those dependent on oneself, and they grow progressively weaker toward more distant acquaintances. Even toward strangers there is some obligation, for instance, hospitality; but toward mankind in general there is none. The utilitarian notion of "general welfare" is meaningless from a particularist point of view. This means that one cannot know how to act toward another person until one has established a relationship to him, since the obligations governing action are always parts of relationships.

Loyalty is an extension of particularism to groups, since it affirms the primacy of obligations toward one's own groups as against other groups.

Both particularism and loyalty express the primacy of social relations as determinants of behavior. They belong to the outlook of people living in a social world, a world in which actions express social relations and are directed toward social objects. In a social world one's obligations are derived from one's particular social relations, rather than from general principles applicable to all men. Such a world contrasts sharply with the world defined by values of universalism and impartiality. In a universalist world one strives to detach oneself completely from the objects of one's actions, and to treat them all as equal, separate, interchangeable entities; in a social world one is the focal point of a myriad of relationships which one strives to maintain and extend, since action takes place only within relationships.

Ascription is another characteristic of the social outlook. It is the opposite of the achievement principle, and means that one's actions and obligations toward people spring solely from their relationships to oneself rather than as a response to something they have done. It characterizes the outlook of a parent who loves his children no matter what they do or fail to do; the householder who offers hospitality to a stranger without knowing anything about him; the patriot who unquestioningly defends his country and stands by his friends. The achievement principle, in contrast, demands that action be taken only in response to appropriate action, as in rewards and punishments, payments for services rendered or for future services. Insofar as actions are governed by the ascription principle, all relations tend to approach the model of kinship relations, since these are the primary example of relations that continue unaffected by achievement of any sort.

The basis for suggesting that the value system of an integrated social organization will be characterized by particularism, loyalty, and ascription is partly logical and partly empirical. Logically, a social relation is inherently particularistic and ascriptive, and groups inherently evoke loyalty rather than impartiality. Therefore a rational social organization, which produces strong social relations, would have to have these characteristics as well. Empirically, the cultures in which the integrative trend has developed farthest are in fact characterized by these value principles. There are some exceptions, especially with regard to ascription-achievement, which throw some doubt on this; but these relate to the status systems of the cultures rather than to their social relations. Status systems will be discussed in chapter 4, since they are of a quasi-legal character. At the same time these exceptions show that the ascription-achievement variable is more complicated and cannot be directly identified with the social-economic distinction.

The contrast between particularism, loyalty, and ascription values and universalism, impartiality, and achievement values is part of a larger contrast between the ideally rational social and economic organization. These two stand as polar opposites in most respects. A social mode of organization relates and unites people with personal ties; an economic mode of organization separates people and things into distinct commodities. Each social relation is unique, personal, irreplaceable; each commodity is impersonal and interchangeable with all others. In an economic organization all human relations tend to become contractual and specific (Parsons, 1949:189ff. and 1951, chap. 3), that is, they become channels of impersonal exchange and allocation which are limited to definite kinds of exchange and definite periods of time. In a developed social organization, on the other hand, social relations tend to become diffuse and to approach the kinship model; that is, they tend to generalize to more areas of action, to become permanent and unbreakable, to obliterate differences of interest and outlook.[1] Actions and objects tend, in an economic organization, to become emotionally and morally neutral; individuals become detached from them and learn to choose them impartially on the basis of consequences. In a society of personal relations, actions and objects take on particularized meanings and particular emotional and moral tones from the social relations which they express or symbolize. The individual is surrounded by special obligations and expectations and by special affects and meanings rather than by neutral, interchangeable means and ends.

The characteristics of an integrated social organization can be summed up in Durkheim's concept of sacredness. Social relations are sacred in that they are unexchangeable and therefore of unique, absolute value. Actions and objects become sacred when they symbolize some relationship or role; for instance, the place in which one has lived symbolizes one's group, work symbolizes one's adult role, and rituals and ceremonies symbolize group life. All developing groups soon establish their own places and times, their own routines

---

[1] For example Gluckman (1955:62) speaks of "the tendency for Lozi contractual relations to expand to the pattern of their kinship relationships. If A lends B a garden, or employs B in fishing his traps, or places his cattle with B to herd for him, he ranks as a senior kinsman of B. As soon as people begin to exchange goods regularly, they aim less at a good or standardized bargain, than at keeping up a cycle of exchanges and reciprocal assistance. This tendency is particularly marked in contracts affecting land, for the two parties begin to help each other in many ways extraneous to the loan."

(ceremonies), their own language, beliefs, and values, as sacred symbols.

The separation of people and things produced in economic progress has been called alienation. A person becomes alienated from his possessions and creations when he learns to regard them as utilities which have value because other people desire them; he becomes alienated from other people when they are perceived as competing with him for scarce goods; and he becomes alienated from himself when he sees his own value as a utility based on the desires of others.

Both modes of organization, economic and social, are ideal types rather than descriptions of actual societies. They represent alternative directions in which societies can develop to become more rational. In determining which model applies to a particular institution the direction of development of that institution is more important than its characteristics at a given time. If it is moving toward greater efficiency it is governed by the economic model of rationality and is part of an economy; if it is moving toward greater integration of personal relations it is governed by the social model and is part of a social organization.

For example, in Southeast Papua (Belshaw, 1955), as in many parts of the world, buying and selling transactions occur, not in an open market between strangers, but between trading partners. When a person grows old enough to begin trading goods he selects a partner, establishes a relation, and from then on trades only with him. In some societies young men inherit their partners, or their fathers arrange suitable partnerships among relatives; in other cases partners are selected from the regular trading area or trading families of the group. When European firms move into such an area, the natives form partnerships with them by opening an account.

So far this practice fits the model of a social relation. Trade appears to be a symbolic act expressing a personal affective relation between partners. This relation is particular and exclusive; it is diffuse rather than a specific contractual relation, since it lasts indefinitely, spreads to other areas of action, and does not demand any exact balancing of accounts. Belshaw remarks of two brothers, "They seem to look upon their account with Buntings, not as a tight financial arrangement which they must balance evenly, but as a loose relationship of a reciprocal kind. 'We give Buntings our copra, they give us what trade we need' is the attitude. To them, the relationship is similar to that common between kinsfolk or trading partners" (1955:37). Once a trading relation is established, it gives acts of trade a special moral and affective tone. Trade ought to be carried out exclusively with one's partner and felt as a gesture of friendship. To treat one's goods as neutral commodities to be sold to the highest bidder would be an act of unfaithfulness and would mark one as a kind of prostitute.

On the other hand, this whole system is currently developing in an economic direction and thus must be understood primarily as part of an economy. Belshaw remarks "The Ware people frankly do not know where to sell their copra; wherever they go they feel they are being cheated. They prefer a standardized relationship with one firm as a trading partner to experimental moving from one firm to another, but they are not sure that the procedure, correct in their own trading system, is correct in modern commerce, and this doubt worries them" (1955:33). The doubt expressed here is a doubt as to whether the Ware islanders will benefit most from a single partnership or from shopping around for buyers; it indicates that the trading relation is becoming neutralized and its economic value is being assessed. The word "correct" means "economically correct," involving a maximum return to the islanders. A further development in this direction would be marked by increased shifting around of partners, depersonalization of particular acts of trading, concentration of partners in efficient centers of trade (this is already happening), and finally a specialization of trading operations and their separation from operations of production, which is just beginning to happen. These changes would indicate the predominance of economic rather than social rationality.

In contrast, one could imagine a highly specialized, impersonal trading system which was changing in the direction of greater social rationality. Changes would include the development of trading partnerships and the decline of exact accounting. Instead of buying wherever price-quality ratios were most advantageous, people would form the habit of patronizing one store regularly. They would get acquainted with the store owner or clerk and talk together while shopping; through conversation the relation would spread to areas of life other than shopping. The storekeeper would contribute in various ways to activities of his customers and would become involved in them. Community affairs might begin to be held in the store or its parking lot, and the owner would plan to set aside more space for such affairs when he remodels. A development of this sort, which actually does occur in isolated instances, particularly in co-op stores, indicates the appearance of social rationality, in the beginnings of an integration of marketing with other activities, and in the personalization of trading.

Because economic and social rationality are so completely opposed to one another, it would seem that an organization which becomes more economically rational must inevitably become less socially rational, and vice versa. And yet each of these forms of reason presupposes the other and is completely dependent on it. Neither can exist without the other; economic rationality is possible only in a socially rational organization, but a socially rational organization cannot survive unless it is also economically rational to a considerable extent.

Economic calculation requires that a plurality of goals be held in consciousness simultaneously so that their relative importance can be compared. It requires that available resources be known so that they can be rationally allocated. And once a decision is reached, the goals must remain constant if the decision is to be carried out successfully.

The integration that occurs in social organizations and personalities provides the stability that enables calculation and rational action to occur. In an integrated system, alternate goals can be held together without destructive conflict and repression, and they can remain constant through a course of action. When insufficient integration exists, the goals of a system are frequently involved in conflicts which prevent them from being directly compared. Some goals may be repressed from consciousness entirely, and others may vacillate so that their value relative to other goals cannot be determined. Resources are similarly tied up in conflicts and repressed from consciousness so they are not available for allocation. And once decisions have been made it is difficult to carry them out because goals and resources tend to change unexpectedly. In such circumstances it is impossible to be economically rational.

When individual personalities are insufficiently integrated, such difficulties appear as vacillating behavior. A disorganized person has difficulty making up his mind; he does not know what he really wants, and tends to choose one goal after another without being able to really face alternatives and decide between them. He may decide on one course of action but be unable to carry it out because of unconscious resistance put up by opposing desires. Sometimes his actions may be largely paralyzed by conflicting goals and at other times they may lead to unexpected, but unconsciously desired, results. Or, if he does succeed in carrying out a decision, the results may be unsatisfactory because they frustrate desires of which he was not aware.

In a group such difficulties appear as failures of communication and of action. A disorganized group is one that cannot communicate effectively due to conflicting values and beliefs and to lack of trust. As a result, the group's executive cannot obtain adequate information about group resources and values, either because information is withheld from it or because information is misinterpreted. The decisions that are reached do not adequately take account of the values and resources of the peripheral, misunderstood members, and these are either isolated from the group activity or thrown into opposition to it. Sometimes a group decision may be completely nullified by covert, diffuse opposition, or it may be radically modified in action through misunderstanding, or willful reinterpretation, or adjustment to actual resources. If the group is divided into factions, each may undo the work of the other, or group policy may vacillate as factions alternate in control of the group executive. All of these difficulties are parallel to difficulties experienced by poorly integrated individuals in reaching and carrying out decisions.

Theories which deal exclusively with economic rationality in decisions and organizations are valid only on the assumption that integrative problems are solved. Theories of economic decisions are relevant only insofar as people know what they really want and what resources they have available, and insofar as their goals are not related to internal conflicts. When people who do not act as economists say they should act to be rational, their behavior indicates not perverseness, but insufficient integration. The classical economic theory of the firm, as well as recent organization theory, is valid only on the assumption of adequate group integration — adequate communication based on ideological identity, no major factionalism or power conflicts, no major conflicts of belief as to group goals.

Just as economic rationality is possible only in persons and groups that are relatively well integrated, so social rationality is possible only if the economic problem of resource allocation is solved to some extent. All societies must adapt to environmental conditions, including physiological needs, and successful adaptation must be based on relatively efficient resource allocation. The less efficiently resources are allocated, the greater the adaptive stress on the society. If physiological needs are not adequately met, for instance, individual ill health will reduce adaptive ingenuity and lead to social malfunctioning. Or the society, in an attempt to satisfy needs, may concentrate on productive activity; but in this case the technical requirements of production will largely determine the forms of social interaction and will severely limit the varieties of social structure that are possible. Or the society may decline because individuals leave it for other more efficiently organized groups. For instance in Homans' "Hilltown" (1950, chap. 13) the main cause of social disorganization seems to be the inefficiency of Hilltown agricultural practices, which drove young people to move to more prosperous localities. Conversely, efficient resource allocation reduces the pressure of physiological needs, geographical circumstances, and hostile military powers, and thus increases the area of choice within which a society or individual can solve its integrative problems.

Theories which deal exclusively with values related to social integration must also assume that economic problems are somehow solved. Thus Aristotle and Plato, in describing the happy man, mention that he must be adequately equipped with external goods, and they locate their ideal societies in favorable geographical locations.

INTEGRATIVE DECISIONS

Social systems are built up, sustained, and adapted to changing conditions by a continuous, though unconscious, integrative process. This process consists of the adjustment or mutual modification of forces. It includes the putting together of things that were separate and the reconciling of things that were in opposition; also negatively, the separation of irreconcilable forces and the exclusion of disruptive elements. Integration occurs in perception, thought, and dreams as well as in action, so that knowledge of its workings gained in one area can be applied to the others as well.

All learning of new roles and relationships, as well as modification of old ones, involves integration. Becoming a parent, for instance, means that dependent expectations formerly directed toward other people, parent figures, must now be perceived as directed to oneself, and that the corresponding obligations and ideals must be taken on by oneself. It also means that one's own hostile and other cathexes formerly directed toward parent figures will now be directed to oneself. Becoming a parent thus involves creating a self which includes both the new responsibilities and the old cathexes, now self-directed, and this is a problem which must be solved by integration.

At least four ways of solving the problem are distinguishable. One is to change the obligations in such a way that they no longer elicit much hostility, to transmute the remaining self-directed hostility into some related feeling such as conscientiousness, and thus to make two formerly opposed elements compatible and partly reinforcing. Or if the hostile feelings are too strong to be completely changed, one can perhaps learn to accept them, taking the attitude that part of a parent's job is to bear undeserved hostility without complaining. Or if the hostility and the obligations are too strong to bear, they can in part be redirected away from oneself on to other parent figures. Or, if even this is too difficult, some of the threatening feelings can be repressed.

All of these changes can be called forms of integration, since in each case the new role is included in the self, though with varying degrees of completeness. In a narrower sense only the first result should be called integration, because only in this case are formerly opposed feelings changed to reinforce one another. The second result might be called "immunization," since it involves the development of a tolerance for formerly threatening feelings. Immunization is always achieved indirectly, by (1) strengthening the self and making it more secure, and (2) isolating and weakening the threatening feelings. In the present instance a new parent becomes immune to self-directed hostility (perceived as coming from others) when (1) integration in other areas of parenthood make him more secure as a parent, and (2) he learns to perceive the hostility as unrealistic, groundless, and therefore not threatening to him.

The third result might be called differentiation or separation because two parent roles are differentiated and kept separated in it — one, the "real parent," being assigned to some patriarch or older parent figure, and the other, a pale imitation, being taken by oneself. In this way the rigors and conflicts of the original parent role are displaced on to a substitute parent rather than resolved, and an easier parent role is created for oneself. In the fourth result, repression, the incompatible hostile feelings are excluded from the self to make room for the new role.

The first kind of change is the most adequate, because the new role is reinforced by a formerly conflicting force. The third change is less effective, because the new role has less support and the personality is partly split up into potentially discordant elements. The fourth change is least effective because the repressed feelings are in actual conflict with the self and are potentially disruptive of the role. Also the energy needed to keep feelings repressed is bound to that task and thus is not available for other tasks. The same kinds of change occur in relationships as in roles, in which case it is the roles and feelings of two people that are made more compatible.

Integration of all four sorts occurs constantly. Personalities and their relations change constantly in small, unnoticeable ways, until one suddenly becomes aware that major changes have taken place. The taking on of parental roles, for instance, frequently is spread over several years, and the more successful adjustments to parenthood are themselves the culmination of further years of preparation with analogous roles. Social parenthood, like all roles, is never taken on directly, but is achieved as the summation of manifold invisible changes.

There is a second sort of integrative process which is conscious, and this process will be our primary concern here. Conscious integration consists of the direction and control of the continuous subconscious integrative process; it is made possible by an understanding of how the subconscious mind works. Control is exercised indirectly, through selection of the environment in which integration occurs. Since the environment provides part of the material available for integration, deliberate selection of environmental factors can have a material influence on the outcome of integration.

The addition of conscious thought to the integrative process has both advantages and disadvantages. On the positive side, conscious foresight can tremendously extend the context of integrative activity. The subconscious mind integrates only the materials immediately available to it — present feelings and drives, present beliefs and obligations, immediately perceived cues and symbols. It has no contact with the future and the distant. But conscious thought can note faraway contingencies, remote opportunities and dangers, and make provision for them. Future difficulties can be prepared for in advance, and future opportunities can be kept open by preventing premature closures that would exclude them.

On the negative side, consciousness can exercise at best only an indirect influence on the integrative process, and cannot of itself produce any particular desired outcome. One cannot, for instance, decide to fall in love with someone tomorrow morning, or choose to give up anxieties one knows to be unrealistic. Such goals can indeed be worked for, but only indirectly and with no assurance of the exact desired result.

The influence of the conscious mind is weak because it is both indirect and incomplete. It affects the integrative process through the selection of the environmental material available for integration, but cannot determine how the material is to be perceived or what treatment is to be given to it. For instance, if one decides to fall in love with someone, that decision can be implemented by seeing a lot of the person (or absenting oneself) and by engaging in pleasant activities together (or sharing hardships). These activities provide materials for integration of an old cathexis with a new role. But they do not necessarily lead to the desired result; they may instead lead to indifference, anxiety, hostility, or a manipulative relationship.

Further, a consciously selected external environment provides only a small part of the material to be integrated at any one time. The major part of the material consists of personality factors which are given and unavoidable, and which severely limit the kinds of results that are possible. Our inadequate knowledge of the unconscious and its workings, finally, makes it difficult to select appropriate, fitting environments out of the narrow range available.

Because of the limitations of conscious thought, its proper concern should be to increase the effectiveness of the unconscious integrative process, rather than to set up specific aims of its own. It should act as an advance scout, resource specialist, and advisor rather than as master in the ordinary sense of the term. This general aim of increased effectiveness is what has been called "growth" by Dewey; it includes increase of integrative power, or mastery, or creativeness, as well as increased complexity of the problems and materials to be mastered. Specific aims may be consciously selected as part of the general process of promoting growth, but they are to be regarded as tentative ends in view, subject to modification if the integrative process moves away from them.

Conscious control of the integrative process with the aim of increasing its effectiveness is a decision-making activity in the ordinary sense of the term. It involves the discovery or invention of alternate action possibilities, estimation of the consequences of each, and selection of one course of action rather than others. Unconscious integration may also be called decision making, since it also involves the selection and modification of presented feelings, expectations, cues, and ideals; but since it is not ordinary usage to speak of unconscious decisions it may be better to reserve the term "integrative decision making" for the conscious supervisory process.

Integrative decisions take a slightly different form depending on whether they are used preventively or curatively. In a preventive use one assumes that the persons and relations concerned are basically sound, able to deal with most ordinary matters as they come up, but subject to occasional difficulties. Conscious decisions are needed only to deal with these unusually difficult situations. In a curative use one assumes that the persons and relations concerned are partly immobilized with continuing inner conflicts which they are unable to master. Conscious decisions are needed to break through deadlocks, resolve persistent conflicts, and restore the effectiveness of the unconscious integrative process. In a preventive use the origin of difficulties is external; in a curative use it is internal.

Preventive decisions involve the application of three basic principles. First, one should *select or arrange situations which are not too difficult to master*. By mastery is meant the successful integration of the varied, potentially conflicting factors of the situation, or at least integration of some and immunization against the rest. If the situation is too difficult, it will not be integrated; instead, one or more of the troublesome factors will be repressed, or rejected, or ignored, and potential conflicts will become real ones. Affective energy will be tied up in these conflicts and a reduction of integrative ability will result, leading to further disorganization in later situations.

Integrative crises are most likely to occur in times of transition, when new roles must become part of the self and be integrated with older cathexes. Consider for example a youngster's first moments at school. Suppose the mother takes him to school and returns home, leaving him to face a roomful of new people and furniture. The situation, like all situations, is composed of varied, ambiguous, potentially conflicting elements. The mother's departure can be perceived as a rejection, or as an expression of confidence, or as a routine separation — mothers and dependency feelings belong at home, children and independent activities belong in school. The children can be perceived as potential playmates like familiar children or as harmless, unimportant strangers, or as enemies, or as rivals; the teacher can be seen as a new mother, or an unimportant stranger, or a threat. Now if the child's fear of rejection is strong, it is easy to perceive the mother's departure as a rejection, and the attendant fear is readily transferred to the schoolroom situation. Once this integration of elements has occurred and the schoolroom comes to mean maternal rejection, an incompatibility between home and school is set up, and the child, as a home self, perceives school and its roles as alien and dangerous. The situation has become too difficult to master and integration has been incomplete and unsuccessful; this results in further weakening of the child's integrative ability and tighter clinging to his old home-dependent role.

Conscious foresight should be directed to simplifying the situation to the point of possible mastery by the child. This may be done by the mother's staying at school a while, so that the fear of rejection cannot readily be attached to anything in the situation, and can easily be excluded by the child if it should appear. The exclusion of this potentially troublesome feeling makes it easier to integrate the remaining factors.

Another possibility would be to make the teacher as similar to the mother as possible, thus making it easy to see the teacher as a new kind of mother and enabling the child to transfer some of his maternal relationship to the teacher. The school would then be a new kind of home, and the school role a variant of the home role.

A different approach would be to emphasize the possibilities of the other children as playmates. This would be easiest if some of the children were already playmates, and would also involve introducing playlike activities into the classroom. Such activities would enable the child to associate the classroom with previous play groups and to develop a classroom role out of his peer group relationships, rather than out of his relation to mother. The teacher would become an umpire and resource specialist rather than a mother figure.

Which schoolroom situation is the right one to select depends on the strengths and weaknesses of the child's personality. A transitional crisis produces its damaging effects by activating and intensifying personal weaknesses. Consequently if one knows the weak points of the child's personality one can predict which of them will be activated by the particular situation, and can structure the situation away from them. If the child's fear of rejection is strong enough to make its activation likely, some protection against it should be built into the situation. If peer group relations are ambivalent and unstable, they should be kept under control; and so on. If the major weaknesses are all guarded against so that they do not become the focus of attention, the child will be able to master the situation.

Weaknesses are usually guarded against by activating and emphasizing strong points which counteract them. Thus anxiety about mother can be counteracted by cues which activate friendly peer relations, or by activities in which the child is already successful and confident. The emphasis on activities and relations which the child has already mastered enables him to extend his mastery gradually into new activities. So the integration of the new role begins most readily in areas where it is similar to earlier roles, and moves only later into unfamiliar areas.

The second principle to be followed in integrative decisions is to *make provisions for future stresses*. If adequate preparation is made in advance the stresses can be prevented from causing disorganization or a blocking of integration. One usual way to prepare for stress is to gradually change present roles in the direction of future role expectations, so that when the time comes to take on the new role it will not be too difficult to integrate. Thus the school role can be prepared for by introducing bits of it into home activities — attention to pronunciation, independence from maternal supervision, and so forth. Learning demands in upper grades can be prepared for by some first grade activities.

Or, if several alternate future roles or relations are available, it may be wiser to direct present changes away from a role or relation which may be too difficult to integrate, and toward easier roles. Still another method is to try to develop such a solidly integrated relation or role that it will be immune to the future stress; or to develop a relation or role flexible enough to absorb required future changes without undue strain.

One class of future stresses which should always be prepared for is that class of factors which have been temporarily excluded from a present situation. For instance in the schoolroom situation, if the child's fear of rejection is temporarily neutralized by the mother's presence, some provision must eventually be made for dealing with this fear, because the mother cannot stay at school indefinitely. In this case it is usually hoped that rapidly developing school relations will support and reinforce the child's new pupil role until it is immunized against attacks of fear. Similarly, if conflicts in peer relations are temporarily excluded by classroom discipline, they must still be prepared for, either by substituting opportunities for new relations, or by developing an environment in which the old relations can gradually be reintroduced and then modified, or by immunization against the cues which would bring on conflict. It is always necessary to make such preparations sooner or later because the temporarily excluded element will not vanish but will continually be ready to re-enter the situation upon an appropriate cue. People too frequently forget this point; they suppose that by repressing a fear or some other troublesome feeling, by forbidding fighting among their children, by setting up a routine that will exclude deviant activities, they have solved a problem. What they have done is to simplify a present situation in such a way as to prevent future growth. They have temporarily excluded disturbing factors without making provision for their eventual reinclusion; but when the excluded factors reappear they must again be excluded, and the cycle of exclusion and reappearance will become the focus of a frustrating and energy-absorbing conflict.

The principle of preparing for future stresses frequently conflicts with the principle of avoiding present factors that are too difficult to master. Preparation for future difficulties usually involves introducing more complicated and difficult factors into present situations; and present situations are often simplified by temporarily excluding difficult factors. For instance, the quickest way to simplify the schoolroom situation is to take the child back home to a familiar life; but this is an escape from future stresses which makes their eventual mastery more difficult. At the other extreme, too much advance preparation for the school role frequently creates such a difficult preschool role expectation for the child that he cannot master it; the school expectations become alien superego obligations which he must meet at all costs, rather than an integral part of the self. Once this has happened, school learning situations readily become fused with this alien obligation, and are responded to by anxious, rigid conformity and compulsive memorization. The integrative decision maker must find a proper combination of these two principles, finding or creating situations which are neither too difficult to master nor so self-contained that they prevent future growth.

Sometimes the two principles supplement rather than contradict each other and combining them becomes easier. The principle of providing for future difficulties enables one to select among several equally easy present situations, or the principle of avoiding present difficulties facilitates a selection among alternate directions of development. For example, in the school situation it may be possible to focus the situation around the teacher's similarity to parents, or around the children's similarity to play groups, or around the school's grownupness and difference from both home and play. If all of these situations facilitate the immediate integration of school roles, choice among them can depend on which contributes most to the easing of future learning problems.

The third principle to follow in integrative decisions is to *hedge against uncertainty*. This principle is important because our knowledge of the dynamics of social situations is inadequate at best and dangerously misleading at worst. Our ignorance is great in dealing with new people and strange situations, because of the defenses people put up against detection; and it is greatest of all in dealing with ourselves, because of the strong defenses we put up against self-knowledge. When knowledge is inadequate it is best not to undertake decisive actions if they can be avoided, because an error in such a case would be difficult to correct. Instead, it is better to postpone irretrievable decisions, either by not acting at all, or by finding acts that would fit into a variety of developments. At the same time, of course, it is necessary to watch for signals that will clarify the situation and permit more decisive action.

A curative use of integrative decisions is more complicated and difficult than a preventive use. A preventive use takes situations as they come up and adapts them, while a curative use involves the sustained study and transformation of a complex set of relationships. Both follow similar principles, but in different ways. In both cases it is necessary to arrange situations that are not too difficult to master, but the preventive situations are those that just happen, while the curative situations are devised to originate and activate a continuing solution to a continuing problem. In both cases it is necessary to prepare for future events, but prevention looks forward to normally expected events, while cure anticipates events that are made necessary by the way in which the solution was started. In both cases uncertainty and error is a hazard, but the one answer is to postpone action while the other answer is to search for error and continually gather new knowledge.

The problems with which curative decisions deal result from a failure of the integrative process to master cultural demands. They are characterized by conflicts in role expectations, obligations, ideals, and beliefs, both within a person and among related persons. Conflicts tie up affective energy inside a person and prevent it from being expressed or used. The conflicts are sustained by various equilibriums in which two integrated sets of factors oppose each other, and are intensified by vicious circles. Individuals are absorbed in maintaining defenses, both passive and active, against perceived threats which they themselves help sustain and which immobilize them.

Integrative problems are difficult to solve because any particular conflict or defensiveness is tied up with other conflicts in an indefinitely ramified network. The whole network, because of its rigidity and the vicious circles within it, resists changes occurring in any small part. For instance, employment discrimination, which is itself a symptom of a much larger problem, causes members of the minority group to miss the experience that would qualify them for better jobs. Lack of opportunities discourages people from going into training for the forbidden jobs; instead they adapt their expectations to the lesser jobs open to them. Presently they develop work habits and attitudes that fit them only for available jobs. They partly internalize contemptuous attitudes of others toward these jobs and develop an ambivalent self-image. This makes it difficult to take on adequate parental roles, and as a result their children have difficulty developing the strong, self-confident personality that would enable them to overcome unusual obstacles. More capable and confident minority group members leave the community in search of better job opportunities. These and other developments present the discriminating employer with an objective justification for his belief in the inferiority of minority group members. Also he is forced to defend himself against the hostility he perceives resulting from his discrimination through further discrimination. He defends himself against his guilt by developing elaborate ideologies which prove his righteousness; but these ideologies demand more systematic discrimination, which increases his guilt.

The most important step in solving a complex problem of this sort is to find some point at which a solution can be started with actually existing resources. (Strictly speaking, the most important thing is to establish a discussion relationship within which a search can occur, but this is an anticipation of the argument of chapter 5.) Three principles are relevant to the search for a starting point.

The first is to *find parts of the problem that can be changed with existing resources.* By "change" I mean not direct resolution of conflicts, but rather simplification of the problem. Conflict resolution and immunization can only be achieved by people involved in a problem themselves; every "sick" person must cure himself. But outside resources make cure possible by simplifying situations that previously were too difficult. They enable the unconscious integrative process to shift from defense and repression to positive integration.

The first principle thus necessitates a study of the resources available for introducing changes, and of the various possible changes that might result from them. Resources might include a variety of things — emotional support, money, education, setting examples, refusing to play an expected role, and many others. Each of these resources is useful only because of the specific ways it can simplify a problematic situation and the specific changes it makes possible. Resources that might be useful at one point could be completely useless at another. For instance, emotional support will not help a discriminating employer cope with his threatening environment, but it may help a minority group member tolerate exaggerated threats to his self-respect. Money will put a person into a vocational school or new neighborhood, but will not help him accept the new concept of himself that he must develop there. Consequently with given resources it may be possible to introduce considerable changes at certain points, and few or none at others.

An inventory of possible changes is not enough by itself to locate a starting point. Changes must not only be introduced; they must also be protected against external pressures until they are stabilized. Otherwise the external pressures will undo the changes and restore the original problem. This is the common experience of social workers, counselors, and so on, who laboriously promote changes in individuals only to see these changes undone as the individuals return to their home environment. A proper starting point, therefore, must be independent enough of its environment to sustain changes *for a time* against outside pressures. Elsewhere (1955) I have called this sort of thing a problem area. A problem area is a conceptually isolated part of a larger problem which is naturally or artificially independent enough to change without changes in its environment and to persist in those changes for a time. Dewey's concept of the problematic situation is the same thing, except that Dewey gives the impression that problematic situations come all neatly packaged and ready for solution, whereas they actually must be carefully searched out or even constructed.

The second principle relevant to finding a starting point, therefore, is to *find or arrange a sufficiently independent problem area.*

Neglect of this principle is the most serious shortcoming in the current use of integrative decisions. Although the theories with which therapists, counselors, social workers, community workers, and such operate stress the interdependence of everything with everything else, they also frequently assume in practice that any conveniently available part of a problem is independent enough to constitute a problem area. Therapists assume that an individual is an independent problem area just because he moves about in space independently and can walk into the office by himself. Remedial teachers assume the existence of an independent place, the school, and an independent time, the counseling hour. Community workers try to deal with ethnocentric attitudes and discriminatory practices as though they exist in a vacuum. The result of these convenient assumptions is initial success, then a reaction and return of the original problem.

The laying out of a problem area is not simply a conceptual process, but has implications for action. When one draws an imaginary boundary around a certain set of relationships one is saying that the whole set is interdependent, that is, that all of it changes together. No single part can change by itself, because the other parts, remaining unchanged, will resist and undo the change in the dependent part. Therefore if the set is to be changed all of it must be changed at the same time. This means that changes must be introduced at all major points of the system simultaneously. By "simultaneously" I mean not necessarily the same day, but rather the same year or two. The allowable time lag depends on the degree of interdependence between the parts.

In other words, the boundary of the problem area determines the number of changes that must be introduced during the first step of a solution. The larger the area, the greater the number of changes to be introduced. The recognition that social problems are widely ramified implies that they are most readily solved by multiple co-ordinated changes. For instance, a job discrimination problem (in which job discrimination is simply the most obviously annoying symptom of a large problem) is most readily solved by simultaneous changes in schools, neighborhood recreation, families, business climate, law, and residential patterns. Even an "individual" neurosis is most thoroughly solved by co-ordinated treatment of several people and their relationships.

The first two requirements for a starting place, that it be changeable with existing resources, and that it be a sufficiently independent problem area, ordinarily conflict. Independence ordinarily varies directly with size — the larger the problem area, the more independent it is likely to be. But the effectiveness of one's resources diminishes with the increasing size of the problem to which they are applied. In terms of available resources the ideal problem area is very small; in terms of independence it is likely to be large. In addition, one's most effective resources may not be located in the areas of greatest independence. For instance a therapist must usually deal with whoever walks into his office. He cannot include related people who refuse to come in and get involved, even though their inclusion in the problem area may be essential to its independence.

Sometimes it is possible to find, or construct, a problem area which fits both requirements. If no such problem area can be found, it is necessary to compromise and begin with slightly inadequate resources in a less independent area, and hope for the best. Compromises are usually made at the expense of the independence requirement. Since the degree of independence of a problem area is a vague and elusive thing, while resources are usually rather definite, it is easier to limit the initial problem to fit the resources on hand, and hope that it is independent enough.

The third principle relevant to the search for a starting point is to *find or arrange a problem area that can expand.* Since the initial problem area is almost always a small part of a larger problem, expansion is necessary if the larger problem is to be solved. Expansion consists of the inclusion of new problematic factors in the initial area and the extension of changes to them. Usually this is a gradual, creeping process but in fortunate cases it may proceed quite suddenly.

Expansion is made possible by the successful integration of conflicts in the initial problem area. Integration releases resources which had formerly been blocked, or creates new resources: emotional energy which has been tied up in ambivalence and repression is released by integration, emotional energy tied up in defensiveness and hostility is released by immunization, money is released by success in meeting financial pressures, the ability to educate is developed by successful education, the ability to set an example is developed by the self-confidence that comes with success, and so on. As these resources are released they become available for the initiation of changes in new parts of the problem. If initial planning is adequate the step-by-step release and reutilization of resources leads to successive expansions which continue until the major parts of the problem are solved.

Planning for expansion, in other words the application of the third principle, consists of predicting the resources that will be released by success in an initial problem area, and determining whether those resources will be helpful in the next larger problem area. If they are not helpful, that initial problem area must be discarded or changed and a new one examined. All selections of initial problem areas must be justified by a judgment that the released resources will be effective in larger areas. Thus demonstration projects in cultural change must be justified by the judgment that the example set by the project will of itself be contagious. Therapy with an individual must work toward development of the emotional strength that will enable him to support related individuals (wife, friends, and such) in their attempts at integration. Attempts to reduce job discrimination must assume that the resources released — money, examples, new self-concepts, new friendships — will reduce pressures elsewhere and reduce the need for defensive ethnocentrism.

Note that the people introducing changes in expanded problem areas are usually different from the initial introducers of change. They are usually the ones who have been released from defensive tasks in the first stage of a solution. In fact, the crucial test of success in social problem solving occurs when the initial introducers of change leave the scene. If the solution collapses, it was illusory from the start. If it keeps expanding of itself, it has been successful. The reward for careful application of the third principle is the sight of an expanding, self-energizing, and self-maintaining solution.

A spectacular example of failure to prepare for expansion of a solution is the Koinonia interracial farming community of Americus, Georgia. From the standpoint of the first and second principles this community was a brilliant success. A small problem area consisting of a handful of people on a co-operative farm was set up and isolated from the surrounding area. It was so small that the available emotional resources of self-respect, affection, and trust were adequate to permit resolution of racial conflicts within the community. It was so independent that the fear, hate, delusions, and helplessness of the surrounding towns could not infect the community. But there was no way of expanding the solution. The emotional resources developed at Koinonia could not be transmitted to new people, precisely because of the original isolation of the community. Emotional resources are transmitted in close personal relationships, but relationships could not develop across the community boundary. The community became a threat rather than a source of support for its environment, and the resulting environmental pressure will eventually destroy it.

Another example of failure to provide for expansion is Baker Brownell's Montana study of 1946–47 (Brownell, 1950). The initial successes in community integration achieved in this study were impressive because the initial problem areas were small, isolated, and adapted to the available resources for change. But the new resources released by community integration, useful as they were for further community integration, could not be applied to the next larger problem area. The next problem area, it turned out, was the state capital at Helena, where the powerful mining interests perceived the study as a threat and destroyed it. The application of the third principle here should have led to a prediction of the legislative struggle and a demand for initial problem areas whose change could rapidly yield large amounts of political power. The communities actually chosen yielded little political power and therefore were the wrong initial problem areas. Indeed the importance of political power in this example necessitates its treatment as a political rather than an integrative problem (chap. 5). This was indeed done within the small communities, but not in the whole state. Perhaps all problems are ultimately political, but this one was more obviously political than most.

The conflicts between the third principle and the first two principles require further compromises and adjustments in the search for optimum initial problem areas. The second principle requires the initial problem area to be independent so that changes can be successfully started; but too much independence violates the third principle by preventing removal of boundaries and expansion, as at Koinonia. The first principle requires changes to start where resources are initially available; but these spots may prove to be dead ends from which no expansion is possible, as in the Montana study. The optimum initial problem area is neither the easiest to change, nor the most independent, but the most fruitful.

Up to now I have given the impression that integrative decisions require a great deal of detailed planning before action can begin. This is entirely false. Detailed prior planning is impossible because the necessary knowledge of what changes the unconscious integrative process will produce cannot be acquired prior to action. What is required is knowledge of how new situations will be perceived by people who have changed in unique ways, how their reactions to what they perceive will be interpreted by other equally changed people, and so on. General and probable predictions can be made here, but not exact and certain ones; the particularism and relativism characteristic of social relations gives all general propositions about them a certain amount of unreality.

Indeed if the course of a solution could be laid out in advance, the successive problem areas all defined, and the final state of affairs clearly described, integrative decisions could hardly be distinguished from technical decisions. Moreover if the introducer of changes supposes he can plot a complete solution in advance he will be making technical rather than integrative decisions. That is, he will be using his resources to engineer people into his desired direction of change, pushing them away from undesired adventures, bargaining them into working toward his goal.

It is not possible to set up integration as a goal and work out the means to achieve it. Integration, immunization, and so forth cannot be forced on people; they must be spontaneous. What can be forced or bargained is external appearances and outward actions, but not the inner reality. Integrative decisions must be goalless, and this would still be true even if the necessary knowledge for purposive decisions could be had.

Consequently the three principles of integrative decisions must be applied continuously during the course of a solution. Every present situation must be treated as a possible initial problem area and tested and modified accordingly. Every foreseen future state of affairs must be treated as the next larger problem area and preparation for it made accordingly. When the course of a solution changes unexpectedly, as it frequently does, decisions must be adjusted to the change. The integrative decision maker figuratively faces the problematic situation and says to it: "You tell me what you could do and I will help you do it if I can."

With this kind of think-as-you-go decision process it is necessary both to continually check for error and to continually search for new knowledge. Each shift of the problem presents a new situation to be studied in detail and requires a new set of predictions. Each action and reaction reveals new aspects of the system under study and checks the validity of previous predictions. The search for additional knowledge is all the more important because the introducer of change cannot, as in preventive decisions, hedge or postpone decisions in case of uncertainty. Once a solution has started it must continue to its own stabilized completion, or it will be undone.

The principles of integrative decision making discussed above are not the sort of principles familiar in mathematical logic or game theory. They cannot be fed into a computer to yield decisions that would help a practicing clinician. Their application requires sensitivity and intuition, and cannot be formalized with any precision. In view of this vagueness, it may be questioned whether and in what sense integrative decisions are rational at all. This question is difficult to answer decisively because there is no universally agreed on definition of rationality, and an answer given in terms of some definition of rationality would therefore beg the question. In terms of the preliminary definition of reason given in chapter 1, these principles are rational because they are derived from principles appearing in trends of social development and therefore represent a type of effectiveness. They are analogous to principles of economizing, since they are effective in creating a type of social organization that produces its own kind of good. But since this conception of reason is not universally accepted, the above argument is not conclusive.

Nevertheless there are several generally accepted characteristics of rational action which fall short of a definition and which can serve as a criterion. Rational action should be deliberate and principled and capable of being taught to at least some people; there probably should be experts who can improve and teach their skills; the results must be objectively testable by unbiased observers, and the connection between action and result demonstrable in terms of some science. On all these counts integrative decisions can be rational. They follow principles such as have been indicated; there are experts, psychotherapists of all sorts, who can teach their skills; and the effectiveness of results, in terms of increased integration and increased creativity, can be objectively assessed to a large extent. The relevant sciences are all those dealing with social systems and personality, and advances in those sciences should lead to increased effectiveness of integrative decision making.

INTEGRATIVE AND ECONOMIC DECISIONS COMPARED

Just as the social and the economic modes of organization are opposed in most respects, so the decision processes associated with each exhibit striking contrasts. They are based on quite different ways of perceiving or defining problems, they involve different processes of deliberation, lead to different action, and usually have different results. In an economic approach the competing desires or habits of which all problematic situations are composed are perceived as simply alternative — there are too many of them, they cannot all be satisfied at once, and some will have to wait. Conflicts are resolved by a process of arranging wants in a hierarchy of importance or relevance for the occasion, and selecting the appropriate means. In an integrative approach the desires and habits are treated as parts and symptoms of a social system or personality in conflict. In this case the conflicts are resolved by an integrative process in which the desires are changed rather than satisfied, and action alternatives are chosen according to how they contribute to this process.

Economizing proceeds by comparing different values, quantitatively if possible, and thus focuses on what they have in common. Economic value or utility is conceived as a neutral, homogeneous quality shared by all goods and services; the commodities allocated by economizing tend to become standardized, interchangeable, and colorless. In an integrative approach, on the other hand, it is precisely the particular qualities of things which are of interest — the particular symbolic meanings which things have for a person, the particular relationships of which he is composed, the particular areas of strength and weakness in his personality. No comparisons need be made, since actions and solutions are built up by combining and recombining the available materials in ever-changing ways.

In an economic approach a problem is resolved immediately, as soon as the various ends can be compared and arranged in a hierarchy of importance. A social problem, on the other hand, takes years to resolve and really is never finally resolved, merely transformed in a series of variations on fundamental cultural themes. An economic problem can be settled rapidly because economizing takes personality and social structure as given and attempts maximum satisfaction rather than change. Or rather, since personality and social structure are continually changing, economizing ignores the changes that do occur and makes no attempt to control them. Integrative decision making, on the other hand, is an attempt to make social and personal change a rational process. Social problems are endless because social change is endless; it takes place in the indestructible matrix of culture from which we never escape. The weakness of integrative decision methods is that they are unable to deal with scarcity, with the unavoidable fact that not all desires can be satisfied and not all values achieved. Life simply is not a continuous process of growth composed of endless ends (Dewey); it is finite, both spatially and temporally, and renunciation is inevitable and continuous. Integrative decision methods ignore the renunciation that is continually occurring; economizing is an attempt to make renunciation a rational process.

These contrasts can come out more clearly in an illustration. Suppose a person settled in one town is offered another job in a distant town. The situation is approached from an economic standpoint if the two jobs are perceived as mutually exclusive alternatives, and a decision is then reached by comparing the two to see which offers more. It is impossible to have both jobs, so one must be given up; the problem is to determine which job is least valuable and can be given up with smallest loss. A list of the advantages of each job is made — one offers more interesting work, a better school for the children; the other offers more pay, better living conditions, and so on. The two groups of values then are compared; this involves estimating the importance of each value that is separable from the others, and adding together the items on each list to see which total situation looks more attractive. If both alternatives have important disadvantages, a search might be made for a third alternative — a different job, or a variation of one of the two available that would combine some advantages of both original alternatives. Or a choice might be made on the basis of which alternative offered the greatest likelihood of eventually opening into the more desirable third alternative. But since no possible job will combine all the advantages of both original alternatives, some renunciation is still inevitable, and the problem is still one of minimizing the inevitable loss.

In making this sort of decision, the individual's preferences are regarded as given, and no attempt is made to change them. Or, if they are questioned, it is in terms of more ultimate preferences or interests which themselves are unquestioned. For instance, faced with a difficult comparison between better living and better working conditions, a person might ask himself, "What do I want out of life, anyway? And how do living and working conditions contribute to it?" Or, faced with a conflict of interest between himself and someone else, children or friends, a person might ask himself how much he was identified with these other people, how far their interests are his own, and how far he should consider their interests in his calculations. These questions enable one to estimate and clarify the relative importance of one's values, but do not lead to any change in basic values.

If the job offer is approached from a social point of view, it is seen first as an opportunity to learn more about oneself and the other people involved. Reactions to the new prospects are clues to unsuspected desires, fears, self-concepts, expectations, obligations, hostilities. Attention is then focused on these personality factors, with the jobs themselves taking the secondary position of symbols and cues. For instance, if an initial attraction for the new job is interpreted as a desire for escape from an uncomfortable deadlock, attention is centered on the deadlock itself, on whether there is some way of resolving it, and if not whether escape is possible in the new job. Once the various clues are followed and the resulting information combined with previous knowledge of oneself and others, a picture of the proposed new situation can be built up — a picture not of wages and hours, but of probable roles and relations. The prospective situation is then evaluated in terms of whether it simplifies some present conflicts to the point of making resolution possible, and whether it offers new difficulties that present (or prevent) an opportunity for growth. For instance, if the new job involves living within visiting distance of relatives, the question will be asked whether this will make possible the further resolution of old conflicts and anxieties, or whether the relations are still deadlocked and close contact would only intensify stress. Again, the question would be asked whether friendships to be broken off by the move contain in themselves possibilities for growth that would be destroyed by moving. If the new situation is seen to simplify some problems and make others more difficult, comparison can be made in terms of which set of problems is a more important obstacle to growth, that is, which set offers the greatest likelihood of a permanent deadlock of energies.

The general objective of an integrative decision process is to project the probable changes in personality and relations resulting from moving or not moving, and then set up rational control over these changes. The move itself becomes an incident in the permanent attempt to grow up and achieve an integrated web of relationships. No loss is involved either in moving or in not moving, since in both cases one's personality continues to exist and to develop in new directions.

The contrast between an economic and an integrative approach to the job offer is most apparent in the different attitudes toward friends and relatives. From an economic standpoint friendships are frozen assets; they cannot be exchanged for anything else or moved to a new location, but must be renounced in a long-distance move. However, the new location offers opportunities to replace them with new, substitute friendships, so that nothing irreplaceable need be lost by the transfer. A person with foresight will not invest too much affect in friends and relatives because they cannot be transferred, but will cultivate more temporary attachments that are more painlessly lost and more easily replaced. From an integrative standpoint, however, friendships are unique and irreplaceable; a new friend is not a substitute for an old one, because each one brings with it a permanent change of the self. Nor are more superficial friendships more readily replaceable, because the cultivation of such alliances is also a change in the self, a change in the direction of decreased capacity for close friendship.

In our culture friends and relatives are more likely to be treated as frozen assets whose value must be compared with the value of career opportunities, climate, and salary. Moreover when the comparison is made they are often outweighed in value by career factors. The reason is that our culture with its strong individual achievement ethic defines career opportunities as more important than friendship; a person is expected to leave friends and relatives if a better job is available. Consequently friendships and kinship relations are not usually so close to the core of the self as is occupation, and they include within themselves expectations of being treated as secondary to occupation. When a person is asked "Who are you?" he is more likely to reply in terms of occupation than by naming his friends and relatives; he thinks of himself as a unique person, distinct from all other people and only peripherally related to them. A contrasting situation is reported by Murphy (1953:30–31) to exist in India; there kinfolk are so much a part of the self that a decision to move is inevitably an integrative decision centering on the effects of the move on kinship relations. When a person decides to move it is not to advance his wealth or career but to escape from intolerable social conflicts. Murphy's adverse judgment on this cultural situation reflects Western achievement values.

SCOPE OF INTEGRATIVE DECISIONS

As with economizing and other forms of decision making, integrative decisions are appropriate only insofar as (1) objective conditions make them necessary by presenting the kind of problem they can resolve, and (2) conditions are present which make successful integrative problem solving possible.

First, integrative decisions are made necessary by a failure of the unconscious integrative process, by which potential conflicts of role expectations, cathexes, ideals, and so forth become real ones. Sometimes the existence of such conflicts is obvious; at other times conflicts are disguised and must be inferred from a variety of signs and indices. Group or organizational conflicts are likely to be overt and obvious, though their roots may be hidden and devious. But conflicts within an individual are usually disguised, and make themselves known only through their effects. One of the most usual signs of a hidden internal conflict is an inability to perform normal tasks, where there is no organic incapacity, and an inability to express affection in a normal manner. Here the normal requirements in action and feeling are those prescribed by a cultural role, and failure to take the role indicates some sort of integrative difficulty. If the difficulty is a common one, it should be traceable back to some discontinuity or conflict in the culture as well. Another sign is the existence of anxiety, accompanied by excessive fatigue in the performance of normal tasks. This sort of sign indicates that action is proceeding in spite of internal blocks, and that excess energy is needed to push action through its internal barriers. Another sort of sign is the occurrence of unrealistic action and affect toward a goal object, or the continued pursuit of unrealistic goals, which indicates that the goal object is primarily a symbolic substitute for other goals which have become blocked. In such cases action cannot proceed to its real completion, so it continues endlessly, insatiably discarding one achievement after another as inadequate. Other signs point to other kinds of integrative problems.

An integrative procedure can be used preventively when those occasions likely to produce conflicts are foreseen. The previous example of a child entering school illustrates a situation in which preventive treatment by mother or teacher can be helpful. Preventive decisions are appropriate in periods of transition to new roles—entering school, the coming of siblings, adolescence, marriage—since these are the times when new conflicts are likely to develop or old conflicts to become reawakened. The development of new personal relationships or a move into a new social environment are also sometimes occasions when preventive decisions are appropriate.

Second, adequate integrative decisions are not possible unless one is in a position to acquire an understanding of the hidden aspects of a problem. Understanding is necessary for any kind of decision, but it is particularly difficult to achieve in integrative problems because they are largely unconscious and disguised. The amount of understanding required is greatest in dealing with long-standing conflicts, since these are likely to involve great complexity, deep repressions, and much symbolism. It is necessary not only to perceive the half-expressed currents of feeling accompanying action, but also to find out what unconscious forces are blocking and diverting action and tying up energy. The special symbolic meanings of the person's environment must be learned in order to understand his reactions to it, and the unconscious meaning of his own behavior must be discovered. All this requires both unusual sensitivity and close association over a period of time; ideally, it requires the specialized conditions of psychoanalysis, where special training and long, intensive study increase the possibility of success. Similarly, long-standing community problems require expert participant observers who can devote a great deal of time to their investigations.

Situations calling for preventive treatment do not require nearly so deep an understanding, since the elements producing temporary stress are usually comparatively simple and obvious. Here a less intimate acquaintance and more superficial involvement is often good enough for a relatively perceptive observer.

A further condition for the successful use of an integrative procedure is the availability of new social resources—affection, confidence, and so on—when these are needed to support changes in the conflict situation. Ordinarily the indigenous resources are already fully involved or are blocked from use, so new resources are necessary if changes are to be successfully produced and stabilized. Moreover, the new resources must be acceptable to the persons involved in a problem, since otherwise no use will be made of them. For instance, a difficult transition from home to school cannot be eased for a child by the love and confidence of neighbors if the child's own parents are indifferent and the teacher is unperceptive and demanding. Neighbors simply are not closely enough involved in a young child's life to provide the security needed in a time of inner crisis. On the other hand, there are times in adolescence when the emotional support of parents is useless or dangerous, because the problem is precisely one of learning to become independent of that support. Here the affection of friends, distant relatives, or neighbors can provide a better basis for the learning of new roles and a new self. In any case, however, a close personal relationship is necessary for the conveyance of effective emotional support. In group or community problems new members often provide the additional strength necessary to make changes possible, though sometimes old members can have the same effect by becoming more deeply involved.

The main limits on the use of an integrative method are set, not by the existence of integrative problems, but by the availability of knowledge and emotional resources. There is no lack of integrative problems anywhere, but the understanding and the resources necessary for coping with them on a conscious level are rare. Inner conflicts or group tensions can be discovered by any casual observer, but the understanding of deeper causes and prediction of reactions to change requires both perceptivity and persistent observation. And even if understanding of a problem is sometimes not too difficult to achieve, the emotional involvement and the inner resources needed to carry out intelligent changes may not be available.

When the conditions for successful use of an integrative method are not present, other procedures must be used to deal with the problem, even though they cannot produce a wholly satisfactory solution. In some personal problems it may be possible to determine that the person's goals are valid in spite of, or in addition to, their irrational meaning for him, and that goal achievement is desirable even though emotional problems remain unsolved. In this case economic and technical decisions are appropriate. In many cases legal and moral barriers ("it's not my responsibility") can be used as protection against involvement in insoluble problems. Group conflict may be approached in a legal fashion (chap. 4) with the hope of achieving a tolerable solution, if nothing better.

A school grading task is an example of a decision that cannot usually be integrative. In an integrative approach the grade would be interpreted as a symbol of acceptance or rejection by the teacher, and the decision would be based on estimates of how difficult it would be for a student to preserve or develop his self-respect in the face of a given grade. Such an approach is usually not possible because in our culture grades ought to be impartial judgments of achievement and the student-teacher relation ought to be relatively impersonal. This means that the symbolic social meaning that a grade does take on will be an idiosyncratic meaning, depending on individual circumstances; and the usual student-teacher relation will be such that the teacher will be unable to learn the individual meaning of a grade. Hence an attempt to grade on an integrative basis will most likely be based on faulty judgments both of the meaning of the grade and of the relationship itself, and will likely lead to more harm than good. Grading decisions are more properly to be treated as technical decisions of an individual's degree of fitness for a standard task, or legal decisions as to whether a set of standard requirements has been fulfilled. On the other hand, an integrative approach to grading may be appropriate in an individual tutorial relationship with young children who have not yet learned the impersonal student role.

In the case mentioned earlier of a person faced with the possibility of moving to a new job in a new town, the appropriate type of decision would depend first on the degree of perceptivity and self-knowledge of the person involved. A thing- and task-oriented person would probably not learn much new about himself even if he tried, so an integrative approach would most likely be ineffective and therefore inappropriate. For a perceptive person the appropriateness of an integrative approach would depend on whether personality conflicts were activated by the job offer. When a conflict already exists in the career area, for instance marriage or family *vs.* career, a job offer can reactivate the conflict and provide a chance to begin resolving it; if no such conflict exists an integrative approach is probably unnecessary.

Quite often social and economic considerations are mixed together in a problem so thoroughly that it would be a mistake to ignore either of them. In this case the most appropriate decision procedure is a mixed one combining integrative and economic elements in some way. I have explored this topic elsewhere (Diesing, 1958).

SOCIAL VALUE

Rational social organizations make action of all kinds possible, so the good achieved by them can be called simply action or social action. Or it could be called shared action or shared experience to emphasize the co-operation of various persons or parts of the personality, all of which are necessary to make action successful. If one wishes to bring out the emotional component of action, one could call it love, friendship, or brotherhood, depending on the kind and intensity of the relationship. These terms must not be understood to refer to a state of private feeling, such as "being in love," but to a complete relation including action, feeling, and mutual understanding. In Fromm's discussion of the term "love" (Fromm, 1947:96ff.) he defines it as an active, productive relatedness between people; this is the sense intended here. "Shared experience" perhaps connotes both the action and feeling components more impartially.

All the above terms are misleading in that they seem to refer only to single acts or single relationships; but integrated social systems also place actions and relationships in a larger supportive setting. The larger setting both insures successful completion without blockage and gives meaning to individual acts. From this standpoint the good is self-realization in the objective idealist sense of participation in an infinite (enduring, self-contained) system of activity, a system which transcends individuals and enables them to transcend themselves. The idealists have often been interpreted in very queer ways as totalitarians, authoritarians, as sacrificing the Individual to the State, and I do not of course intend any such meaning here. Subjectively, self-realization involves something on the order of a sense of belonging, of inner security, and of the meaningfulness of life. Dewey's categorical imperative "so act as to increase the meaning of experience" (1930:283) expresses this. The individual participating in an integrated system is confident of the rightness of his acts, since everything—tradition, his inner standards, the expectations of others —support them. He senses the existence of a larger whole in which he moves and which carries his acts along to insure their completion. This is a sensing of the sacred as Durkheim, and Dewey, describe it. And he is aware of the meaningfulness of his actions in that they contribute to an enduring activity. Meaningfulness here is a blend of cognitive and cathectic elements; it includes a feeling of the importance of the enduring activity as well as an understanding of how one contributes to it.

A disorganized society produces people who are insecure in that they do not know what is right, and feel helpless, unsupported; people with a sense of the meaninglessness of life in that they feel no connection between their acts and feelings and anything else. Participation in segmental organizations has much the same effect, since here the system of action is incomplete; it does not involve the whole person and indeed can take up only the more superficial part of the personality.

Shared experience differs from utilities in that it consists not of distinct objects but of active participation in a system of relationships. It cannot be possessed by an individual as his personal property, since it transcends the individual. It cannot be bought, sold, or exchanged, since it is not an object distinct from other objects, and cannot therefore be measured, compared with other objects, and assigned a price. It does not satisfy a desire or need as utilities do, but is constitutive of the personality and its needs. Utilities exist in relation to a self that is separate from them; social actions are an expression of the self, and of its solidarity with others.

Chapter 4

Legal Rationality

Every society develops a set of fundamental rules for the guidance of its members. These rules are made necessary by conflicts among the many normative elements that pervade social life, the day-to-day expectations, personal obligations, commitments that govern behavior. When conflicts occur, the fundamental rules are called on to resolve them by setting boundaries of validity, determining priorities, or canceling invalid norms. Subgroups and organizations within a society also develop fundamental rules applying only to members and centering on the special concerns of the group. In this chapter we shall deal with the rationality to be found in fundamental rules.

The fundamental rules of a society may be called its legal order, or perhaps its moral order, or perhaps its status system. Of these three, I choose the term "legal" with some hesitation, first, because rules are not the whole of law, and perhaps not even the most important part of it. At least equally important are the special institutions which service the legal order, such institutions as courts, jails, police, lawyers, law schools, and legislatures, with which we shall not be concerned. These institutions cannot be considered here because they develop into complete organizations which embody a variety of types of rationality in addition to "legal" rationality. But the fact that I am not dealing with the whole of law is certain to lead to misunderstandings which the reader must try to avoid.

Second, there is no general agreement on the definition of the word "legal" and on the boundary between legal and moral rules. Rules which are called legal by one person are called moral by another, and even when there is agreement on terminology the words have different connotations for different people. But the term "moral" has a still greater variety of meanings, and is almost unusable without elaborate and systematic definition. The same is true of the word "status." My purpose here is not to argue for any particular terminology or boundaries in the field of the normative, but to discuss the special kind of rationality appropriate to fundamental rules, whatever they may be called. Consequently if anyone objects to my use of legal terminology he should substitute his own terms wherever necessary.

NORMS AND THE LEGAL ORDER

The legal order is not sharply distinguishable from the ordinary norms which it regulates. The countless norms which come into existence in every society are never arranged in a perfect hierarchy with exact priorities and clear distinctions between levels. Instead, the scales of priority shift with time, place, and circumstance, and the more fundamental rules shade into the less fundamental without any break. However, it is possible to indicate in a general way what kinds of norms usually belong to the legal order and what kinds do not. Let us survey several kinds of norms for this purpose.

First, there are the expectations and obligations (chap. 3) which are parts of all social relations. These are the most pervasive, but also the most fluid and the most particularized of all norms. Every relationship between two people grows its own expectation-obligation norms, which change continually as the relation develops, and which may be unique to that relation. Only rarely do people become aware of the web of expectations in which they move; ordinarily it remains completely unconscious. Awareness occurs, as a rule, only when expectations are regularly thwarted, or when one contrasts one's own rules with those of a different person, and often not then.

Second, one can speak of essential expectations and obligations in contrast to secondary or peripheral ones. The essential expectations are those which individuals must be able to count on in performing their own part of the relation. For example, parents in our culture must be able to count on some measure of obedience from children if they are to carry out their own obligation to protect and train their children. Children in turn must be able to count on some amount of care from parents if they are to be free to play their roles as children. Friends who have arranged to meet at a certain time must be able to count on each other's presence at that time in making their plans. In contrast, the obligation to accept the invitation of a friend is not as crucial and may occasionally be avoided for sufficient reason, and the expectation that the friend will sympathize and agree with one's point of view is even less crucial to the performance of one's own obligations.

The distinction between essential and ordinary obligations is usually not drawn very sharply, and often it represents two poles of a continuum rather than two kinds of obligations. Also, the determination of which obligations are essential varies from one relation to another, even when the same pairs of cultural roles are involved. The degree of obedience that one parent absolutely insists on will be regarded as unnecessary and optional by another; and where failure to keep appointments might break up one friendship, it might be readily forgiven in other cases. Yet since all the individual relationships exemplifying a pair of cultural roles tend to be similar, they also tend to be similar in their definitions of essential obligations.

Third, one may speak of authoritative norms, namely those norms that people have agreed will prevail over ordinary norms in case of conflict. The agreement that a norm will prevail over others gives it an additional strength and dependability. If A recognizes the importance of B's expectation to B and undertakes to fulfill it, B can count on A's performance and can insist on it in case of nonperformance.

Though the distinction between essential and authoritative norms is clear in the abstract, it is very difficult to make in practice. In the abstract the distinction is between mutual agreement and more or less unilateral insistence. However, in practice agreement is frequently a tacit matter, as Hume pointed out long ago in his account of the ground of obligation (1888, bk. III, pt. 2, sec 2). Now a tacit, unconscious agreement may be perfectly dependable and even unbreakable, but often it is hard to distinguish a real agreement and a pseudo agreement. A may assume an agreement on B's part because of continual performance, but B may have been performing for reasons of generosity, carelessness, coercion, or other reasons, without accepting any obligation at all. In this case there will be an eventual nonperformance, followed by a dispute. In labor-management relations, for instance, labor may come to expect as a definite right some Christmas bonus, time-punching arrangement, work rule that management has acquiesced in for many years, while management may regard the practice as a freely revokable policy rather than as a binding obligation.

Authoritative norms are much more clearly distinguishable when they follow a dispute. A dispute draws attention to a norm, brings it into consciousness, dramatizes it; and any resulting settlement must necessarily be conscious and explicit for both parties involved. Clarity can also be achieved when agreement is public and explicit, or when an official spokesman for a group announces that from now on a certain norm will be binding on all.

Authoritative norms are usually accompanied by sanctions of some sort, either the diffuse sanctions of social approval-disapproval, or the specific sanctions of public officials, both part time and full time. In addition the inner sanctions of guilt, shame, and conscientiousness frequently support both authoritative and nonauthoritative norms. Sanctions serve to render the performance of duties more secure and dependable, partly by deterring delinquents, partly by dramatizing duties and reaffirming them, partly by excluding, reforming, or readmitting offenders to society. All sanctions differ from plain coercion in that they are accepted as legitimate, at least by some of the people to whom they apply. Indeed, in many cases a delinquent will invoke sanctions on himself as a way of making amends, reaffirming the duty, and getting himself reaccepted into the group.

The existence of different kinds of sanctions enables one to make further distinctions among authoritative norms according to the kind of sanction which supports them. Some norms are supported primarily by diffuse sanctions, some primarily by specific sanctions, and some by specific sanctions of officials of a sovereign state.

Each of the above types of norm, except the first, have been regarded as legal by some people and nonlegal by others. Ehrlich (1936) and Petrazycki (1955) seem to regard all essential expectations-obligations as part of the living law, since they apparently locate law in the habitual insistence of individuals rather than in public agreements. Or one may base law and legal obligation on tacit agreement, as Hume does. Or, as with Llewellyn and Hoebel (1941, chap. 2), one may limit law to those authoritative norms agreed on after public dispute, and relegate tacit agreements to the borderland of law. In this definition the existence of a court of some sort, that is, a public dispute-settling place, is essential to the existence of law. A still narrower definition is that of Weber (1954:11ff.) and of Hoebel (1954: 28), in which law is limited to those norms supported by specific sanctions of specific public officials. The officials may have a general enforcement function, as in the case of the military societies of the Plains Indians and the secret societies of West Africa, or they may act as public officials on special occasions only, as in the obligatory retaliation by specific kinsmen for murder. Finally, in the definition of John Austin (1954) and his followers, only norms sanctioned by full-time officials of a modern state are legal. One may also distinguish two or more kinds of law; thus Ehrlich distinguishes the living law, or essential expectations-obligations and tacit agreements, from the norms applied by official state courts, and Weber distinguishes law in general from state law.

The narrower one's definition of law is, the more remote from daily life the legal order becomes. With wide definitions such as those of Ehrlich and Petrazycki the legal order is an intimate part of life; with narrow definitions such as those of Austin and Gray (1909) the legal order is reserved for lawyers and judges, and ordinary people have almost no contact with it.

Morality is often conceived to include some or all duties that are less than legal; but if several definitions of the legal are possible, the boundary line of the moral is also not a fixed one. What is moral in one theory is legal in another. In addition, if law is defined narrowly as all commands of the sovereign or judgments of state courts, there are several kinds of morality that are as different from each other as they are from the legal. There is the social morality of sensitivity to broad ideals and shifting expectations and feelings; the legal morality of respect for authoritative norms embodying the recognized rights of others; the political morality of taking responsibility for one's own present and future development; and perhaps the morality of group codes supported by diffuse sanctions. To these must be added the economic morality of impartial attention to costs and consequences and avoidance of waste. Each of these kinds of morality has been championed by some philosopher as the only possible kind of morality. In the social morality of T. H. Green (1883) and perhaps F. H. Bradley (1951), the morally good man is the one who learns to form ever wider and deeper emotional attachments, centered in family relations but extending to larger groups, whose self is constituted by social relations and whose experience is consequently shared with others. In the legal morality of Kant the good man is the one who can be absolutely relied on, though he might have difficulty in relating to people emotionally. The moral theories of Westermarck (1932) and of Bentham exemplify group code and economic morality.

If the legal is defined broadly as all rules explicitly agreed on as binding by a group, the line between law and morals is again a changing one, though in a different way. Each group, beginning with siblings in a family, has its own legal code and is in turn subject to the legal code of the larger group which includes it and also the codes of still larger, more inclusive groups. But the rules treated as binding by one group, such as a family, are not necessarily important to the larger community which includes it. They may be recognized as ordinary obligations but not as definite legal duties. In other words, the rules that are legal for one group are moral for a larger group, and the law of this group is in turn part of the morality of some still more inclusive group. Only the law of the final group, the whole society, is law for all.

Social status is somewhat easier to distinguish from both law and morality, at least in the abstract. Ordinarily social status systems are defined as only those rights and duties that arrange people in a hierarchy of some sort *and* are supported primarily by diffuse sanctions. In Western culture at least, this makes for a superficially clear distinction: moral codes are supported primarily by internal sanctions, social status systems primarily by diffuse sanctions, and legal systems primarily by specific sanctions. The distinction is even clearer if the hierarchy of status supported by courts (legal status) conflicts with that supported by diffuse sanctions (social status) as Barber (1957:55f.) observes was the case in medieval France. However, where specific and diffuse sanctions support the same status hierarchy, legal and social status may be indistinguishable in practice; and where moral codes are supported by shame and social approval, morality and social status may also be indistinguishable.

Fundamental rules, the subject of this chapter, undoubtedly belong in the class of authoritative norms, since those norms whose importance is denied by some persons can hardly be used to regulate other norms, but are themselves in need of judgment and regulation. Among authoritative norms, those tacitly agreed on are probably not fundamental either, because the use of a norm to regulate other norms tests and makes explicit the extent of its acceptance. Explicit authoritative norms also may have varying degrees of priority and generality, and some may be regarded as relatively localized and nonfundamental, belonging to the fringes of the legal order as I am using the term.

This rough classification is perhaps sufficient for the present. Our primary purpose is to discuss legal trends and legal rationality, and all that is needed to begin is a general area in which one can look for trends of legal development. Once these trends have been located and analyzed, the ensuing conclusions about legal rationality apply to anything in which those same trends occur, no matter how it is classified. The question of the scope of legal rationality will be taken up again toward the end of the chapter.

However, we shall see that legal rationality and legal trends are most clearly apparent in the narrowest type of norm, the rules enforced by Western state officials. This narrow kind of law will turn out to be paradigmatic for all law, and can be called law in the strictest sense, as I am using the term. The characteristics of this strictest law will be found to a lesser extent in social status systems, externalized moral codes, and rules of formal organizations, to a still lesser extent in the law of stateless societies and in internalized moral codes, and not at all in tacit agreements and nonauthoritative norms. To avoid confusion, I shall use the term "Law" for law in the strictest sense, and the terms "law" and "legal order" for everything in which a legal trend may occur, following Llewellyn's terminology (1940). The latter two terms thus will refer to much that is sometimes thought of as morality or social status. I shall also use the right-duty language to refer to legal rules, to contrast with the expectations-obligations of nonfundamental norms.

The legal order, law in the wide sense, constitutes a kind of skeleton of the group's social structure, which individuals can rely on and around which they can build a detailed system of roles. The authoritative rights and duties comprising this skeleton are the same for a whole class of persons, while the ordinary expectations and obligations surrounding them vary with circumstances and the inventiveness of individuals.

Rules of law are a framework, not only for the details of role obligations, but also for the roles themselves. As long as individuals recognize and carry out their duties, they can take a variety of roles consistent with those duties without risking sanctions. For example, as long as children stay within the basic structure of duties toward siblings, they can take a variety of roles with one another — nurturing, dependent, competitive, supportive, and so forth — and as long as they recognize the basic duties of obedience to parents, they can develop similar variations in relations with parents.

The total set of rights and duties attributed to an individual constitute his legal status. A status is a general, basic position in society; it determines which roles are open to a person, what range of variation is possible in each role, what roles he must take, what kind of response he can definitely count on in each role, and what additional range of responses he may try to elicit. For instance, a person with the status of child in our culture cannot get married, cannot participate in many adult activities, except in a few limited roles, cannot usually take a role of authority toward adults; but he may have friends of his own status, may take dependent roles toward adults, and must take a dependent role toward his own parents. Once he discards his status as a child and is given a new status as adolescent or adult many new roles are open to him and the old roles are no longer available, even if he wanted to retain them.

If law is defined narrowly, as Law, one can distinguish between Legal status, or one's position in the formal courts, and social status, or one's position in society. But in the wider conception of law that we are using this distinction becomes irrelevant. One must merely remember that some cultures contain two or more semi-independent legal systems.

Statuses are the component parts of legal systems just as roles are of social systems; and the rights and duties which make up a status are analogous to the obligations and expectations which partly make up a social role. Since each system of roles exists in the framework of a status system, a person cannot participate in one without also participating in the other. He cannot actively occupy a status except by taking some appropriate roles — in this sense role is the dynamic aspect of status (Parsons, 1949:43) — but he cannot take any role unless he has the status which will make that role available to him. The two systems are so closely interdependent that in some respects they must be studied together as a single compound structure. Indeed, it is only the difference of developmental trends in status systems and role systems that enables one to distinguish them as different modes of social organization.

So far the legal order has been treated in relation to social action; but it can also be related to economic activity in quite parallel fashion. In social life rights and duties are the basic framework for expectations and obligations, as people engage in role-playing activity; in economic life they provide the basis for allocation and exchange. Just as people cannot carry out the requirements of a role unless they can count on certain responses from others, so in economic action people cannot allocate or exchange resources unless they can count on the availability of the resources. No allocation of resources can be successful unless there is some measure of individual control over resources against the actions of others. Hence people making economic decisions must inevitably make claims on some resources with the intention of excluding other people. As in the case of social expectations, claims are either tacitly acknowledged or are disputed by counterclaims; if the disputes are resolved some claims are accepted and sanctioned, and eventually specialists are created to judge disputes and apply sanctions. The result is a system of property and contracts, property being direct control over resources and contract representing exchange of resources. Both property and contract are expressible as complex sets of right-duty relations.

Probably the basic form of property is one's own time, since all allocations involve some use of one's time. People who do not own their own time are slaves, and slaves can hardly exercise any property or contractual rights unless they acquire the right to at least some of their own time. In addition to time, all commodities are forms of property, and anything that becomes a commodity during economic progress is subject to ownership and exchange.

A system of property and contract forms a framework for all economic life, just as a status system is a framework for social life. It determines what allocations and exchanges are possible by prescribing the exact degree of control each individual has over resources. People cannot make any economic decisions unless they have a place in some system of property and contract, and they cannot exercise property and contractual rights except through economic activity.

Law thus has a double function of providing a basis for both social and economic activity.[1] Quite different characteristics are required for performing these two functions. Insofar as a legal system has a social function it concerns itself with status differentials; insofar as it has an economic function it concerns itself with property and contract. The value standards of a social legal system carry over the social emphasis on a hierarchy of obligations and on the importance of discovering priorities of obligation (for example, "women and children first") while an economic legal system carries over the economic emphasis on impartiality and universality (for example, "first come, first served"). Legal relations in a socially functioning system tend to be diffuse (status relations) while in an economically functioning system they tend to be specific (contractual relations). Punishment in a social legal system tends to deal with the whole person rather than with a specific offense. Many infringements of norms may be passed over with little or no sanction, till at a certain point total punishment occurs. The offender is either excluded from society altogether, or an attempt at thorough rehabilitation is made, or both. In an economic legal system punishment tends to be partial and limited to the specific offense, for instance a monetary fine. This type of punishment has nothing to do with ostracism or emotional rehabilitation; even corporations can be punished by fines, though they have no social personality at all. The conflict between these two kinds of legal systems is one of the most important sources of trouble in culture contact. This is particularly noticeable when Western legal systems, with their drive for universality and impartiality, for equality of all men before the law, come in contact with the localized, particularistic, status-conscious legal systems of many preliterate peoples.

The American legal system as it now stands is primarily economic in function. It primarily centers on specific, contractual-type relations, and strives to provide impartial treatment for all. Status elements exist but are of secondary importance, and are continually threatened by the drive for impartiality. Such statuses as those of women, children, more recently labor, aliens, inferior races, are recognized because of their importance for social life, but they are treated as exceptions to a basic impartiality of treatment. The social

---

[1] Northrop (1960) discusses a third legal function, which he calls mediation, but this is identical with integration.

function of law is performed in American law primarily by the non-Legal parts of the system, often in disguised form to avoid conflict with Law. Officially, Americans deny or are unaware of status differentials; unofficially, status symbols and race prejudice are pervasive. Officially, Americans believe in equality of opportunity and impartiality of treatment; unofficially, family, ethnic, regional, and personal loyalties are stoutly maintained as rights and duties. Official punishment tends to be specific and quantitative, though there is some fragmentary interest in basic rehabilitation; but unofficially, total exclusion is the more usual form of punishment in social life.

Needless to say, this particular distribution of the economic and the social orientations of law, the economic orientation dominant and the social orientation concealed or located in non-Legal morality, is by no means universal. Consequently, students of legal organization who study only Western Legal systems get a distorted picture of the nature of law, which would be remedied by study of primitive and non-Western law. An interesting example is provided by Hegel's *Philosophy of Right.* Hegel gives an excellent exposition of the necessary relation of law to elementary economic activity in his part I, but falls short in his treatment of the social side of law in part II. Instead of discussing the relation between status and role-playing activity, he works through the categories of a subjective, individual morality, dealing with such things as intentions, purposes, the will, and conscience. Morality of this sort is the subjective counterpart of a status system, just as utilitarian morality is the subjective counterpart of contract and property use; but subjectivity alone is not a proper social basis for law. Not subjective morality, but rather a status system provides the legal framework for the family social life of part III, just as the property and contract categories of part I rather than rules of calculation are the legal framework for the economic life of civil society. Hegel's shortcomings are remedied by Bosanquet (1930:187ff.), who gives a particularistic, socially oriented account of legal rights.

In spite of the intimate connection of legal systems with both social and economic life, they possess one characteristic which is neither social nor economic, but is a true emergent. Legal transactions are always public in a way that social and economic activities never are. They always concern the whole group sharing a particular legal system, never only the two individuals involved. This is obvious when law is interpreted and enforced by special public officials; but it is also true when specialists are absent.

The reason for the public character of law is that rights and duties are not effective unless they are recognized by an entire group. Individuals cannot be secure in their legal rights unless they know that all members of the group acknowledge them. Property is not securely owned unless all group members recognize ownership or can be made to recognize it; status rights are not secure unless all potential partners in social relations recognize them. The difficulty of securing general agreement in a large group is what makes specialized public officials and police forces necessary, since in this way a group can guarantee its members rights even against dissenting members.

For the same reason rights and duties cannot be changed except by a public act acknowledged and accepted by all group members. A decision accepted only by some members and denied by others would not really establish new rights and duties securely, because the dissenting members could not be relied on to act according to them. Thus the settlement of a legal dispute must necessarily be a public act of a public official, even when a private citizen is acting. Unless his action is public, that is, accepted by all, it does not settle the dispute.

For example, in a society without full-time legal officials murder is often avenged by kinsmen, who have a duty to kill the murderer or a substitute of equal status. The difficulty of this system is that unless the relatives of the murderer accept the avenging act of the kinsmen as a public act, they are duty-bound to retaliate, and a feud begins. A settlement of a murder-dispute can be achieved only by a public act. Public acceptance transforms the kinsmen into temporary public officials and their murder into an execution; it changes the murderer's status into that of an outlaw who has no rights, and the kinsmen's status from that of outlaw murderers to blameless citizens.

Legal systems are the public setting of social and economic life. They are the means through which the whole of a society participates in each individual action, offering its acquiescence or support. At the same time, they set the limits of individual action, indicating what actions are necessary and what range of action beyond this is possible.

LEGAL TRENDS

The discovery of legal trends is somewhat more difficult than in the case of other modes of social organization because of the close interdependence between legal and socioeconomic organization. Several suggestions on the nature of legal trends have been made at various times. The most famous suggestion, Maine's dictum that the law moves from status to contract, has been recognized to apply only to Western law. It summarizes the shift of Western law from a social to an economic function that accompanied the rapid economic progress of recent centuries. Writers have noted that this trend has in some degree been reversed in the last fifty years as public attention has been drawn to problems of social disorganization and accompanying problems of status insecurity brought about largely by economic progress.

Several other suggestions are closely related to the status-contract distinction and, like it, apply only or chiefly to Western legal history. Two examples are the theory that law moves from collective to individual responsibility and that it moves from ascription of liability for acts to ascription of liability for intentions. These developments need not be further considered, since they are by no means universal. They represent the influence, not of some universal selective process, but of some factors peculiar to Western culture.

Another suggestion is that made by Hoebel (1954) and also by Barton (1949) that law moves from private to specialized public enforcement. This suggestion is supported by numerous examples in primitive law and must be seriously considered. It appears not to apply to legal systems that are already backed by a full state apparatus; but if one includes lawyers in the category of nascent public officials, it may even be extended to apply to Western legal systems. One could say that law becomes ever more specialized in its personnel, that legal personnel become ever more explicitly public figures, and that this trend continues today.

Another trend that is discussed by many writers is the trend toward legalism, which looks promising except that it is always condemned whenever it is mentioned. In the case of social status systems, stratification appears to be a universal trend and must be seriously considered. Perhaps all three of these trends can provide some clues to the nature of legal rationality.

There may be other legal trends which I have not considered; if so, my analysis is incomplete to that extent. However, it must be remembered that I am dealing only with trends that are universal, automatic, and inevitable in the same way that technological progress is. I am not interested in developments that occur only through conscious effort, but only in developments that continue even against the most determined opposition, since only such developments point to natural selective systems. This requirement is met by both legalism and stratification.

Let us begin with legalism. To make matters more specific, consider the development of legalism in labor arbitration in the United States. Labor arbitration is an extremely new area of law, less than fifty years old in the United States. It began as a protest movement against the excessive legalism of United States' courts, and yet already the first traces of legalism can be discerned in it and the first protests against legalism in arbitration have appeared (MacPherson, 1949; Davey, 1955:85, 88–89; Sembower, 1957:98–111; Domke, 1958). Thus we should be able to see in labor arbitration the very first beginnings of legalism and perhaps find the dynamics and the rationality, if any, underlying it.

Among the trends that have been noted are, first, an increase in the complexity of labor contracts (Updegraff and McCoy, 1946:136; Dunlop, 1949:68). The first contracts with new unions in the thirties were usually very simple affairs, stating that a certain union was the official representative of the employees in matters pertaining to wages, hours, and working conditions, and adding a few details. But soon disagreements arose and were carried to arbitration; and the resulting distinctions and clarifications were embodied in succeeding contracts. Other disagreements were declared inarbitrable and were resolved in later bargaining sessions. Within ten years contracts had become little booklets full of details and distinctions, and are still becoming more complex.

A parallel development is the increasing detail of job specification. This includes not only statements of what a worker ordinarily does and what he may occasionally do, but also what he cannot be asked to do and what he must not do. This development results partly from disputes about pay differentials, in which a worker complains that his job is substantially the same as that of a higher paid worker and that he is therefore entitled to the higher rate of pay. Partly it results from workers' complaints about gradual job speed-ups and employers' complaints about slow-downs; these disputes are resolved by establishment of standard rates and amounts. And partly it results from workers' fears of job scarcity and attempts to exclude others from their jobs. Each new piece of machinery or technical improvement produces, or threatens to produce, a new dispute, and leads to further specification of standards, equivalences, and differentials.

Accompanying this specification of both jobs and contracts is the development of technical meanings for ordinary terms and the invention of new technical terms. These terms are more exact and precise than ordinary terms and thus prevent disputes over whether or not they apply to a particular case. Such crucial terms as "overtime," "seniority," and "base pay" of course take on technical meaning; but also the detailed terms used to define them, terms like "consecutive," "successive," and "average," become technical. And with the technical terms come the specialists in terminology, the lawyers. Originally any worker could become a "shop lawyer" with a little study; he could learn the brief contract by memory and apply it confidently to a variety of disputes. But with technical terms and increasing length and complexity, contracts and job specifications tended to become baffling and even unintelligible to ordinary workers and had to be interpreted by specialists. These same specialists had to be called in to draft contracts after the crucial general issues had been settled by collective bargaining.

Legalism also appears in the procedure of arbitration hearings. The ideology of arbitration originally defined it as an informal problem-solving process, freed from the artificial rules and technicalities of courts. But the need for rules became apparent immediately. Even such a simple question as who should present his case first could lead to a dispute which threatened to wreck the hearing (Seward, 1957:147); so procedural rules promptly appeared and soon became standardized. These procedural rules, in turn, tend to become more complex. Sembower (1957:100ff.) notes the following legalistic procedural developments: increasing exactness of the initial submission by the plaintiff, the use of prehearing investigations, increasing reliance on rules of evidence, use of written records, increased length and importance of posthearing briefs. Complexity of procedure brings with it the need for lawyers, who will know how to avoid mistakes of procedure; today both sides of an arbitration case ordinarily employ lawyers, though twenty-five years ago this was a rarity. Lawyers in turn demand written records, so they can check for mistakes and possible bases of appeal; and when a stenographer is listening, men's words become formalized and precise, as they become aware that their words will be scrutinized by eager opponents.

Perhaps the most familiar aspect of legalism is reliance on precedent, and this too is increasingly evident in arbitration. Precedent becomes more important in arbitration hearings as a lawyer's argument; but it also serves to settle grievances short of arbitration. One arbitrator observes, "Increasingly in recent years one finds both sides referring to prior arbitration decisions in third and fourth step meetings, and there are many instances in which grievances are settled on the basis of such precedents" (Killingsworth, 1953:130). Indeed, some writers have expressed the belief that arbitration decisions are yielding a growing body of case law which will resolve incipient disputes and diminish the need for arbitration in the future. The publication of arbitrators' opinions facilitates the reliance on precedent. Publication of select opinions (by Bureau of National Affairs, Inc.) began about 1945 as a private, informal venture; but demand was considerable, and it is to be expected that the number of opinions published will increase. A warning against such an increase has been given by one writer who cites publication as one contributing aspect of legalism (MacPherson, 1949).

Finally, there is a trend toward uniformity in the legislative statutes and court decisions dealing with arbitration (Updegraff and McCoy, 1946:154). This is partly achieved by direct borrowing of existing statutes from state to state. The writers who cite this trend and who predict it will continue argue that it eliminates arbitrary differences across political boundaries.

An extreme, if questionable, example of the rapid appearance of rules and precedents to structure an originally fluid situation is provided by the War Labor Board. Alfred M. Ross states (1948:58 quoted in Braun, 1955:182):

The Board enjoyed thinking that it operated strictly on a "case-by-case basis" with every dispute decided on its own merits, but in practical effect this was only a pleasant fiction. The "merits" of a case rested on the application of rigid and uniform policies which gradually developed during the first two years of experience. This was not the result of choice but of necessity. It would have been extremely difficult to grant more to one union than had been granted to another under similar circumstances.

It may be argued that this rapid development was due to management pressure, based on the expectation that definite rules would freeze the status quo and eliminate labor's wartime bargaining advantage. However, even this pressure probably only speeded up a process that would have occurred in any case, for the reasons Ross gives. One side or the other would have complained if it had received any worse treatment than anyone else under similar circumstances.

Note that all these developments have occurred in direct opposition to the original and still prevalent ideology of arbitration, which defines it as a flexible, particularized problem-solving process. Arbitration began in part as a protest against the excessive legalism of United States Law, but it is increasingly coming to resemble its opponent, just as equity did some centuries earlier. This does not mean that arbitration law will inevitably become indistinguishable from Law, and indeed this is unlikely; but it does indicate that the same natural selective system is at work in arbitration as in United States Law.

Legalism, as here revealed in outline, seems to consist of (1) a trend toward complexity of distinctions and clarity of detail, such as highly technical terms, (2) a trend toward clear and distinct hierarchical differentiation, for example, job specification, (3) a trend toward uniformity, equality, and universalization where differentials are not involved, and (4) more generally, a trend toward rigidity, unchangeability, action according to rule. Once rules are made, they may be clarified, made more precise, extended, but not changed. Of these trends, (1), (3), and (4) have clearly occurred in Western Law, and their effects are also obvious in Roman Law.

Social stratification is not a distinct trend, but is rather another example of legalism. In the most highly developed case of stratification, the caste system of India, (1), (2), and (4) are characteristic; and in less developed status systems (2) and (4) at least are evident, with (1) appearing in status symbols. This identity of trend further justifies classifying law and social status as the same mode of social organization.

Bureaucracy is another area in which legalism occurs. A bureaucratic organization typically develops a code of rules and a set of forms (4); the rules and forms become more complex and detailed (1); and applicants are treated uniformly according to unvarying rules (3). The bureaucratic personnel themselves often develop an increasingly detailed hierarchical differentiation (2).

In what circumstances does legalism occur? Although a definitive answer to this question would be hard to give, we can at least derive some suggestions from labor-management relations, and from other sources. First, legalism occurs only in the presence of permanent and clear differences of interest. Labor and management are examples; the economic process operates to create and maintain differences of interest between labor and management, whether in capitalist, socialist, or communist economies. Legalism occurs only slightly in small families and small groups, where differences of interest are vague and shifting, though it does occur to the extent that differences are clear and persistent, for instance in the assignment of irksome tasks. It occurs only slightly in the law of many small primitive tribes which are highly integrated. On the other hand, in large, highly differentiated social systems such as those in India and in West and South Africa for example, Bantu tribes, Fulani-Nupe, Yoruba — which are loosely integrated, there is a considerable amount of stratification. Similarly, stratification develops rapidly in areas where different races and cultures mix and accommodate but do not assimilate. Here the cultural differences produce persistent, clearly defined differences of interest. Thus one could venture a general proposition: as integration increases, legalism decreases, and law — including morality and status — declines in importance, though it does not disappear.

A striking case of the relative absence of legalism is described by Harbison (Harbison and Dubin, 1947). The case is the Studebaker plant in South Bend, Indiana. The authors mention, for instance, that shop rules remained unwritten for many years. The Studebaker contract was a relatively unused document; grievance discussions often bypassed it, and shop lawyers did not flourish. Company-union relations at all levels were largely informal and friendly. The authors suggest several reasons for this relative absence of legalism, such as the size of the town, the unique position of the plant in the town, the competitive position of Studebaker in the auto industry, the position of local 5 in the UAW, and the flexibility of top officials. All of these circumstances tended to reduce, though not eliminate, differences of interest and to increase solidarity.

Second, legalism occurs only when the distribution of power among different interests is relatively stabilized by checks and balances. Legal systems tend to reflect the general power distribution of the society they serve, so that any considerable shift in power distribution induces a corresponding shift in law. If the change in power is sudden and drastic it will lead to a rapid writing of new laws, as in the case of the New Deal, the accession of Socialist, Fascist, or Communist parties to power, and the appearance of new union-management contracts in the thirties. If the change of power is gradual and prolonged, it will be reflected in subtle but cumulative shifts in the interpretation of existing laws and in the unobtrusive slanting of legislation. Thus the growth of corporations and of corporation power from 1850–1900 was accompanied by shifts of judicial interpretation which strengthened the legal position of corporations, as many writers have observed.

When law is subject to external pressures coming from shifts of power its own internal dynamics are blocked or concealed. Its changes become part of a general social change and cannot therefore have any uniquely legal characteristics. Thus the first union-management contracts, the New Deal legislation, the acquisition of legal personality by corporations, the Supreme Court decision on segregation are not examples of legalism, though they provide the foundation for later legalistic developments.

The expectation of an imminent change of power can have the same deterrent effects on legalism as an actual change of power. If one interest group believes its power is going to increase, it will concentrate on helping to bring about the expected increase rather than on protecting its present position by legal arguments. If, for instance, an interest group has a Marxist ideology which promises radical changes in the near future, it will not accept the enmeshing devices of legalism but will rely rather on its own clear intuitions of justice and right. Only when the hope of further expansion of power dims does power subside in importance and law begin to develop.

A third prerequisite for the occurrence of legalism is the existence of common values, other than the legal norms agreed on, and some slight degree of trust and solidarity among the different interests. The common values strengthen the sense of rightness, the legitimacy, of the rules and sanctions that do develop. Without some such sense of community, some "general will," however slight, it is difficult to find rules that are accepted as legitimate by all parties, judges that are accepted as impartial, and sanctions that can be borne without resentment and retaliation. An example is provided by Harbison and Dubin (1947). The authors note that though GM-UAW relations were on the whole bitterly hostile and devoid of legalism, legalism did develop rapidly in certain small areas in which both sides could agree on general principles, and where agreement did not affect bargaining positions. The authors also note that the extreme legalism that occurred in these areas provided no effective drainage for many frustrations, which built up into "human relations problems."

To sum up these tentative suggestions, legalism seems to appear when there are permanent, clear differences of interest; it acts to stabilize the resulting conflict-situation, *if and only if* there are already other bases of stability — stable power relations, solidarity, common principles — but it does not resolve the conflicts, remove the frustrations and hostility, integrate the opposed interests. Gouldner (1954) makes the same observations about bureaucracy of the "punishment-centered" variety. He generalizes that bureaucracy develops in response to rising levels of tension resulting from conflicts of interest, that it controls and stabilizes the tensions, but that it also preserves them and prevents tension reduction through integration.

From the standpoint of the integrative ideal, law is a distinctly third-best solution to conflicts of interest, since it stabilizes conflicts without resolving them. In the ideal family state there would be no law; short of the ideal, law must be tolerated with regret. But it is a mistake to apply the integrative ideal too enthusiastically to many modern situations such as labor-management relations, where differences of interest and outlook simply will never be resolved. The economic process is continually renewing differences and increasing individuation, and the integrative trend cannot develop to any extent against such opposition. Hence the legal ideal is the appropriate one, and law is not a third-best but the best solution.

The selective process producing legalism can be discovered by considering the circumstances in which it is most likely to occur. If the foregoing conclusions are correct, legalism develops most rapidly in relations between opposed, evenly matched and mutually checking powers which have achieved a precarious stability. In such a situation disputes themselves are the selective forces which change or eliminate some rules and allow others to survive. These rules which can prevent or eliminate disputes will survive; those rules which produce disputes over their proper interpretation will eventually change. This does not mean that a rule of law must always be obeyed by everyone to survive, but it does mean that rules which themselves produce frequent disputes tend to drop out of use or get modified.

This point is apparent in each of the aspects of legalism mentioned above. Rules, concepts, clauses which are vague produce disputes over interpretation, and these disputes are settled by clarification, by increased precision, by finer distinctions. Vague terms such as negligence, due process, ordinary working day, are interpreted differently by people of different ideologies and interests; as these disputes are settled, the terms take on a more precise technical meaning which is less open to dispute. Again, rules or changes of rules which appear to give one person or group a differential advantage over others lead to disputes in which others try to get the same favorable treatment. These disputes can be settled by showing that no one has gained any advantage, and that all are in the same relative position as before. This in turn can be done either by clarifying status differentials to show that they have remained the same, or by applying a rule which gives equal, impartial treatment. For instance, bureaus, agencies, and personnel departments can minimize trouble by carefully applying the same rules to everyone, regardless of circumstance. It then becomes difficult for any individual to complain about the treatment he is getting, because everyone else is getting the same treatment. Impartial rules are effective in impartial situations where the abstract identity of all men comes to the fore because particularizing differences are unnoticed — in queues, in managing large masses of men, and generally in casual contacts. Clarification of pre-existing differentials is effective in situations where the concrete differences between persons are recognized — in marital disputes, disputes between employer and employee, and generally in long-standing, complex relationships. In such situations the idea of equal treatment makes no sense because of the obvious differences between the parties involved.

Finally, any change of rule tends to be regarded with suspicion when differences of interest and ideology are important. If one party proposes or supports a change, others will suspect that he is benefiting by it, and will object. Even changes which are of obvious benefit to all parties involved do not necessarily avoid dispute, because then people will dispute over who benefits most. So it is difficult to gain general acceptance of any change of rule. On the other hand, rules to which all parties have already agreed are not likely to become subject to dispute. Disputants will not readily attack rules to which they have already committed themselves, because this would threaten to destroy whatever stability does exist and produce renewed and indecisive strife. Instead, they will try to show that the rule does not apply in their case, or that, properly interpreted, it really favors their claim. Even changes of rule are more likely to survive if they can be made to appear as an application or clarification or extension of already accepted rules.

The selective process producing legalism operates apart from any conscious plan or intent of the parties involved. Conscious attention is ordinarily focused on the immediate situation, and people's energies are devoted to getting what they want, protecting what they have, avoiding trouble, preventing others from taking advantage of them. As a result of these varied efforts, some rules and principles get established and clarified while others are rejected, and a trend occurs.

The trend is given special impetus by the efforts of mediators, judges, and arbitrators to settle or to avoid disputes. The same reasons that operate in the selective process also influence mediators in their selection of rules and in their choice of procedure. For instance, the trend to rigidity and reliance on precedent is accelerated by mediators anxious to find the most reliable grounds of settlement. Since the rules most likely to be accepted are those to which the disputants have already agreed, mediators appeal to those rules as much as possible. They apply the rules directly to a dispute if possible, or, if the rules are not immediately applicable, they make them applicable by appropriate interpretations, clarifications, deductions, or analogies. In so doing they contribute further to the authority of established principle, and circumscribe further the area of discretion of later mediators.

FUNCTIONAL RATIONALITY

If one considers the conditions associated with the growth of legalism one can see that a form of rationality is involved. Given clear and persistent differences of interest among people who must work and live together, disputes arise which hinder joint activity. These disputes must somehow be settled or, if possible, prevented, so that activity can continue. Integration is one way of settling and avoiding disputes, but with sharp differences of interest and outlook and a finite amount of time, integration fails. Force is another conceivable mode of settlement, but without a preponderance of power or the determination to work for one at all costs, that too fails. Nor can positive working relations be established by force. Frequently bargaining and negotiation can uncover a compromise position which is of at least minimum acceptability to all; but when conflict is acute, negotiation is slow, difficult, and inconclusive. A legal order is able to provide solutions and prevent disputes when other methods fail, and this is its claim to rationality. If a system of law produces good results of this sort, it can be called rational.

Legalism is the gradual development of a system of law. Therefore the ideal of a functionally rational legal order can be obtained by projecting the trend of legalism to its completion. Such an order would be, first, a system of rules, that is, prescriptions which apply to a class of situations rather than to particular situations. In judicial procedure based on rules the individual case is treated as an example of a class and as identical with all other members of that class. The circumstances and persons which make it unique are ignored as irrelevant and do not affect the disposition of the case.

This rejection of particularizing circumstances and persons is what Max Weber fastens on as the mark of formal rationality in judicial procedure (Weber, 1954). The opposite of formal rationality is what Weber calls "khadi justice," that is, a system in which each case is treated as unique and disposed of according to the unique demands it makes and problems it presents. In khadi justice there is absolute reliance on the intuitive judgment of the khadi. He applies no rules, recognizes no precedents, and therefore there is no standard by which his judgment can be criticized or corrected. One could conceivably evaluate the judgment by its long-term results, but such a judgment would arrive too late to affect the case and could only affect the khadi. Whether such a judicial procedure ever existed or could exist is a historical question which does not concern us here. What Weber describes is, of course, an ideal type which could not actually exist. Probably anything even remotely approaching it could occur only in a highly integrated society in which power was also highly centralized; in any other kind of society legalism would set in and limit the judge's discretion.

Each rule must specify the kind of situation to which it applies, as well as the action prescribed, or forbidden, or permitted for that situation. In order to act according to rule, then, one must first classify one's present situation and then apply the rule designed for that class. The rules, in turn, must be explicit and clear enough so that any situation likely to occur can be classified precisely and unambiguously.[2] But since the variety of human actions and circumstances is infinite, the rules must be extremely detailed and complex, employing terminology especially designed for clarity and precision and requiring interpreters specially trained at making exact distinctions. Unless all this clarity were present, ambiguity in the application of rules would arise, and people would get into disputes over whether the rules had actually been followed or not. But when people get into disputes over rules, one can no longer say that the rules are effectively regulating behavior, so an ideal set of rules must be clear enough not to produce disputes.

In judicial procedures, inadequate clarity of rules produces a similar result. Ambiguity in the application of rules to cases would provide room for human judgment and khadi justice; different judges would resolve ambiguities in different ways; even the same case might be decided differently by different judges; and the formal requirement that all cases of the same class should be treated the same would be defeated.

Just as each rule taken by itself must be clear and precise, so all the rules together must be consistent. That is, the scope and requirements of one rule must not overlap with those of any other rule. If this were not the case, and two rules required different actions in the same circumstances, ambiguity would again result, with the further consequences mentioned before. Alternatively, if two rules did overlap in scope, one must clearly have precedence over the other. Any hierarchical relations between rules must be clear and unmistakable.

The consistency demanded of an ideal set of rules should not be confused with the integration required of role expectations, obligations, cathexes, and ideals. In a self-consistent set of rules each rule is still completely independent. It explains itself, states its own scope, and carries its own validity within itself. There is no mutual clarification, mutual adjustment of scope and meaning, mutual support and justification. The rules can be independent because they are supreme; they prescribe categorically, and are not conditioned by

---

[2] Cf. Cardozo, 1921:143: "No doubt the ideal system, if it were attainable, would be a code at once so flexible and so minute, as to supply in advance for every conceivable situation the just and fitting rule."

outside circumstances — except in the sense that the whole system is supported by the nonlegal elements of public acceptance, power distribution, solidarity that makes its existence possible.

On the question of whether the rules should distinguish different kinds of persons or whether they should classify all persons in a single class, legalism is ambiguous. In some places one can find a trend toward the breaking down of distinctions between persons and an extension of the same rules to all persons; but one can also find a trend toward greater clarification and systematization of distinctions between persons and groups of persons. These two trends correspond to the two orientations of law and morals described earlier, the economic and the social.

Perhaps from a purely legal standpoint a self-consistent, rational system of rules could be of either sort. But if the system is to perform its dual function of providing a framework for economic and social life, it must contain rules of both sorts. Both contractual relations and interpersonal relations are necessary in life, but each requires a different kind of framework. Contractual relations require a framework of rules which apply impartially to all persons, which define all persons as identical and interchangeable members of a single class, and which also define times and places as identical and interchangeable. Interpersonal relations require a framework of rules which distinguish several different kinds of persons, each with its own unique set of rules, and which also differentiate several kinds of times and places.

Contractual relations are impersonal and specific, in Parsons' terminology; they are consciously established between specific people at specific times for a definite, limited purpose. But selection of specific persons, times, and places implies rejection of others, and this is impossible unless others are actually available. Therefore contracts are impossible unless alternative persons, times, and places are legally available. Moreover the wider the selection of alternatives is, the better people are able to make the exact contract which best suits their purposes. Any limitation of alternatives, in fact, is a hindrance to the making of contracts. For example, if the law distinguishes between citizens and foreigners and enjoins priority of treatment for citizens, contracts with foreigners are more difficult to make. Therefore in an ideally rational system of rules there would be no limits on the availability of persons, times, and places. Instead, all persons would be defined as interchangeable members of the same class, and similarly with times and places.

Interpersonal relations, on the other hand, are diffuse, without any definite boundaries. They do not develop through the efficient selection and rejection of definite alternatives, but adapt whatever material is available, and thus do not require a set of interchangeable alternatives.

Indeed, persons who were interchangeable could hardly form any but a most superficial attachment, since neither would have anything new to contribute to the experience of the other. Each would mirror the other, and there would be nothing to communicate and to share. As in all relations, the two poles must be opposite and complementary; the two persons involved must each bring something unique to the relationship which the other must accept and respond to. Even persons who are basically similar must become different from one another, take different roles, when they relate to each other. But deep and complex relationships can only develop between people who systematically complement one another.[3]

Therefore any system of rules which serves as a framework for social relations must define and sustain differences between opposite classes of persons. The basic and deepest opposition is between men and women; when this is adequately sustained, it forms the basis for the deepest kind of relationship. Other oppositions, between parent and child, brother and sister, older and younger, teacher and apprentice, leader and follower, provide bases for other relationships. When the legal system maintains proper differences among these statuses, each person is faced through life with a variety of opposites, each bringing out a new phase of his personality and developing it further.

A framework for social relations must also provide some kind of underlying unity within which opposites can come together in a relationship. This is done by defining groups whose members are supposed to share some common identity — "blood" relatives, clan, peer group, race, social class — and by encouraging and demanding fre-

---

[3] The requirement that the people involved in a relationship must be opposite to one another and therefore different does not apply to contractual relations, because their personalities are not involved. All that is necessary is that the property of the two people be different; they can then still exchange goods even though their personalities are identical.

quent in-group interaction. Members of such a group can then feel a kinship with one another that enables them to synthesize their opposition into a social relationship, and are thrown together enough so that relationships can form. Group membership does not of itself suffice to provide material for a relationship, however; in order to relate, people must take roles in which they become opposites to one another. The "we" group provides the background, and the sets of opposite statuses provide the basic content for social relations.

A system of statuses must, of course, satisfy other considerations as well as legal ones, such as the technological requirement that there be enough places to staff a complete productive system, the economic requirement that each status provide rewards sufficient to attract an adequate supply of personnel to it and to ensure a willing performance of its duties, and the integrative requirement that abilities and values developed in one status be usable in the next succeeding status.

The socially oriented type of law has been criticized (by Karl Popper (1950), for instance) as implying a closed society in which people are locked into place and there is no freedom. This criticism is based on an overextension of the contractual ideal. It is true that a status system limits the range of voluntary actions. For example, when a legal system differentiates men's and women's status and assigns different "work" to each, it is very difficult for women to do men's work and vice versa, and it is also difficult for men and women to make voluntary agreements with one another. So it might seem to some men that they were locked into place and prevented from being women, and vice versa. But if men and women were both assigned the same duties and in consequence became pretty much indistinguishable in their personalities, how impoverished their relations would become!

It is also a misconception to think of status as something inherently unchangeable. Though a status system limits the range of voluntary activities and shapes the personality, it is not necessary for a person's status to remain the same throughout life. Indeed, from the standpoint of social rationality it is desirable for some though not all of a person's statuses to be changeable, to permit personality growth. And actual status systems do allow for changes of status, though perhaps not always to a sufficient extent. Age status is always changeable, class status frequently so, and in some cultures change of sex status is also possible, taking sex in the social rather than in the biological sense.

In summary, a rational legal system is a system of rules; these rules must be complex, detailed, and precise enough to apply unambiguously to all cases; they must be consistent; some of the rules must apply impartially to all persons, while others must apply differentially to different statuses or classes of persons.

Such a system is rational because it is effective in its functions of preventing and settling disputes. It prevents disputes by providing a framework for economic and social relations, concentrated on just those spots where disputes might arise. It defines the basic rights and duties of each type of relation and supports their performance. Also it defines, shapes to some extent, and maintains to some extent, the basic material of which relations are formed, to help insure performance of duties. When disputes do arise it provides a procedure of settlement.

Actual laws are good, or reasonable, or effective, to the extent that they conform to this standard and perform these tasks. Rules which are inconsistent, or vague and general, are bad because they make correct action difficult and lead to confusion and dispute. Rules which are discriminatory in their prescriptions for specific voluntary acts are bad because they arbitrarily limit the range of voluntary agreements. Rules which fail to differentiate the rights and duties of different kinds of people are bad because they limit the range and depth of personal relationships. In each case the rules are bad because they are ineffective.

Rational legal systems undoubtedly have additional characteristics which have not been brought out in the foregoing account. That account was based primarily on a study of legalism in United States labor arbitration, and cannot therefore claim to be complete or free from error. Developments in arbitration have undoubtedly been influenced by temporary or local conditions, such as the legal training of some arbitrators, peculiarities of union and management ideologies, and peculiarities of Western industrial organization. Studies of legalism in other areas, and of stratification, would correct overgeneralizations based on local conditions and might bring out additional characteristics. In particular, studies of legal trends in other cultures would correct distortions based on the peculiarities of Western culture. Also further studies of cases in which legalism did not develop, on the model of the Harbison and Dubin work (1947), would provide helpful evidence on the conditions of legalism and the functions of legal systems.

Some people may wonder how the study of legalism can produce any useful information at all about judicial rationality. Legalism is frequently regarded as a sign of degeneration rather than of growth in law, something to be studied only with a view to preventing its recurrence, as a biologist might study some loathsome disease. The very word has become a term of abuse, designating a procedure so lost in technicalities that it fails to achieve justice. Consideration of this objection may clear up some possible misunderstandings.

First, a person who objects to legalism should consider the fact of its persistence. Why is its occurrence so persistent and so widespread, in spite of opposition? There must be some reason; it must accomplish something for somebody, or it would die out. If legalism constantly produced injustice for all, people would cut through it and establish an effective judicial system.

The case of legalism is quite similar to that of bureaucracy, which is also widely condemned. The bureaucrat, like the legalistic judge, is widely regarded with loathing and contempt; in fact, the legalism of the bureaucrat is precisely the reason for which he is condemned. Yet bureaucracy continues to develop. It develops because it is a rational form of organization in certain circumstances, and in fact exemplifies more than one form of rationality. It is an efficient form of administration (chap. 1) and a decision-making structure (chap. 5) adapted to large organizations; and, I would add, its rules exemplify judicial rationality and illustrate the growth of legalism. In fact, Blau (1956) and Gouldner (1952) have shown that it is precisely the rationality of bureaucratic organization that produces dislike. Perhaps their remarks apply to legalism in general as well as to this particular manifestation of legalism.

Second, I am not advocating legalism as a procedure for developing a rational legal organization. The study of legalism was undertaken only to see what sort of structure of rules develops by itself, spontaneously, and why it develops that way. This should throw some light on why rules are necessary, since they appear even when people do not want them, on what the minimum characteristics of a workable system of rules are, and by extrapolation, what a judicially good system of rules would be like. Once one has gotten some answers to these questions it is possible to take up the further question of how an existing system of rules might be improved. Conscious revision or construction of a legal system is an entirely different and, potentially, much better procedure than merely waiting for a slow, spontaneous growth.

The case is analogous to that of technical rationality and technological progress. Study of technological progress throws light on what efficiency is and why and under what conditions it is desirable; but the best way to increase efficiency is by scientific research, not by unconscious trial and error.

Third, I am not saying that judicial rationality is the only form of rationality relevant to concrete legal institutions and actual judicial procedure; nor do I believe that a highly legalistic procedure is necessarily better than one exemplifying other forms of rationality. Legal institutions, like all concrete institutions, have a variety of functions and exemplify several forms of rationality. Consequently a good legal system must not only be judicially rational, but rational in other ways as well. Specifically, economic calculation and bargaining, integrative processes, political decision making, and sporting contests, among others, go on in United States' courts. All of these are more desirable at times than strictly legalistic procedures. But they are not always possible, and there are cases in which legalistic decisions are both possible and desirable. In general, the question of what sort of procedure is possible depends on the kind of decision structure (chap. 5) that exists, since different kinds of structures make different kinds of decision procedures possible. The desirable procedure depends on the kind of problem that exists; this point will be developed later in the present chapter.

As for terminology, I have already indicated that I am not advocating any particular terminology. If anyone wishes to call any or all of the other forms of reasoning occurring in courtrooms judicial I have no objection.

One could call legal rationality a form of technical rationality if one postulated a goal of structuring human relationships and settling disputes. Law then would be both a technique and an instrument for doing these things. Such a goal would be an odd one, though. It is never held as a whole by any one person; even judges, mediators, and legislators are concerned only with parts of it, and they are assigned those parts as public agents rather than choosing them as private persons. One could perhaps call it a public goal, implicit in private goals as well as in nonpurposive relationships, and law-morals could be called a public technique. But this, too, is an odd way of speaking.

If one did call law a technique it would be differentiated from other techniques as public is from private. This is an important difference. Ordinary private techniques are servants of people's desires; they are tools, to be used at will and discarded at will. Law, as a public technique, is supreme over individuals and their desires. It is not used by anyone; even public agents are its interpreters rather than its masters, since it is supreme over them too. It achieves its purpose, not by being used, but simply by existing. Nor can it be laid aside when one does not wish to use it — it is always in force.

Nor finally, can it be changed at will, like ordinary techniques. The difference between law, the ruler, and technology, the servant, is shown vividly when one compares the way techniques develop and the way a legal system develops. Technology progresses by constant change; old techniques are replaced by new and better ones, and the people who cling to old techniques are themselves replaced by those who adopt new ones. A legal order develops by denying change. All the developments that constitute legalism involve the clarification, strengthening, extension, or narrowing of old rules, but not their elimination. Disputes are settled by applying old rules to new situations, not by inventing new rules. Indeed, a judge who attempted to settle a dispute by declaring that the old rules had that day become invalid and that he would invent new ones for the occasion would himself be replaced.

The reason for this difference lies in the different settings in which law and technology develop. Technology develops when goals are given, settled, and agreed on, while law develops when interests are separate and opposed. Law provides a neutral meeting place or framework which enables opposed interests to deal with each other without overt conflict. But in order to be truly neutral, it must stay beyond the reach of any interested party; it must be immune to manipulation and change by a private interest. It must be supreme. This does not mean that it must come down from some transcendental source. Law grows out of ordinary social and economic intercourse; but it becomes law when people set it up above themselves and thereby give it an official immunity to manipulation and change.

JUDICIAL DECISIONS

One may include under judicial reasoning both the reasoning of the man of action who wishes to act in accordance with the law, and the reasoning of the judge (impartial spectator) who wishes to determine whether someone else has acted in accordance with the law. Though both are essentially the same, I wish to deal here with the reasoning of the judge. Since law is a public order, it is the public reasoning of the judge which affects the growth of law, rather than the private reasoning of the man of action. Consequently the reasoning of judges is more directly relevant to a study which focuses on the development of law.

The approach to law through legalism draws attention to one aspect of the judicial process, the applicational aspect. If law is treated as a system of rules, the judicial process must consist of an application of rules to cases. Rules are statements that a certain class of persons has a duty to perform (or not perform) certain actions, or conversely, that a class of persons has a right to a certain treatment. The task of the judge is to classify the case before him so as to determine which rule applies to it. He takes definitions of several classes, as clarified by examples, then sees which definition best fits the case, and with which examples it is most analogous. Then, by applying the rule proper to that class of cases, he determines what ought to be done. For example: 1. (case) This man is (ought to be) a machinist first class, because his work fits the definition of machinist first class; it is more similar to the work of A and B who are machinists first class than it is to that of C and D, second class machinists. 2 (rule) All machinists first class ought to receive $1.87 per hour. 3. (ruling) Therefore this man ought to receive $1.87 per hour.

The reader is referred to Ladd (1957, chap. 8), Levi (1949), and Stone (1946:139ff.), for several schematizations, as well as further arguments, details, and examples.

Judicial reasoning is easy and requires no casuistic skill when only one rule obviously applies to a case. In such cases a judge's decision is automatic and predictable, and parties seek it out only when facts are in dispute. But frequently two or more rules can be applied to a case with equal initial plausibility and with opposite results, and here a real judicial problem exists.

One way to deal with the problem is to interpret and clarify the conflicting rules until one clearly stands out as the most appropriate one. The judge can, for instance, draw out the implications of key terms or specify from the context which of several possible meanings is appropriate. Or he can clarify meanings by seeking out the original context of the rule: the problem it was designed to deal with, the expressed or unexpressed intentions of the rule makers (to be discovered in what they deliberately left out of the rule as well as what they put in and what supporting arguments they used or did not use), the meanings the terms originally had, the qualifications that were left unstated because they were common knowledge or taken for granted, and so on. Or he can clarify by seeking out the present, living-law context of the rule to see how people who live by the rule customarily interpret it. These three procedures are what Cardozo (1921) called the methods of philosophy, history, and tradition. (Cardozo's fourth method, the method of sociology, is nonjudicial from our present standpoint. Its uselessness for legal problems has been cogently argued by Alf Ross (1959, chap. 13)).

Instead of working directly on the stated rule, the judge can proceed by comparison of cases. If two rules are in question, he can take one case which was decided by rule A and one decided by rule B to see which one is most similar to the case *sub judice*. Or rather, since there will be similarities and differences with both, he will see which similarities or differences are crucial for determining the relevance of the rule. A number of variations of this approach are also possible.

The continual application of rules to cases has the effect of clarifying the rules. The range of applicability of each rule is more precisely defined, both by the cases which are judged to fall under it and by those from which it is excluded. The hierarchical relationship between rules is established by cases in which one of two conflicting rules is excluded and the other applied. Also the meaning of each rule is clarified by the various cases which are judged to fall under it, each case bringing out some particular shade of meaning. This judicial clarification of rules is an essential part of legalism. As Berman observes, "We can speak intelligently of legal decision-making as the 'application' of 'rules' to 'facts' only if we recognize that in each application to new facts the rule changes — and that it is by this subtle and gradual process of change that true consistency is maintained" (1958:376).

The judicial application of rules is also a testing ground for the rules themselves. When several rules are available for use in a given case, a judge will pick a rule which gives a clear result over one which is ambiguous, and a rule which can be clarified over one which is intrinsically vague. But if a rule is ambiguous in case after case its use will decline and it will eventually drop out of the legal system altogether. For example, the rule that in cases of contributory negligence the party who had the last opportunity to prevent the damage is responsible has nearly dropped out of use because of incurable ambiguity, according to Jensen (1957:46ff.). Some rules may be clear only in a limited area of cases, and their use will gradually be confined to that area. The scope of other rules may be continually broadened because they yield clear and consistent results again and again.

Perhaps I should add that a judge may pick an ambiguous rule over a clear one if he is using nonjudicial reasoning in his decision, because the ambiguous rule gives him a greater space in which to operate. If nonjudicial reasoning is prevalent, as in khadi justice, it may produce a trend toward ambiguity and generality of rule which is counter to the legalistic trend toward clarity.

As rules are clarified and selected it becomes easier to use them in a legalistic judicial process. The more vague a rule is, the more difficult it is to determine what it means and to what it applies, and the more scope there is for argument as to whether a rule has been correctly applied. To be sure, any rulelike statement can be put into a deductive sequence, but when the rule is vague its selection is relatively arbitrary from a judicial standpoint and depends on nonjudicial considerations. Thus the development of clear rules through a long tradition of judicial decision is an aid to later decisions within that tradition. Similarly, when new rules are constructed by people with legal experience, they are likely to be framed with a view to easy and exact judicial application.

So far we have dealt with only one part of the judicial process, the most superficial part according to some. The account has been based on the assumption that the written opinions of judges reproduce the actual reasoning that led them to their decisions. But this may not be the case. Judges may reach decisions by some entirely different line of reasoning, or prejudice, and then justify them by some plausible interpretation or analogy. They may concern themselves with the effects of a decision either on the plaintiff and defendant or on society, or its acceptability and its effect on their own position, or they may intuitively feel that one decision is the right one. And apart from conscious reasoning, judges undoubtedly also are influenced by subconscious factors to prefer certain rules or certain conclusions over others.

The actual process, both conscious and subconscious, by which judges reach decisions may exemplify a variety of modes of rationality, or may be irrational or nonrational in varying degree. Certainly political reasoning (chap. 5) is sometimes present to a considerable extent; integrative considerations are also likely to occur in some rudimentary form, and other kinds of reasoning as well. However, we are not concerned in this chapter with how judges actually reach decisions, their private reasoning, but only with the public reasoning which they set down officially for all to examine. This public reasoning is and must be judicial, whether or not the private and subconscious reasoning also is.

SCOPE OF JUDICIAL DECISIONS

Since the application of rules to cases is only one of several ways of reaching a decision, it is necessary to define the conditions in which this sort of reasoning is appropriate. Or, in the language of problem solving, it is necessary to indicate the kind of problem that can be solved by the application of pre-existing rules.

One condition is that both relevant rules and some person qualified to apply them be available. This condition is perhaps self-evident, yet it is sometimes neglected. A person is qualified to make judicial decisions only if he is accepted as neutral on the question at issue. The judge, or umpire, is conceived as a spokesman for rules which are regarded as superior to all parties involved; but if the judge is thought to have a bias for one side he becomes an ordinary participant rather than a spokesman for superior rules. His decision is treated as an incident in a continuing conflict, to be resisted, evaded, or overturned as circumstances permit. If the rest of the legal system is still regarded as neutral the conflict may continue through other courts or with other arbitrators or umpires. But if the whole structure is regarded as biased the frustrated party will turn away from it and try politicking (chap. 5) or other procedures.

A similar requirement of neutrality holds for the rules; if they are regarded as biased by one side, a decision based on them will not be accepted as final, and the dispute will continue. In addition rules must be clear enough to justify one relatively determinate conclusion in a given case. If a rule is so ambiguous that opposite conclusions are made equally plausible by it, it cannot be used to produce acceptance of a decision. Unless the available rules are clear or can be clarified by the methods of history, philosophy, or tradition, nonjudicial reasoning must be used to fill the gap.

Other conditions necessary to the use of judicial reasoning can be discovered by considering the circumstances in which legalism develops. The occurrence of legalism indicates that judicial decisions are being selected and rewarded and therefore that they are appropriate. By examining the circumstances, then, one can discover why judicial decisions are appropriate, and state these reasons as general conditions. In the analysis of developments in labor arbitration, it was suggested that legalism develops most rapidly (1) when there are clear and continuing differences of interest, (2) when there is relative stability of power among the different interests, plus the expectation that stability will continue indefinitely, and (3) when there are other bases of stability — mutual understanding and trust, common interests — present to some extent. Let us consider these points, remembering however that any error in them will lead to corresponding errors in the conclusions based on them.

(1) The differences of interest clearly are the continuing source of the problems with which law must deal. These problems, moreover, are such that it is difficult to deal with them by either a calculating or an integrative approach. A calculating approach would consist of the comparison of various, alternative resource distribution patterns to see which one promised to yield the greatest aggregate utility; but this procedure would be difficult and perhaps impossible because it would involve interpersonal comparisons of utility. And even if it were possible, the judgment would be difficult to carry out in practice, since the loser would have no motive to give up resources for the sake of an aggregate in which he had no interest.

Bargaining avoids these difficulties, since it is based on a recognition of continuing differences of interest. It drops the impossible goal of maximizing utility and substitutes the goal of agreement. Consequently bargaining can often be substituted, combined, or alternated with judicial reasoning. One difference is that bargaining is private while judicial reasoning is public, but this difference disappears when the whole public is divided into two opposed interests, as in labor arbitration.

An integrative approach has been excluded by definition, since the problems have been defined as consisting of continuing differences of interest. Continuing differences might be produced by a variety of factors. The most important one is the economic process of calculation and exchange, which sets people into permanent competition with one another, as in the case of labor and management. The impersonality involved in such competition, for instance in job competition or applications to formal agencies, prevents people from developing the personal relations and mutual understanding that would enable them to adjust to one another. Similarly, differences in age and sex are often such as to prevent people from fully understanding and sharing each other's point of view. To the extent that interests can be integrated, law is usually unnecessary; but when interests defy mutual adjustment, they must be dealt with by legal means. Judicial decisions resolve conflicts of interest, not by adjustment, but by setting up boundaries and procedures for coexistence.

It is important not to assume too hastily that integration of interests is impossible. Quite often continuing differences of interest in some areas are compatible with the development of common interests and co-operation in other areas. In these cases a too hasty reliance on judicial procedures is mistaken because it shuts out the possibility of integration. When people insist on their rights and focus attention on the exact scope and meaning of rules they lose sight of the underlying feelings and motives which must be the center of attention in an integrative procedure. Only when integration is obviously impossible, or has been tried without success, is it advisable to rely on a judicial procedure for solving problems.

(2) Stability of power supports the growth of law by making possible the development of a system of mutual checks on the use of power. When power positions remain constant over a period of time the opposed parties can develop knowledge of each other's position and possible strategies, and can devise checks and counterstrategies. The resulting deadlock makes it generally disadvantageous to resort to force, and offers an inducement to turn to other ways of resolving disputes. Law is one such way. Of course, if differences of power are extreme no adequate check on the superior power can be devised and law cannot develop; but exact equality is not necessary either. There are a number of checking devices available to inferior powers — harassment, coalition, escape, passive resistance, protest to superiors in a hierarchy, and so on.

In labor-management relations law and its adjunct, arbitration, began to develop when the superior power of management was checked by the organization of unions, supported by a friendly government. Before unions became effective, managers could, and sometimes did, act arbitrarily in relation to employees. They could issue any sort of work orders, raise or lower wages arbitrarily, levy fines, change work hours without advance notice, all under the threat of firing for disobedience. But when this power to fire was countered by the power to organize strikes, managers yielded some of their prerogatives by accepting contractual obligations and work rules, and industrial law became possible. Similar examples from national and international politics have been described by Carr (1948) and others.

When shifts of power are gradual, the expanding power has less and less incentive to continue accepting the rule of law, and more and more opportunity to achieve its aims by force. This poses a political problem which cannot be adequately met by further legalistic development, but requires a political decision process. One solution is to shift the intepretation of the rules to make them more acceptable to the rising power; another is to build up counterpowers. If the problem is seen in legal rather than in political terms, the resulting legalism becomes more and more a partisan device to artificially contain the rising power, and respect for law declines. One such example of artificial containment has been cited in the text (p. 139); others have been cited by Carr (1948) and other writers. This political use, or misuse, of legalistic devices is what some critics have in mind when they condemn legalism for artificiality.

(3) Factors such as mutual trust and common interests help produce acceptance of judicial decisions. They counter the hostility and suspicion that might otherwise be produced by continuing conflicts, and substitute a disposition to get along peaceably and work things out. Without some small disposition to get along peaceably, the solution produced by a judicial decision remains precarious, because each side will search for some way to outwit the other side and evade the decision. Also each side will concentrate on ways to increase its power so it can overcome the other side and do away with legal restraints. The result will be a power struggle and open warfare, with force rather than law providing a solution.

The second and third points together are the basis of effectiveness of law. They provide the two kinds of reasons that induce people to obey law: self-interest and identification through common interest. Although both kinds of reasons are necessary to a successful law, the proportion of each can vary considerably.

To sum up: judicial decisions are appropriate in situations involving clear and relevant rules, an acceptable judge, clear and continuing differences of interest, and the two kinds of inducements to obedience, self-interest and identification. Unless the rules and the judge are available, judicial decisions are impossible; unless both inducements to obedience are present, decisions will be ineffective; unless the continuing differences are present, decisions are unnecessary or harmful.

To say that judicial decisions are appropriate in these conditions does not imply that no other kind of decision is appropriate. Economizing and integrative decisions have indeed been excluded, but bargaining and political decisions have not. In fact, it will become apparent in the next chapter that political decisions are always appropriate and often necessary when judicial decisions are called for.

If the above argument is correct, judicial decisions are rarely if ever appropriate in a legislative assembly. The reason is that no neutral is available to act as judge; the members of the legislature act as representatives of various interests and points of view and cannot therefore be accepted as impartial. Legislatures are capable of making political decisions, which deal with problems of common interest, and also economic-bargaining decisions where there are conflicts of interest, but they cannot adjudicate disputes like a judge. The same point applies to constitutional conventions.

Actual legislative procedures certainly do not resemble a process of applying rules, nor can the bills which legislatures produce be understood or evaluated as deductive conclusions from basic rules or principles. The legislative process is a political one, as will become apparent in the next chapter, and it largely results in policies expressed as statutes or as authorizations.

In classical natural law theory, legislatures, or constitutional conventions, or sovereigns, were conceived as interpreters of the natural law who deductively applied it to existing circumstances. This view, besides being contrary to fact, exaggerates the ease with which impartial interpreters can be found, and also exaggerates the suitability for applicational purposes of the vague, general social ideals which were called natural laws. It also makes the mistake of supposing that laws can be justified only as deductions from still other laws. Actually the justification of laws is a political question, as will become apparent in the next chapter, and laws need not be deduced from anything to be valid. Natural law theory thus represents a radical overextension of the scope of legal rationality.

In contrast to natural law theorists, recent critics of legalism have underestimated the importance of what I have called judicial reasoning. In one respect, indeed, they are correct, and that is in rejecting judicial reasoning as a device to contain a rising power. Such an attempt merely leads to a loss of respect for law and a diversion of conflict into nonlegal channels, until a new system of law that adequately reflects existing power relations can be built up. But to say that judges should never be passive, neutral interpreters of preexisting rules is to underestimate the depth and reality of conflict in society.

LEGAL VALUE

The characteristic value produced by legal systems has traditionally been called "justice," though people have disagreed as to what justice is. At one extreme, justice has been defined by Hobbes as obedience to law: whatever the law commands is just, and whatever it forbids is unjust. By this definition any set of commands backed by legitimate force, and any judicial decision, automatically produces justice. At the other extreme justice has been conceived as an indefinable, ever-changing ideal, the perfect solution to disputes which judges and law makers quest after but never find. By this definition, or lack of definition, justice is never fully achieved.

We need a definition somewhere between these two. Our subject has been legal rationality, rather than concrete legal institutions in all their complexity. Consequently we need to define justice as a product of legal organization, that is, a system of rules which are clear, consistent, detailed, and technical. We are interested in *legal* justice, that peculiar to a rational legal order, and not in an ultimate justice which is the summation of all goodness. In Weber's terminology, this is formal rather than substantive justice, the justice regularly produced by a formally rational legal order, rather than that produced by the inspiration of khadi judges. Neither of the above definitions is appropriate for this purpose, though each of them is valid and important in its own way. Hobbes's definition is inappropriate because it eliminates reason from law altogether. The ideal conception is inappropriate because this sort of justice is achieved by social and political reasoning, not judicial reasoning. The writers who conceive of justice in this fashion, such as Stone (1946), Llewellyn, and Garlan (1941), are emphatic in declaring that it can be achieved only by forsaking the mechanical analysis and interpretation of rules and considering broader social issues.

Several somewhat narrower traditional definitions of justice are relevant to our present, limited treatment of law. First, justice has frequently been defined as impartiality, or fairness, or equality. These terms have been understood, not in the tautological sense that all cases which are the same should be treated the same, but in the practical sense that all persons should be treated the same by a court. The opposite of impartiality is discrimination, that is, treating two cases differently just because of the people involved in them. Impartiality is part of the universalist-utilitarian value system associated with economic progress (chap. 2); it provides a basis for contractual relations by removing barriers of personality, sex, status, class. If all persons are legally indistinguishable, then all can establish relations by mutual consent with anyone. When a system of law has been strongly influenced by economic development, as Western systems have, it moves toward impartiality in treatment of persons, so the definition of justice as impartiality is appropriate for these systems.

An impartial legal order does not necessarily enjoin people to treat each other impartially; people can be enjoined to be self-seeking or anything else. What is necessary is that the injunctions, whatever they may be, apply impartially to all persons, and are impartially applied by a court.

Though impartiality is a form of justice, it cannot be the only form. Contractual relations are important, but they are not the whole of life. Society is not simply a set of independent persons who relate to each other voluntarily for specific purposes at specific times. The deeper, more diffuse personal relations are also essential and must also be provided for. Law in the wide sense must also differentiate classes of people and demand different things from them; it must discriminate. A socially oriented legal order provides a hierarchical system of statuses with a place in it for everybody. When the system is operating smoothly everyone is in his own place, doing his own work (Plato, *Republic*, IV). "Work" here means not just an eight-hour job, but the whole set of appropriate activities toward others that defines one's personality in outline. Most people have their own relatively unique status and deal mainly with people of different statuses. For instance, there can only be one eldest son in a family, or one eldest son of eldest son in a patriarchical family, and the various eldest sons in a village have few occasions for joint dealings. In such a system the concept of impartiality has little relevance, because it applies only to dealings with people of the same status, and such dealings are rare.

Justice, in a socially oriented legal order, is reciprocity (Malinowski, 1926; Gouldner, 1960). To reciprocate means to pay back; reciprocity exists when people pay back contributions with return contributions. A legal code is just when all its rights and duties are so arranged that the duties of status A to status B are matched by equivalent duties of status B to status A. An individual is just if he consistently pays back with equivalent actions all the things done for him. He need not pay back each specific action with another specific action as in a contract; since relations are diffuse in a socially oriented legal code reciprocation is required only in the long run over a whole range of actions. For instance in some legal codes it is thought that children pay back the parental care given them by supporting the parents in their old age. If the legal code is just a person can reciprocate simply by doing his duty, or "doing his own work," in Plato's terminology, since the system is so arranged that his duties eventually balance others' duties to him.

Reciprocity is not exactly equality, since it applies to relations between different statuses where comparisons are difficult to make. For instance in Malinowski's example of reciprocity between the duty to provide fish and the duty to provide taro, one cannot ask whether the fish and taro are of equal exchange value, since there is no common unit of measurement; economic progress has not extended to these items. Similarly, one cannot ask whether the duties of a husband equal the duties of a wife; they are just different. And yet there must be some rough equivalence, or one cannot speak of paying back. The inability to be exact about equivalences often contributes to the diffusing and deepening of relationships, since when people cannot be sure their moral debt is discharged, they overreciprocate to make sure, and this leads to an ever-increasing cycle of exchanges (Gouldner, 1960).

The opposite of reciprocity is exploitation, that is, continually taking without giving back sufficient in return. Ordinarily, though not always, a person of higher status exploits one of lower status — parents exploit children, teachers exploit students and graduate assistants, upper class exploits lower class — because the lower status person does not have enough power to enforce reciprocity on the higher. Even if enforcement is centralized, the superior power of the upper statuses is not easy to neutralize completely; they ordinarily run the judicial system, make the decisions, and enforce them. When exploitation is widespread and continuous it becomes right in the minds of the exploiters, and the whole legal system becomes unjust.

In Greek philosophy reciprocity was formulated as "giving each person his due." What is due a person are the rights belonging to his status, and one gives by performing one's duties toward that status. Each person is due something different, because each person to whom one is directly related has a unique status in relation to oneself. If the notion of giving a person his due is intepreted in terms of modern contractual morality it becomes an empty tautology. When the notion of special statuses drops out and everyone is treated the same, "giving his due" can only mean to do what is right, impartially, to everyone. The Greek definition must be interpreted in the context of a socially oriented conception of law to be intelligible.

The whole notion of reciprocity is irrelevant in a contractual legal code. All contracts are automatically reciprocal since otherwise the contracting parties would not have agreed to them. If a contract is obviously and extremely unbalanced, there must have been some misunderstanding or deception and the contract is invalid — it does not exist. Similarly exploitation of a continuing sort is hardly conceivable, since no one would voluntarily agree to be exploited and it could occur only through continuous, open, illegal coercion.

Since law has both a status and a contractual aspect, both definitions of justice must be accepted as partly adequate. Justice is impartiality in those areas where relations are defined as contractual in a given society. Here discrimination would be unjust. But justice is reciprocity in those areas where the society defines relations as personal; here exploitation is the evil to be avoided.

Justice in both senses provides an absolute which limits the infinite relativity of integrative decisions. No solution or part of a solution to an integrative problem which is unjust can stand, because injustice is a continual source of conflicts. An unjust society or legal system could survive indefinitely, but only in a state of chronic conflict, repression, and integrative failure.

If one were to construct a more general definition that includes both previous definitions one might employ the concept of dependability (Alf Ross, 1959, chap. 12) or predictability. A system of law provides assurance that other people can be depended on to perform at least their basic duties. It does this partly by specifying the duties so that people know what is expected of them, partly by calling public attention to them and teaching them, and partly by focusing sanctions of various sorts on them. A just man is one who can be depended on to carry out his duties and keep his agreements. Fairness is a special case of dependability; it means that a person can expect with assurance that he will be given the same treatment that anyone else in his circumstances would receive.

Predictability results directly from the nature of law as a body of rules. Rules stand above individual cases; they are timeless, and therefore are as valid in the future as in the past. A person who lives in a society based on rules knows in outline how other people will act, and he knows that his expectations will not basically be thwarted by the arbitrary whim of others, including judges.

And yet there is a difficulty in the conception of justice as predictability. Legal theorists of past decades have emphasized and amply documented the essential unpredictability of courts. We have been told that certainty generally is illusion, that many areas of law are such that an equally good argument can be made on either side of a case, and that judges actually are motivated into a decision by everything but the ambiguous rules and precedents they actually cite. Their decisions may sometimes be predicted, but only on the basis of knowledge about individual judges — personalities, political views, sympathies and prejudices — and not on the basis of any knowledge about law. Consequently if justice is predictability, we may wonder whether there ever is any such thing as justice.

We must distinguish here between the unpredictability of judges and the unpredictability of juries. In a large percentage of court cases the doubt centers on questions of fact; once these have been settled by a jury the judge's decision is clear and predictable within narrow limits. These cases do not concern us, since the rules involved in them are clear. The important cases for us are those — a large percentage — in which the unpredictability results directly from the rules involved. They are cases in which two rules or two systems of rules conflict, cases of ambiguity of rules, or situations not directly provided for by the rules. In these cases law is not a timeless body of clear, consistent rules, but a guess as to what the courts will do.

But these cases are precisely the ones that represent the breakdown of the legal order. Predictability disappears because the rules have failed in their job of providing a clear guide to conduct. The task of the courts is one of garage repair work, in Llewellyn's phrase, or sometimes of more basic clarification and reconstruction.

To find justice, then, one must look at the legal-moral order when it is working successfully. Success is marked by the fact that people do not need to go to court because they do not disagree on the interpretation of the rules they live by. And in these areas, where the legal order is successful and people are in agreement, justice is achieved. Behavior is dependable and predictable in essentials, even in spite of unbridgeable differences in interest and outlook.

One can also find predictability in courts, but this is primarily a predictability of procedure, based on clear and detailed procedural rules, and also to some extent a rectification of wrongs when individuals have disobeyed a clear rule. Such kinds of predictability are important, but only as supplementing and reinforcing a basically successful legal order at its weak points. The justice of a society is not located primarily in the spasmodic excitement of its courts, but in the calm assurance of its ordinary members in their daily activities.

Chapter 5

Political Rationality

In previous chapters I have indicated how rationality in the decisions of individuals is made possible by the rational organization of society. The organization of society produces materials which are shaped to be usable in decisions; unless such materials were available, only the crudest of decisions would be possible. Economic organization produces resources which are measurable, divisible, interchangeable, and morally neutral. Such resources are necessary for allocation decisions; they have the characteristics which make exact comparison of alternatives possible. Social organization produces materials — personalities — which are unified, adjustable, accepting, and tolerant of strain and frustration. Without such personal qualities, only the most elementary and limited integrative processes would be possible, and integrative decisions would be empty and useless. Legal organization produces rules which are clear, detailed, intelligible, consistent; these rules make possible the exact classification of actions and the specification of rights and duties.

In addition, each mode of organization produces the habits of thought and of observation which enable individuals to take hold of the materials made available to them. People living and working in an economically organized society learn to look for alternatives, to measure, compare, and estimate costs. People living within a socially organized society learn to be sensitive to feelings, to meanings hidden beneath the surface of overt action, to frustration levels and limits of tolerance, to possibilities of acceptance and growth. They learn to communicate feelings, provide emotional support, find specific ways of reducing or redistributing frustration. People involved in a judicial system learn to make exact classifications and distinctions, to draw inferences, and to find analogies.

In this chapter we shall deal with the organization of thought itself, the system of communication within which particular habits of thought are applied to materials to result in decisions. Thinking is not an uncaused, self-generating activity, as some classical philosophers seemed to think; like everything else, it has determinants. If the determinants of thought are properly structured, thinking can be rational, but if they are improperly structured, thinking is irrational. I shall use the term "decision-making structure" to refer to the set of sociocultural determinants of practical thought, since decisions are its product. Not all the determinants of thought are included, but only those which can be controlled and structured. Biological determinants, for instance, are not included. Decision-making structures occur in both individuals and groups; we shall be concerned primarily with group structures, though what is said about groups will apply to individuals as well. Political rationality is the rationality of decision-making structures.

I call this type of rationality "political" because politics is concerned with decisions and how they are made. The politics of a country or group is the process by which the group decides on its own activity and on the part to be played in that activity by members. The political structure of a group is the organization of forces which determines how its decisions are made, that is, its decision-making structure. Political science is the study of decision-making structures.

Politics is also concerned with the carrying out of public decisions and the achieving of a group's goals, but this activity embodies only technical and economic rationality and so does not concern us here.

A parallel concept used in cybernetics is that of a control system. The control system of an organization is the structure within which decisions governing the activity of the organization are made and transmitted. Though this concept is frequently used in connection with machines such as the thermostat which makes programmed decisions, it is also applied to the analogous structures governing human beings, and in this latter usage is probably identical to the concept of a decision-making structure. One difference is that cybernetics has up to now been concerned more with the initial stages of information processing and the terminal stage of result evaluation in a control process, and less with the intermediate stages of discussion and formulation of action programs.

DECISION-MAKING STRUCTURES

A decision-making structure is composed in the first place of discussion relationships — talking and listening, asking questions and answering them, suggesting courses of action and accepting them. These relationships are combined in a set of roles which, in a settled group, get recognized and assigned to individuals. In Western groups, some usual roles are those of an idea man, a critic, a moderator, a technical expert, a foreign relations man, a conscience figure, and a leader who crystallizes decisions. In small groups one person usually holds several roles: the crystallizing leader may also be a moderator and a foreign relations man, or he may also be the idea man or the factual expert. Official groups may consciously recognize certain roles and give them titles, such as Majority Leader, Chief Whip, Speaker, and so on. Ordinarily, however, roles are not consciously recognized; and even when there are official parliamentary roles, an informal structure of roles may appear that differs from the conscious, official structure.

A decision-making structure is composed, second, of a set of beliefs and values, more or less held in common by participating members. These define the kind of ideas that can be seriously considered during discussion and decision. Beliefs about the world, about man and society, determine the kind of factual propositions that are acceptable to the group, as well as the kinds of evidence or support that make them acceptable. Values determine the goals that are acceptable within the group, the possible desires, needs, external pressures, obligations, and so forth, that can be considered in selecting a goal or goals, and the ranking of goals, desires, needs, and obligations. Legal-moral norms define available and proscribed means, methods of combining ends, techniques of relating means to ends, and guides to selecting means. Beliefs and values, in short, determine the general content and order of the universe in which discussion and decision takes place, while the roles define the participants and their manner of participation.

There is always some variety in the beliefs and values held by members of a group. As a result, ideas that are plausible or desirable to some members are unthinkable for other members; ideas that seem extremely plausible or highly desirable and important to some will seem barely possible and of little interest to others. Such variations are the cause of many of the disagreements occurring in discussion.

A third component of a decision-making structure is the commitments already accepted by a group, and the courses of action in which it is already engaged. All decisions have to be made in an actual context of actions and commitments resulting from previous decisions. This is a context of "givens" to which any new decision must be adapted. It provides continuity and stability and helps to make vague goals and values more specific. Ordinarily there is also some disagreement among the members of a group as to what its commitments and present actions are, and this is a further source of discussion.

The three components appear in all decision structures, though in a great variety of forms. In general, the larger structures are more highly differentiated, more formalized and rigid, more explicit and self-conscious, while the smaller ones are simpler, more fluid, and unself-conscious. A brief survey of some typical structures will illustrate the range of variations in decision structures.

A governmental structure represents the extreme of differentiation, explicitness, and consciousness, and perhaps also of formalization. Decisions result from interaction among a wide variety of specialized roles. There are specialists who consider the effect of a course of action on the economy, others who consider its effect on the budget, others, on the party, others, on the courts, others, on foreign relations, and so on. Each specialist has his own subspecialists; some of these are factual experts, others idea men, others liaison men, still others mediators. Most of these roles are explicitly assigned to specific persons, who continue to hold the role for a long time and until they are explicitly and formally removed. Communication and discussion among these roles is mostly explicit, formal, and conscious. It may take the form of written memoranda or official meetings in which people sit around a table and speak in turn. With written communication and large meetings it is the literal meaning of words that count, rather than the gestures, inflections, and concealed attitudes of the speaker and listener; discussion moves on an abstract, impersonal, intellectual level. Informal discussion also occurs, but only in smaller subgroups within the main structure.

With such a wide diversity of roles, there will also usually be a great variety of beliefs, values, and norms operative in the different parts of the structure. Persons assigned a specialized role for a long period of time tend to develop specialized beliefs, values, and standards appropriate to the role, so that role differentiation also brings ideological differentiation with it. This in turn causes difficulties of communication, which must be solved by intermediary interpreters and moderators.

Finally, the commitments and active programs of so large an organization must also be many and varied, even to the point of being contradictory. Besides the commitments of the present government there are the leftover commitments and actions of past governments, which may spring from an entirely different background but which cannot simply be canceled. They must be continued in some fashion, modified if possible, and new decisions and actions must be made to fit in with them.

Judicial structures stand out among decision structures as being formalized, explicit, and conscious in the extreme, though they are much less differentiated than governmental structures. There are only three main groups of roles, two opposed positions and a neutral center position, with perhaps assisting factual-expert roles. Sometimes the central position is elaborately divided and subdivided, as in the Lozi courts (Gluckman, 1955), but this is unusual. The formalization appears in the governing ideology, the explicit procedural rules as to what can be said, how, and when. This formalization is part of legalism; it occurs less in young judicial systems and more in advanced systems.

In contrast, most small decision structures — groups of from roughly three to a dozen people — are much more informal, inexplicit, and unself-conscious. Roles are not explicitly recognized, and may shift from time to time, also without conscious recognition. One person may often hold two or more roles and may shift from one to another without knowing it. Often a leader is consciously recognized, and occasionally some other specialists; but there are many kinds of leadership and usually a group has several leaders in addition to the recognized one.

Beliefs, values, and interests are much more homogeneous in a face-to-face group, since in small groups an integrative process occurs in which divergent beliefs and values are either incorporated more and more thoroughly or ejected completely. Consequently people can understand each other more readily, and there is less need for interpreters and intermediaries. Also, since consciousness usually results from contrast or opposition, people tend to be less aware of their own beliefs and values. When everyone shares the same beliefs (except those oddballs that no one listens to) these come to be taken for granted as self-evident; they need not be discussed or even mentioned directly; and soon they move into the background of awareness.

Discussion in small groups is largely nonverbal and unconscious. People communicate emotions and attitudes through subverbal vocal inflections and through gestures and bodily postures which are not consciously focused on. Barnard (1938:90) uses the term "observational feeling" to describe this kind of unconscious, nonverbal communication. Morever, even in the verbal part of discussion it is not the literal meaning of words that counts but their unspoken implications. People who know each other personally can perceive the personal implication of words and also of silence, and learn to reply to underlying attitudes rather than to literal statements. Discussion may move on several levels at once, conscious and unconscious, and leadership roles fall to people who are sensitive to happenings on several levels at once.

Discussion in an individual decision structure is entirely nonverbal and almost entirely subconscious. The participating roles are taken by the various parts of the personality — let us call them habits. Each habit is activated or inhibited by appropriate stimulus features of the environment; when it is activated, it makes a demand for action on the whole person. Some habits make demands for small, immediate actions, such as sitting down or putting on one's coat; others safeguard long-run goals; still others act as moralists and censors, approving or disapproving a particular action after it has been suggested. Some habits have authority, that is, are acceptable to other habits; some are not acceptable and are refused membership in the structure, that is, they are repressed, whereupon they continue to offer subversive suggestions in disguised forms.

Demands for action are reacted to, partly in terms of other internal demands, and partly in terms of the perceived possibilities of the environment. The same habits that demand action also structure the perceived environment in its dimensions of reality, unreality, and possibility. They determine what can be perceived and how it is perceived, what can be looked for, expected, perceived even when it is not there, and what will not be perceived even when it is there.

Altogether, then, habits do three things: they make demands for action, they offer statements of fact and possibility, and they react to the demands and statements of other habits. In these senses they have the same functions that individuals have in a group decision structure.

The final integration of all demands and statements into a decision is the work of the ego (or is the ego). The ego is the I which finally says, "It shall be done." In reaching a decision, it placates some habits, cautions others, compromises with some, refuses to listen to others, but tries to stay on the good side of as many as possible. Ego activity will be discussed further in the section on political decisions.

There is, of course, enormous variation among personalities conceived as decision structures. Some are highly differentiated, others simple and undifferentiated; some have a strong central leader, others a weak leader or leaders; some are highly unified in beliefs and values, others are torn by ideological conflict; some are relatively self-conscious, others almost entirely unconscious; some exhibit high tolerance and little repression, others are marked by extensive repression and subversive activity. The range of variation in individual decision structures is probably as great as the range of variation in group decision structures.

Several kinds of processes occur within decision-making structures. March and Simon (1958:129–131) have distinguished four of these, which they call problem solving, persuasion, bargaining, and "politics." In problem solving the participants assume that they share relevant goals and criteria; they work out a course of action through a joint examination of the problematic situation, assembling information, making predictions, giving and weighing suggestions, and continuing until everyone is satisfied with the result.

If participants find that they differ in beliefs, goals, or criteria, they may resort to persuasion in an attempt to eliminate the differences. Persuasion involves mainly the testing of disputed beliefs and values by reference to more general criteria shared by the participants, according to March and Simon. Emphasis is on the views of the persons involved rather than on the immediate problematic situation.

In bargaining, the participants work out their own objectives and strategies privately before meeting together. They assume that their objectives, or at least their immediate objectives, are not shared by the other participants, and that persuasion will be ineffective in producing agreement. Instead, agreement is reached by exchanging concessions or pretended concessions, with each side trying to gain a maximum and give up a minimum. Politics is a preparation for bargaining; participants assume that bargaining will eventually be necessary, and try to establish as strong a bargaining position as possible in advance. They do this by forming coalitions, marshaling or increasing their resources, and diverting or destroying the opponent's resources. Warfare is an extreme example of politics in this narrow sense.

In practice these four kinds of process are usually combined in various ways. People may bargain on some points, use persuasion on others, and engage in problem solving on still others. Bargaining and politics, or persuasion and problem solving, are frequently combined in continuous oscillation. Shifts occur too; people may begin with intent to bargain, find increasing areas of agreement over time, and gradually shift to problem solving; or the reverse may occur. Also, as March and Simon point out, bargaining frequently takes place disguised as problem solving or persuasion. So it may be difficult to determine, in a given case, which of these processes or which combination of them is taking place.

The reasons for the occurrence of one process rather than another do not directly concern us here. One possibility is that the amount of bargaining and politics depends on the degree of ideological differences between individuals in the organization, and also on the extent to which goals are in conflict. In addition the very size and complexity of an organization may make bargaining necessary by producing constant differences and conflicts between organization members. In any case, we shall be concerned with all four types of process, since all of them occur in decision structures.

FUNCTIONAL RATIONALITY

The developmental trends of decision-making structures have not yet been isolated and described by scientists, perhaps because the concept of a decision-making structure or control system is a relatively recent one. This makes it necessary to proceed in a more nearly *a priori* fashion, with occasional references to empirical evidence. Any

POLITICAL RATIONALITY   177

such approach, in which fancy is only remotely limited by fact, is highly untrustworthy, so the following account must be regarded as only preliminary speculation to be corrected by more thorough investigation later.

Any decision-making structure must have two characteristics to exist at all. First, it must make possible the presentation of a plurality of facts, values, norms, and action alternatives. At least two of each one of these is necessary, otherwise no decision is possible because there are no alternatives to decide about. This characteristic will be called "differentiation" in the ensuing account, following Bales's terminology in his experiments on role differentiation in decision-making groups (Parsons and Bales, 1955, chap. 5). Second, it must make possible a unified resolution which incorporates at least some of the presented material. This characteristic will be called "unification" in the ensuing account.

Consider, for an example, a small group of men with the common purpose of moving some heavy piece of furniture. Immediately they will differentiate their tasks by each stationing himself at a different spot around the furniture, selected by reference to the other spots. This differentiation, though originally undertaken as a technical division of labor, also creates a decision structure. All during the moving there will be a constant series of decisions, to turn, avoid an obstacle, slow down, and so forth, to which members contribute by virtue of their specialized positions. The decision structure exists because there is a unifying purpose, to move the furniture, and different roles from which a variety of perceptions and suggestions are contributed.

Both characteristics together are irreducible prerequisites for any decision, since together they constitute the meaning of "deciding." Therefore any structure that does not embody them both is not a decision structure, since no decisions can occur in it.

A decision structure yields improved decisions as it embodies both of these characteristics to a greater degree. First, the greater the variety of the presented facts, values, and norms, and the greater the variety of proposed alternatives a structure is able to produce, the more effective its decisions are likely to be. The reason is that decisions are made necessary by problems, and complex problems require complexity of treatment for adequate solution. An adequate decision on farm price supports, for instance, must be based on consideration of a wide variety of factors: facts about the main determinants of prices, production, costs, and returns; facts about voting patterns and their determinants; predictions about the effects of alternative support programs on a variety of factors both economic and noneconomic; values of alternative consumption patterns, alternative income patterns, alternative patterns of population distribution; abstract norms such as efficiency, equality, justice; more particular theories about the proper functions of government in the economy, and so on. Omission of any of these factors from consideration means that the decision will have unanticipated consequences and perhaps quite different total results from those intended, and will be rational only by accident.

Second, the more intricate and subtle the ways of unifying presented factors are, the more effective the decision is likely to be. This again is true because of the complexity of the problems most groups must be prepared to face. A complex problem is likely to give rise in discussion to a variety of contradictory factual reports, differing values and norms, and conflicting suggestions for action. An adequate decision will have to note and embody most of the contradictory material and also relate it to the previous commitments of the group; but this is possible only through an intricate process of combination, evaluation, modification, and elimination. To be sure, some decision can always be reached by a series of arbitrary coin flips or majority votes, but such a decision, proceeding by simple elimination without discussion, will be adequate only by chance.

As the two characteristics are progressively embodied in a decision structure, they come increasingly into conflict with each other. The greater the variety of suggested facts and opinions, the harder it is to reach agreement; and the swifter and more certain the resolution process is, the harder it is to get varied and unusual factors presented to group awareness.

The general requirements for a functionally rational decision structure have now been stated. A functionally rational structure is one which yields adequate decisions for complex situations with some regularity; but only structures which embody the two characteristics of differentiation and unification to a considerable degree will regularly yield adequate decisions. Therefore only such structures are functionally rational. Let us now consider these two requirements in more detail.

A structure is differentiated to the extent that it provides positions for people with different ideologies or points of view. Since a person's ideology determines his perceptions, interpretations, and evaluations, the greater the difference of ideology the greater the variety of ideas a structure will produce. People of differing ideology will ordinarily disagree on the nature and importance of a problem under discussion, and even on the factual situation. They will interpret agreed-on facts differently, make different predictions, and invent different proposals for action. During and after a course of action is taken, they will evaluate its success differently and even disagree on what is happening, why, and what is likely to happen next. When differences are considerable, not all the descriptions and predictions are likely to be correct; but presentation of a variety of descriptions and predictions makes a group more alive to the many facets of what is, or might be, happening, and more alert to what is coming or could come about. As time passes some of the predictions are plausibly verified and others quietly forgotten, but even the unfulfilled predictions are useful as indicators of what could have happened and may even happen yet. When a variety of norms, goals, and ideals is presented to a group not all are likely to be equally relevant to the problem under discussion; but even the less relevant ones may be useful as indicators of alternative possibilities of action if the preferred course of action encounters unexpected difficulties. In addition, as Mill argued in his *On Liberty*, even a quite false theory (or quite irrelevant value) is useful as a stimulus to more vigorous development and more vital awareness of one's true theories and values.

It may be argued that ideological differences are necessary only because human rationality is limited. If human beings could think objectively, biases and ideologies would not exist, and all thinking men could eventually agree on everything; but since this is impossible, the next best thing is a multiplicity of biases so they cancel and counteract one another. If human beings had enough perceptivity, one man could discover all the facts relevant to a given problem; but given limited and fallible perceptive capacities, it is better to gather several factual reports so they can supplement and verify one another. If one man knew the whole truth his predictions would always be correct; but since all existing theories are incomplete and partly false, it is better to bring together a variety of partial theories to better approximate the whole truth.

To some extent this is correct; ideological variety is necessary as a corrective to partiality. But in some respects partiality and bias are even helpful. Partiality makes possible a division of labor in describing and interpreting, in that each person will look at a problem from the standpoint of his own beliefs and values. His standpoint will enable him to see and predict things that others would not be able to see or expect, and to exaggerate things that others can just barely see. If a unified picture can be built up out of exaggerated partial statements, it will be more complex than the picture an imaginary impartial observer would construct. Further, even though some of the things described and predicted may not exactly be there, they represent possibilities that should not be ignored. A group that is continually being reminded of what might happen or is perhaps already happening, or can be made to happen, can be better prepared to meet changes as they occur, than can a group which only knows what is now happening.

Further, the division of labor throws the full weight of a total personality behind each partial approach and allows it to be carried through with greater vigor. This is especially important where criticism and critical revision are necessary. A person who has devised a program of action is less likely to see its defects than someone who is opposed to it. A vigorous opponent can be relied on to bring out all possible shortcomings of a proposal, including some that are not there but may yet come about with bad luck. And when a program is being carried out, a vigorous opponent will be alert to the first small signs of failure which zealous advocates of a program would not notice or would brush aside. On the other hand, enthusiastic partisans will try to salvage a program in difficulty where a disinterested observer might advise giving up, and will try to revitalize a temporarily discredited theory that more impartial thinkers would abandon.

When I say that a decision structure should provide positions for people with different ideologies I mean that they should actually participate in decision making, not merely be included on official membership lists. Many groups have a large and varied official membership without an equally large participation in decision making. A person actually participates only if he has authority within the group, that is if his ideas and feelings are accepted seriously by other group members. Thus differentiation implies a wide distribution of authority. In addition, authority must be of relatively equal strength, since otherwise a member with great authority could, by his opposition, nullify the contribution of a member with little authority.

I use the term "authority" here to refer only to the fact that a person will be listened to carefully, whatever he says. There are two bases for authority, respect and fear. Though these two may ultimately be the same and certainly shade into one another, they are at least superficially different. A person is listened to out of respect when he has personal qualities which are admired — qualities which may be useful to the group, or are highly valued as symbols. A person is listened to out of fear when he is powerful enough to punish inattention.

Respect alone is not a sufficient basis of authority in a highly differentiated structure. Personal qualities are admired only when they are recognized and valued by a group; but group recognition and acceptance are always conditional. The eminence of a group member is readily recognized when he states ideas that are agreeable and familiar, but appreciation diminishes when he regularly disagrees with other group members and expresses novel ideas and valuations. An authority based on respect is strongest when its possessor contributes only ideas which are acceptable to other group members. When his ideology is different and his suggestions startling and disturbing, his authority is likely to be weak and uncertain. Yet this is just where authority is most necessary. Wide differentiation exists only when a group accepts a variety of ideas based on diverse ideologies. Hence authority must be secure enough to compel consideration even of disagreeable facts, needs, obligations, norms, and suggested actions. Such an authority must be based at least partly on fear, that is on power.

By "power" I mean the ability to inflict unpleasant consequences at will. In some children's gangs the unpleasant consequences may be a beating. In more formal organizations consequences such as dismissal or demotion, fines, jail, or vetoes are at the disposal of the formal leader, and the threat of these consequences forces people to listen to him. But the most usual kind of power is the contribution a person makes to an organization's activities. The more important a person's contributions are, the more dangerous their removal would be, and the fear of removal forces people to listen to his views. The contributions a person can make depend on the needs of the organization — money, influence over votes or customers, administrative skill, labor, special knowledge or information, high status or prestige, patronage, and so on. Once an organization has become dependent on a person's contribution, the threat of withdrawal is usually enough to force admission into the organization's decision structure.

Though power is usually a dependable basis for gaining a role in a decision structure, it does not always have that effect. To be effective, it must in addition be respected or acknowledged as legitimate (moral) by the organization members. Use of illegitimate power may gain a momentary hearing, but at the first opportunity the organization members will try to free themselves from its influence and get rid of the power holder. For instance, the leader of a street corner gang may be listened to respectfully because he can beat up anybody in the gang, but a cabinet member would get nowhere in attempting to use such power. At one time industrial managements regarded the strike, that is, the withdrawal of labor contribution, as an illegitimate (immoral) form of power, and consequently thought they had a moral duty to resist even at great expense to their organization. But when striking came to be respected as legitimate it enabled labor representatives to gain participation in decision making.

A decision structure is differentiated, then, when both admirable personal qualities and power are widely and evenly distributed, since this makes possible the equal participation of many people with different ideologies.

Unification of diverse proposals in a decision structure is based partly on mutual understanding, identification, and trust. The various suggestions made during discussion cannot be taken up at all unless they are understood, and improvement of a suggestion usually requires a rather full understanding of it. But even if a suggestion is understood it will not be accepted and developed by others without some sense of mutual identity; and a person will hardly be able to accept the change or elimination of his own proposals unless he identifies with and trusts those who make the changes.

Understanding is made possible by the sharing of a common ideology which is detailed and consistent enough so that it is not susceptible to widely divergent interpretations by different people. Identification and trust are products of integrative processes, and thus cannot be produced at will according to any formula. They frequently are strong in small groups where people are in intimate and continuing contact, but small groups are also prone to fierce hostility and competition. Sharing common experiences, especially ceremonies, may produce trust and identification; and attraction for a common leader, common cause, or common ideals, are often effective. But where anxiety or frustration levels are high these factors may be ineffective, and may be so misperceived as to produce competition or suspicion instead.

When trust and sense of identity are weak and understanding is impaired by ideological diversity, some further basis of unification is necessary. The most dependable basis is centralization of authority. This may be achieved by giving someone the role of making the final decision, with other roles being chiefly advisory, or by narrowing the range of participation in discussion, or by entrusting procedural decisions to some central authority, or by creating a court of last appeal in substantive disagreements, and in other ways.

The basis of a central authority may lie in the role itself, if the group selects people to take the role. An authority derived from the group delegation, however, rests on group solidarity and ideological unity, and is therefore almost as undependable as they are. When these other sources of unification are weak, central authority must be partly based on respected qualities (charisma) and on superior centralized power. Power is not of itself a sufficient basis for adequate central authority, but it is sufficient and dependable when supplemented by group delegation and by personal qualities.

When stated in these abstract general terms, the conflict between the requirements of differentiation and unification comes out clearly. Ideological unity conflicts with ideological diversity, and centralized authority based on unequal power conflicts with widely dispersed equal authority based on dispersed and equal power.

This means, in practice, that an increased unification usually decreases differentiation. All the easy ways of unifying a group involve either exclusion or integration of discordant beliefs, and both of these decrease differentiation. For example unity may be increased by expelling "subversive" elements, or more simply by not listening to any extreme ideas, or by more sharply defining the creed that everyone in the group must accept. These devices increase ideological unity by excluding discordant persons and beliefs. Centralization of authority also unifies through exclusion, since it involves removal of authority from peripheral elements of the group. For instance, central control of communication channels or of discussion procedure can be used to shut out disruptive ideas and valuations. Integration of discordant beliefs, which accompanies increase of group solidarity, also decreases differentiation. Integration implies the loss of conflict and novelty, because if everyone agrees with everyone else, not many disagreeable or surprising ideas will develop.

Similarly, increased differentiation tends to destroy unity. Increase of ideological variety makes it more and more difficult for participants to understand each other and therefore also harder to trust and tolerate each other. In addition, as the stock of agreed-on beliefs and values declines, it becomes harder to resolve ideological differences by persuasion, so differences harden and become permanent. It also becomes more difficult to sustain a single system of authority, maintain agreed-on rules for fair bargaining procedures, or even to agree on what kinds of power are legitimate. But without some agreement on the last three points resolution of differences is very difficult.

As long as the available ways of increasing unity also decrease differentiation, and vice versa, no appreciable increase in an organization's rationality is possible. There is merely a movement back and forth along a unity-diversity axis. A rational structure, therefore, must somehow resolve the conflict between the two.

The standard way to do this in large, highly differentiated structures is to unify in several stages. Instead of funneling all the observations, predictions, proposals, and criticisms directly to one central authority for disposal and decision, which would put an impossible unifying task upon him, the task is shared among a hierarchy of subordinates. Each subordinate acts as a unifying agency for one section of the organization's activities, working out tentative action proposals on the basis of the reports and suggestions developed in that sector. Higher level authorities then co-ordinate the various subproposals, and the central authority limits himself to resolving final disputes or indeterminacies. In other words, different kinds of decisions, each requiring a different kind of unification, are made at different levels. Technical decisions, requiring goals given by higher authorities, are made at the lowest level; economic decisions, involving a co-ordination and comparison of the goals of different sections, are made at higher levels. Socioeconomic and integrative decisions are made at still higher levels, since these involve the modification of organization goals; and political decisions, involving the preservation and correction of the total structure, are made at the highest level (cf. Parsons, 1960, chap. 2). In this way the various lower-level sections can be highly specialized and differentiated, though each section can be well unified internally. Since the sections have no direct contact, they need not understand or trust one another and can develop considerable ideological differentiation. The higher authorities mediate differences among the lower sections, prevent active conflicts, and preserve the general goals of the organization amid differing interpretations.

Though a hierarchy of unifying centers allows for greater differentiation than a single center, it does not automatically resolve the conflict between unification and differentiation. The rationality of the structure still depends on achieving a balance between central authority and sectional autonomy, ideological conformity and diversity. In fact, the problem is more complicated than in a simple structure, because it is necessary to achieve a gradation of authority throughout the hierarchy of subcenters, and a gradation of ideological diversity from the center outward. If too much power is concentrated at the center, ideological diversity can be largely nullified even against the central authority's wishes, because the subcenters, instead of mediating, will eliminate ideas they think will displease the center, and the local initiators of ideas will soon see that they must conform to get their ideas approved. If the subcenters are too powerful the central authority will be unable to maintain the primacy of the organization's basic goals and will be reduced to mediating the conflicting programs of the subcenters. The organization will dissolve into suborganizations related by bargaining and politicking. If neither central nor subcentral authorities are strong enough the organization will be indecisive and may dissolve entirely.

A more basic solution to the problem of increasing political rationality is to base group unity on toleration rather than on complete identity. Toleration is an incomplete form of unification; it consists of accepting the divergent beliefs and roles of others as valid phases of the group culture without taking them up into one's own ideal self. It is based on partial unifications and conditional loyalties, that is, on a feeling of underlying identity combined with a recognition of continuing irreducible differences among group members.

When a group is unified through toleration, divergent points of view can be included in common discussion without having to give up their diversity. If, on the other hand, a more complete identity of ideology were required for participation, the differences in point of view would be eliminated, and with them the sources of fresh ideas and valuations.

Several degrees of toleration may be distinguished, ranging from (1) the bare agreement not to interfere with one another through (2) an occasional offering of suggestions to (3) the full attempt to understand one another and work together without destroying one another's differences. The third degree of toleration is possible only when ideological differences are so small that they can confront one another directly without destructive effects. This frequently, though not always, is the case in small groups. But when differences are so great that direct confrontation would produce only misunderstanding and hostility, they can still be preserved by mutual noninterference.

A large hierarchical structure ordinarily requires the first two degrees of toleration among subsections to preserve the necessary degree of differentiation. This is achieved in practice largely by the voluntary self-restraint of the various authorities in dealing with one another and with subordinates. They must accept, and sometimes even support, ideals and goals with which they disagree, while refraining from a too insistent urging of ideas with which they agree. From the standpoint of a central authority toleration is habitual restraint in use of one's authority, while among subordinates and peers it is the preservation of loyalty and identification in spite of differences.

The political party system is made possible by toleration. Parties can alternate in power only if the majority party restrains itself from using tactics that would perpetuate it in power, and the minority parties refrain from obstructing policies they think are mistaken and dangerous. In this way the ideas of all the parties are preserved for eventual use, though at a given time the ideas of only one party are available for decision making.

Toleration does not provide sufficient unity by itself. It must be supplemented by some common ideology as a basis of mutual understanding, and some centralization of power as a basis for leadership. These requirements conflict with the differentiation requirements of divided ideology and wide distribution of power. Thus any rational decision structure, even one containing a high degree of tolerance, will always remain unstable and in inner conflict.

Ideally the differentiation and the unity in a structure should balance each other without negating one another. That is, there should be enough bases of agreement to handle the most varied reports, proposals, and valuations that the structure can produce, and there should be enough differentiation to tax the powers of unification to the utmost. Anything short of a balance means unused capacity and decreased likelihood of adequate decisions.

Though all decision-making structures must conform to the above general requirements, the kind of problem which a group regularly faces imposes additional, more specific structural demands. Formal organizations, which make primarily technical and economic decisions, tend to require, and to develop, a strong central authority. This development may occur in a variety of ways and for a variety of specific reasons, but partly it occurs as a response to pressures resulting from economic progress. In a progressive economy there is a continuous pressure on organizations to become more efficient, to rationalize; those which do not do so lose out to more efficient competitors and shrink or disappear. Rationalization is achieved by calculating the productivity of existing productive processes, comparing them with alternative processes, and changing those which are less efficient. But attempts to change existing organizational practices frequently meet resistance, since organization members have become attached to them. The practices may have survived because they yield unrecognized, unofficial satisfactions to members, or they may have become integrated into an informal social structure within the formal organization, or both. Consequently, if the affected members participate in organizational decisions they will try to eliminate the particular changes which affect them, and the more widespread the participation in decisions is, the more difficult it will be to work out an effective rationalization plan. Organizations with a loose, decentralized decision structure often find it impossible to reorganize, until the mounting pressure of capital losses forces a decision either to go out of existence or to drastically centralize authority for a radical reorganization. To be sure, organizations with strongly centralized decision structures do not thereby succeed in avoiding resistance to change, but the resistance cannot prevent a decision. Instead, it can be taken into consideration and the decision modified to allow for it. On the other hand, without strong central power the resistance can entirely prevent a decision and paralyze the organization.

The faster the rate of economic progress, the greater the pressure for continuous rationalization, and the higher the survival value of a strong central authority. Individual organizations can cushion the pressure and postpone reorganization in a variety of ways — protecting markets, exploiting local resource monopolies (for example, reputation, loyalty, labor and managerial skills, credit) getting government assistance — but on the whole the advantage lies with centralized organizations.

The direct pressure of competition is not the only factor which leads to centralization of decision structures. Individuals on the lookout for chances of profit can have the same effect. In this case individuals perceive possibilities of rationalization which are unrealized due to entrenched opposition; they buy out the opposition and thereby substitute a new, narrow decision structure for the old paralyzed one; and they proceed with the reorganization.

The advantage of a narrow centralized decision structure accrues also to governments faced with the desire or the necessity for rapid rationalization of the whole economy. For example, the technological demands of modern warfare have been met by drastic resource mobilization carried out through extremely centralized decisions. The centralized structure of the USSR has been at least partly a rational response to the Communist party's desire for extremely rapid economic and technological progress, which requires unusual resource liquidity. Similarly, the desire and necessity for rapid economic progress in underdeveloped countries imposes a requirement of strong central government authority, and perhaps even dictatorship. Entrenched religious practices, caste systems, tribal loyalties, agricultural practices, prevent the necessary resource liquidity and must be rapidly eliminated, and those governments which do not succeed in persuading or forcing their elimination will fail. Indeed, it may be that with the extension of economic and technological progress all over the world, the future will see a continual narrowing of participation and centralization of authority in decision structures, both governmental and nongovernmental.

On the other hand, centralization conflicts with an opposite requirement of widespread participation in the decision structure of formal organizations (Baker, 1948). In large organizations many people are necessarily involved in carrying out a decision, and success partly depends on their understanding and approving the policies they are carrying out. Lack of understanding leads to errors in lower level implementing of decisions; disapproval can lead to covert obstruction and nullification of policy. In either case the result is a concealed indecisiveness in that the organization does not actually carry out its own decisions. Concealed indecisiveness is a problem in labor unions and in managements, where friendly, collusive (Selekman's terminology) top-level relations are nullified by lower level militancy; it is a problem in political parties, where high level party control is nullified by local opposition or apathy; it is a problem in armies, where captains and majors revolt against decisions of generals and politicians; it is a problem for everyone whose noble resolves are inexplicably frustrated by unknown, repressed desires.

There are two kinds of remedies for concealed indecisiveness. One is to break up the execution of decisions into a set of completely routine, mechanical actions so they require no understanding at all. This procedure is standard in armies and industries—privates and workers are trained to perform a series of mechanical acts "by the numbers." The difficulty is that many policy executions can be routinized only to a limited extent, and beyond this limit discretion is unavoidable. Nor does routinization take care of opposition or apathy among lower ranks; it may increase it. Consequently over-dependence on routinization severely limits the efficiency of an organization and also limits the range of actions open to it.

The other kind of remedy is to increase participation in decision making, by increased toleration, distribution of power, and so forth. The participation of lower ranks in decision making means that they will be better able to understand what is required of them by seeing how it fits into a whole plan of action. Also if they understand the general intent of a decision and the problem it is designed to correct, they will be able to exercise discretion intelligently. Opposition to a decision can partly be prevented by taking objections into account during decision making and by considering local circumstances which might produce later opposition.

The conflict between the requirements of centralization and the requirement of wide participation, both as a means of increasing efficiency, is a special, acute form of the basic political conflict between unification and differentiation requirements. Since all large goal-oriented organizations are faced with this conflict, it is safe to say that no such organization ever has a completely satisfactory political structure. The nearest thing to a solution of the conflict is to vary the amount of centralization and the degree of participation according to the kind of problem being faced and the amount of discretion needed to solve it.

Structures concerned primarily with integrative decisions must have widespread participation and a relatively permissive central figure. Integrative procedures and decisions are the opposite of economic decisions; they involve the bringing out of hidden feelings and expectations, of anxieties, hopes, self-concepts, symbolic meanings. All these factors are included in the developing set of social relations as far as possible, through appropriate modifications, and the relations are built up out of them. But if feelings and expectations are to be brought out and made known, the people who have them must be able to express them. They must be able to participate in the discussion by communicating feelings, making and criticizing suggestions for action. Moreover, the participation must be intimate, the more so as the feelings and expectations to be expressed are deep and personal. This means that the task of the central authority is one of encouraging participation, rather than one of shutting it out. He must be accepting, supportive, sensitive to half-expressed feelings, and should interpret and transmit the more hesitant statements to the rest of the group. Instead of making the final decision himself, as the leader in goal-oriented structures does, his task is to express a developing group consensus and thereby bring it into group consciousness. Even this may be done indirectly, for instance by asking a question of the right person at the right time.

Socially oriented structures are found in families and among friends, in some types of small groups, in psychotherapy, and in some small preliterate societies. Read (1959:431–432) provides an example of a socially oriented structure:

> When a gathering convenes, the clan orator usually opens proceedings. He stands in the center of the assembled people and launches into a speech which is partly a panegyric upon himself and partly a sermon in which he may stress such group values as restraint, cooperation, and friendship. . . . When the clan orator concludes, he retires to the sidelines and the debate is open to any adult man who wishes to express himself. . . . On most occasions he waits on the sidelines. . . . Then he may intervene with another

homily or an extensive digression . . . the essential task of the clan orator is to reconcile the many different points of view which are presented at a gathering. He does not command the necessary instrumentalities to enforce a decision, and in consequence his role is to choose from among the possible alternatives and to encourage consensus. Perhaps it is not too far from the truth to describe him as the voice of the group's collective conscience. The orator requires time in order to gauge the temper of the gatherings, and characteristically these proceedings are lengthy and somewhat desultory. An observer often loses track of what is occurring and tends to become impatient with the apparent lack of control or direction. . . . After the best part of a day's discussion a resolution may appear to be no closer than when the gathering convened, then suddenly, at the right moment, the clan orator stands up and presents the assembly with its course of action. The meeting dissolves and a somewhat bewildered observer finds upon enquiry that everyone knows what is required of him.

The phrase "he does not command the necessary instrumentalities to enforce a decision" is a negative and misleading description. A better statement would be "a decision is not thought to be a good one unless it is voluntarily accepted by all." Bohannan (1957:64–65) gives a parallel account, which concludes "Judging, like all other activities of Tiv leaders, consists largely in the timely suggestion of what the majority thinks is right or desirable."

In a structure which produces judicial decisions, the neutrality of the center is the most prominent requirement. Legal problems occur in their most characteristic form when there is a clash between strong and continuing differences of interest. If any decisions are to occur at all, these opposed interests must somehow be included or represented in the structure. Since they can meet only on neutral ground, the decision structure as a whole must be ideologically neutral; and its neutrality must be both symbolized and safeguarded by the center, the spokesman for the whole structure.

Within the general requirement of neutrality there is room for much variation in the degree of authority of the center. This variation, in turn, produces a variation in the kinds of moral and judicial decisions that are open to the center. When central authority is weak, the judge must be strictly legalistic and applicational in his official reasoning. His decisions must carry the whole grounds of acceptance within themselves if no external basis of acceptance—personal power, charisma, the backing of higher authorities—is available. Moreover, the same decision must commend itself to two different and opposed viewpoints to be successful. The surest way to meet these requirements is to show that the decision is directly deduced from principles which both sides have already accepted, and this is an applicational decision. When the judge has considerable personal authority or is the representative of higher powers, his decisions do not have to stand on their own internal persuasiveness. He can act more like a khadi and can aim at substantive rather than merely formal justice. Of course, even the strongest judge can also be legalistic if he wishes; and all judges, even the weakest, must also use political decision procedures in their private reasoning, as I shall indicate later.

Judicial structures also vary in the degree of opposition that typically occurs between the two contending parties. When the opposition is not so strong and not so basic, the neutrality of the judge is less important, and he can be more integrative in his decision procedures. This is often the case in primitive law, where disputes occur within a context of numerous shared values, beliefs, and symbols. The judge, as the representative of the shared culture, is not walled off from the contending parties, but can enter into their private worlds and find the materials for integrative decisions. Preliterate judicial structures provide the connecting link between integrative and judicial structures and show that there is really a continuum between the two, the variable being the degree of opposition present.

The variations in the type of structure required for different problems create difficulties when a group is faced with a variety of problems. Shifts of problem call for, and tend to produce, structural shifts in the group; but these are not always easy to manage. In general, structural shifts are easier to make in small, informally structured groups and more difficult in highly differentiated or highly formalized structures.

For example, Zelditch (Parsons and Bales, 1955, chap. 6) points out that the nuclear family must constantly alternate between economic and integrative, or in Parsons' terminology instrumental and integrative-expressive, decisions. It typically handles the required structural shifting by developing two leaders, one instrumental and one integrative-expressive. When a goal-centered problem occurs, the instrumental leader becomes the group center. He (or sometimes she) corresponds to Bales's "idea man"; he has considerable authority, is task- and goal-oriented, object-minded, universalistic, and so on. When integrative decisions are required, the integrative leader becomes the group center and the instrumental leader takes a subordinate position. The integrative leader corresponds to Bales's "best-liked man"; she (or sometimes he) is nonauthoritarian, sensitive to group attitudes and feelings, expressive of group feelings, supportive, group-oriented. The successful persistence of the family depends on the solidarity of the two leaders and on their ability to alternate leadership without conflict. Solidarity is probably facilitated if the two leaders are occasionally able to exchange roles and thereby better appreciate each others' points of view. If the differences are polarized, one leader being almost entirely task-oriented and the other almost entirely group-oriented, successful communication is likely to be more difficult.

The same kind of structural shift is desirable in large formal organizations but is much more difficult there. Such organizations are primarily and overtly goal-oriented and so require a basically centralized decision structure. But any group of human beings working together regularly develop social relations, and these require integrative decisions for their maintenance and therefore some sort of socially oriented decision structure with an integrative leader or leaders. Structural shift requires solidarity and alternation of leadership between the powerful executive hierarchy and the shifting, permissive, integrative leaders in the work groups. But here, unlike the family, the differences between the two are polarized to the extreme. The disparity in ideology and power, as well as the social distance, is usually so great that communication is not possible. Consequently two separate decision structures develop and produce two separate and opposed series of decisions. The integrative process develops without reference to the formal goals of the organization and thus becomes more opposed to them than would otherwise be necessary. From the standpoint of the executive hierarchy the informal organization which controls the integrative process appears as purely negative, an organized opposition to the organization's goals and a stubborn resistance to the requirements of efficiency. The resulting conflict produces both a loss of efficiency and an impoverishment of the informal organization. The same thing happens in families whose leaders are extreme opposites.

In some cases foremen can facilitate structural shift because they are closer to the integrative leaders and can develop some communication channels with them. However when the foreman merely transmits technical decisions made elsewhere and has no discretionary power, he is not a real leader and so cannot shift leadership.

A second example of structural shift is provided by judicial structures. Judges frequently realize that the legal questions—crime, delinquency, divorce—which come before them are only disguises for much more complicated social problems—social and personal disorganization, marital conflict. They also realize that the highly formalized structure developed to solve legal problems is not adequate to deal with social problems. But when they try to shift the structure in order to deal with the social problem, they find that it is not easy. A very considerable change of role is necessary for the judge and also for the other participants. The judge must abandon his detachment and become personally involved with the other participants. He must become attached to the law-breaker, take his side and share his point of view, in order to bring out the hidden conflicts which constitute the social problem. The litigants, in turn, must abandon their opposition and develop some common ground on which to work out new relationships.

Much of this new participation and involvement is, strictly speaking, illegal for the judge. More important, the old role of the judge conflicts with and inhibits the required new roles. The authority which clings to him even when he tries to be informal and friendly inhibits development of rapport. The judge remains a conscience figure in spite of himself; the conflicting problematic factors tend to be repressed by his authority, so that an appearance of harmony rather than a true reintegration results. The delinquent promises to reform and means it, but the root conflicts are still there; the married couple promise to try again, but still stay within their old pattern of relationships.

The same difficulty of shifting occurs in family structures which have taken on a judicial shape. When parents pay too much attention to moral problems in relations with their children—when they are primarily concerned over whether the children's behavior is right or wrong, and when they try to guide conduct by prescribing duties—they become judicial figures, and take on the detachment proper to judges. The entire family decision structure is legalized, and attention is focused on the exact scope and meaning of rules, consistency of parents' judgments, rules of evidence, and so on. This means, from an integrative standpoint, that attention is focused on the surface aspects of behavior rather than on the underlying personality (integrative) problems. But because of their judicial role, the parents are rendered incapable of dealing with these problems. They are too detached to enter into the hidden meanings of the child's life and too much of an authoritative conscience figure to be able to help the child. They have become the prisoners of their own moralizing.

Less formalized judicial structures, such as that of labor arbitration or some preliterate judicial systems, are easier to shift to integrative problem-solving shape. For example in Cheyenne law the same judges who had just punished some delinquents could shift roles, become friends and benefactors, and rehabilitate the criminals (Llewellyn and Hoebel, 1941:112f.). But even these structures must be constantly protected against overformalization. Any structure which deals regularly with legal problems, or in which the conditions of legalism are present, is in danger of becoming more and more formal. Probably the worst thing about legalism is that whenever it is allowed to continue unchecked it renders a decision structure incapable of dealing with nonlegal problems.

One way to check legalism is to reduce the influence of lawyers in a decision structure. For instance Golden (1955:44) notes that the various firms with good union-management relations which he has surveyed have, as a matter of policy, excluded lawyers from contract negotiation sessions. On the other hand, it is well to have lawyers available to take charge when an inescapably legal problem occurs, as long as they do not so dominate the structure that they prevent the recognition of other kinds of problems.

In general, we can say that structures which must predominantly handle one kind of problem only should be adapted to that problem, but structures which must handle a variety of problems should retain a great deal of flexibility. Families, kinship groups, and informal small groups are most likely to require flexibility, though it is also needed in larger formal organizations. The easiest way to stay flexible is to maintain a plurality of leadership roles and leaders, each ready to take charge when the appropriate kind of problem comes up. But it is also desirable to have alternative roles available for other participants as well, so they can shift when necessary (Gearing, 1958).

A final requirement for rationality in decision structures, particularly large, complex ones, is that they be adapted to all types of political processes, problem solving, persuasion, bargaining, and politicking. This requirement has largely been taken care of in the preceding pages, but it is well to bring it out explicitly. The four processes differ both in the type of unification and in the type of differentiation they require.

In problem solving and persuasion the differing viewpoints are held together chiefly by shared beliefs and values and by mutual trust, though some degree of power centralization is helpful as well. Participants in a problem-solving process ordinarily believe that they share the same general goals and values, but differ somewhat in their thought processes, their conception of the immediate objective and of the problematic situation, and their other values. The differences are not so large as to destroy understanding and good will, and agreement is reached by mutual modification of views. A bargaining process, in contrast, is held together primarily by power distribution, by a few shared rules of procedure, and often by some form of mediator. Bargaining participants usually believe, whether right or wrong, that they do not share the same objectives; their differences are such that they neither understand nor trust one another, and what they do understand they do not approve. Usually they resort to bargaining only because they cannot get what they want by force, though the reluctant recognition that they need each other's good will also plays a part.

Bargaining structures are most effective when they are differentiated into a few, ideally two, clearly defined groups. Bargaining takes place between two opposed groups, so the more subgroups there are in a structure the more difficult it is to work out a series of agreements satisfactory to all. Morever, if agreements are to be kept the bargaining groups must have enough continuity of purpose and of responsible leadership to carry out an agreement over a period of time. When groups are fluid and ill defined the groups that make an agreement lose their identity before it can be carried out, and bargaining becomes meaningless.

Problem solving, on the other hand, is very difficult in a structure dominated by strong, rigid, opposed groups. In a rigid structure all problems are forced into the same basic mold, and all suggested solutions fall into the same opposed categories. Nor are the two sides likely to accept and develop each other's suggestions, so discussion fails. This effect has been noticed, for instance, in the polarization of power between the United States and Russia, where the variety of world and local problems are all treated as phases of a capitalist-communist struggle and the solutions urged by the two great powers are monotonously uniform. The flexibility inherent in problem solving requires a flexible decision structure, composed of a wide variety of shifting, partly opposed points of view, with a relatively strong stabilizing central authority and/or widely shared beliefs and values.

A structure adapted to all four processes must therefore provide multiple alternative forms of unification — common beliefs and values, trust, tolerance, rules of procedure, and also power distribution and centralization. Multiple leadership roles are also necessary to operate these different kinds of unification. Differentiation should vary with the issues raised; some issues should divide the structure into clear and continuing groups for bargaining, and others reduce it to multiple shifting points of view for problem solving.

It may be objected that in a perfectly rational structure bargaining and politicking would be unnecessary, as people would all share the same goal, the general welfare, and would understand each other well enough to reach agreement through friendly discussion and persuasion. This view is erroneous on several counts. First, even the most rational men will continue to have different objectives in specific circumstances; the general welfare is too vague to be an operational goal, if indeed it means anything at all. Second, human cognition is too limited for any one man to understand and properly evaluate all the considerations that are relevant to a complex decision. The inclusion of differing ideologies is necessary to provide adequate coverage of complex problems, and this inevitably means some misunderstanding and disapproval.

Third and most important, problem solving, persuasion, bargaining, and politicking are all necessary to some extent for the preservation of complex decision structures; complete reliance on only one or two processes leads to structural deterioration. Continuous use of bargaining tends to weaken and destroy unity and to emphasize differences. Differences of goals and values are brought out and legitimized, so that people no longer expect to be able to agree. Consequently mutual trust also diminishes and misunderstandings increase, and bargaining takes place in an atmosphere of suspicion and fraud. As the bases of understanding diminish, it becomes more and more difficult to reach a mutually satisfactory agreement, so that unresolved frustrations remain behind to poison each new decision process. This result occurs most readily when a structure is dominated by two persistently opposed groups, because all differences are polarized and hostilities are cumulative.

An opposite kind of deterioration can occur when people engage only in problem solving. Working together on common problems tends to bring people's views closer together, and the friendliness that develops makes it easier to remove remaining differences by persuasion. The increasing agreement among participants tends to convince them of the correctness of their views and to silence doubts. Thus an ingrown group of this sort tends to get more and more narrow and rigid in its outlook, and increasingly unable to correct its own errors of judgment.

Each type of deterioration, whether loss of unification or of differentiation, can be prevented and to some extent corrected by the neglected decision process. In a structure which is in danger of losing unity because of excessive bargaining and is splitting into two fixed groups, careful politicking may prevent the consolidation of the groups and preserve more fluid coalition arrangements (Coser, 1956, chap. 4). Each coalition must engage in problem solving, the problem being to frustrate the opposition, and this joint action may preserve or develop bases of unity — partial understanding, trust, shared values — and partly dissolve suspicions. A structure which is growing too unified must be shaken loose by the preservation or reintroduction of differences. These must be preserved against resolution by some degree of suspicion, misunderstanding, and fear, and by power distribution, as otherwise the group will again grow friendly, unified, and narrow in its outlook. So we see that power, hate, fear, and suspicion are not always evil or a product of man's irrationality; indeed, they are essential ingredients in the structure of political reason.

POLITICAL DECISIONS

The type of decision which I shall call "political" is that which is concerned with the preservation and improvement of decision structures. All decisions occur within a decision structure of some sort, but political decisions in addition have decision structures as their special subject matter.

Political decisions are ordinarily made by the central authority of a decision structure. In formal organizations and in small groups, central authorities are leaders; in judicial structures, judges, arbitrators, or administrators play the central role; in bargaining structures one finds mediators, brokers, chief negotiators, or sometimes even "fact-finding" committees or "neutral bystanders" in a central role. The central role is the one that is most closely involved with the whole structure. Any changes anywhere in the structure affect the center; improvements of any sort simplify the tasks assigned to the central role and structural deterioration complicates them, as I shall show. Because of this actual identity of fate, it is easy for persons playing a central role to identify themselves with the structure and to develop a personal concern for its improvement.

I do not mean to say that persons in central roles make nothing but political decisions. The main concern of a person in a central role may often be the achievement of group or personal aims, with the preservation of the decision structure a secondary issue. This is particularly true in comparatively rational structures, which present few structural problems to the person in the central role. Nor is it the case that only central persons make political decisions. Anybody participating in a structure can concern himself with the rationality of the structure in addition to other matters. But political decisions are made more frequently by those in central roles than by those in peripheral roles, because the condition of the structure affects the central role more directly. Consequently in this section I shall treat political decisions as though they are being made by someone in a central role, and shall show how they contribute to the workability of the central role as well as to the improvement of the whole structure. In a later section I shall discuss the principles of political decisions for those not in a central role.

The central role differs from other roles both in content and, usually, in timing of activities. In formal organizations where the central role is a leadership role, the leader is the one who has the final word in a decision process. Subordinates do the preliminary work of gathering information, making predictions, drawing up initial proposals, evaluating, criticizing, and modifying them; then the leader makes the final decision, and the process is completed. In judicial structures the same time sequence occurs in an even sharper form. First the contending participants develop their cases and criticize each other's assertions, and then the judge delivers the decision which completes the process. In informal and socially oriented structures, the leader also usually has the last word, though in this case he expresses a developing group consensus rather than actively making a decision himself. But he may also be active in a subtle way throughout the process, in bringing statements into greater clarity, steering away from irrelevances or insoluble controversies, and gently nudging participants into consensus. In bargaining structures the mediator does not ordinarily have the final word, but, like the informal leader, is concerned with shifting opposing viewpoints until they are acceptable to each other.

If there is any common element in these various types of central role, it is the concern for achieving a firm, unified decision out of the variety of presented materials. A strong central authority makes the final firm decision himself, while a weaker authority helps others to move toward a final agreement. In this sense the central authority is spokesman for the whole group rather than for a particular fraction of it. His task is to find the words that will enable the group to speak as a single voice.

The noncentral roles are the locus of differentiation in a structure. In bargaining and judicial structures they are taken by the opposed sides, so differentiation is present from the start; but in other kinds of structures these roles also become more differentiated, of necessity. Participants who take a specialized role, for example foreign affairs, and become responsible for problems in that area, develop a special point of view related to their role. Their problems are clear and important, while the problems of others are more vaguely perceived. Consequently disagreements develop over priorities in resource allocation, and over the relative importance of problematic factors. A policy suggestion or factual interpretation coming from one point of view will be criticized for distortions and errors by holders of other points of view. Also, apart from immediate problems, participants will try to promote their particular point of view in order to increase acceptance of their suggestions. In complex groups where power is important a struggle for power is a further consequence of differences in point of view.

From the standpoint of the central role, all these activities expressing the differences within the group appear as pressures or potential pressures. The policy suggestions all demand some response from the person in the central role (hereafter known as "the center"). Either they are directed immediately at the center in a bid for acceptance as group policy, or they will eventually be so directed as they gain more general support and move up the organization hierarchy. If the center does not accept them he risks incurring displeasure or hostility; but if he does accept them he risks the displeasure of opposed members of the group. Only suggestions which are acceptable to all sides present no risk to him.

Ideological discussions and factual interpretations do not produce the same immediate pressure because they do not demand any official action at the center. But they are also pressures, of a more subtle sort; they define the field of ideas within which the central role is set. If a particular idea or interpretation is accepted by the whole group, the center must express this acceptance in his reasoning and decisions, even though the idea may be repugnant to him personally. If it is accepted by only a part, his reasonings must still be so formulated as to be intelligible to this part, as otherwise they will feel alienated. More generally, the center has to accept in some fashion all points of view represented in the group, since he is spokesman for the whole. But he cannot completely identify himself with any one point of view without risking the hostility of those holding other points of view. (An exception to this for political parties and similar action groups will be noted later.)

The power struggles again may not concern the center directly but are certain to affect him eventually. Whoever increases his power in the group will be able to direct this increased power toward the center in advocating policies, and must be listened to accordingly. If any subgroup achieves enough power it may even be able to dictate policy, in which case the center will become a figurehead. In general, any shift in power relations affects the pattern of responses which the center must make.

In short, the center of a decision structure is the focus of a variety of pressures coming from particular parts of the structure. The constant task of the person taking a central role is to maintain some independence in the face of all these pressures. If he yields completely to any one of them, he begins to be identified with the particular standpoint to which he yields, and to lose the confidence of the rest of the group. Consequently he loses his role as spokesman and symbol of the group, and becomes instead spokesman or figurehead for one point of view within the group. Someone else is assigned the role of group center, someone who has maintained independence.

Pressures can be resisted and independence maintained in only two ways, either by balancing the pressure coming from one part of the group against the pressure coming from another part, or by a direct assertion of the central authority against the pressure. Either way presents some danger if used exclusively, so a combination of the two is necessary.

The balancing of parts of the group against each other is a mediating process in which the center acts as interpreter, moderator, referee, rather than as a direct participant. In this way pressures aimed initially at the center are shunted off to someone else; the center withdraws from the argument and stands above it.

Mediation can take a variety of forms. A suggestion coming from one quarter can be countered by a request for comment or suggestion from an opposing quarter. Or it can be countered by a statement of what the opposition would think of the suggestion, as grounds for deferring action or making changes. Or, if opposing views are already available it is only necessary to call attention to them and to ask for further consideration. Still another way is to suggest changes that make concessions to opposing views. These changes might range from a modification of detail to an entirely new compromise proposal. When the center suggests changes, he is not opposing a suggestion and getting into an argument; rather he is helping make the original proposal acceptable to its main opponents. Thus he avoids both direct opposition to the proposal and direct identification with it. In general, the weaker the authority behind a particular proposal, the more active the center can be in mediation.

At times when no immediate decisions are necessary, the center can mediate by interpreting opposing points of view to each other, always with the purpose of helping each understand the other rather than to proselytize for a particular point of view.

While mediation is the simplest way to evade pressures and shunt them away, too much mediating activity tends to isolate the center. He takes on the appearance of withdrawing from the group, of having no interest in or opinion about the group's activities. He is so far above the argument that he becomes an outsider. To avoid this result, it is necessary also to stand for something positive, to defend it, and to assert authority in its defense.

However, this something cannot be a particular interest within the group, as that would involve giving up the role of spokesman for the whole and taking on the role of spokesman for one part. Instead, the center must stand for the goals and principles of the whole organization as against the concerns of any part. He must stand for the shared beliefs and values which hold the group together, as against the values which divide it. These shared values then become a source of respect and therefore authority for him, as he comes to be recognized as their spokesman and symbol. Armed with such authority, he can safely resist special pressures without losing anybody's confidence and without losing his independence.

The kind of pressures which can safely be resisted are those which sacrifice the values of the whole to private concerns. Against such pressures the center can assert the overriding importance of shared group values, and can call for loyal subordination of private interest.

An authority based on shared values has inherent weaknesses which prevent a too frequent use. Even shared values tend to be interpreted differently from different points of view. They inspire the greatest unity of feeling if they are left vague; if they are defined too specifically, the divergences of interpretation come into the open and provoke disagreement rather than expressions of loyalty. But if the center continually acts on behalf of shared values, his treatment of them tends to degenerate into a particular interpretation from a special point of view. He becomes a spokesman for a special point of view, who provokes resentment because he pretends to speak on behalf of all. Hence the best way to preserve and extend an authority based on shared values is to hold back its use judiciously. Only in cases of clear disregard for group values is it completely safe to exert authority.

The political procedures outlined above are quite clearly different from the procedures used in reaching economic or legal decisions. Both of these nonpolitical procedures are directed to some problem lying beyond the decision structure, while political procedures are concerned only with relations within the structure. Nonpolitical decisions are reached by considering a problem in its own terms, and by evaluating proposals according to how well they solve the problem. The best available proposal should be accepted regardless of who makes it or who opposes it, and a faulty proposal should be rejected or improved no matter who makes it. Compromise is always irrational; the rational procedure is to determine which proposal is the best, and to accept it. In a political decision, on the other hand, action never is based on the merits of a proposal but always on who makes it and who opposes it. Action should be designed to avoid complete identification with any proposal and any point of view, no matter how good or how popular it might be. The best available proposal should never be accepted just because it is best; it should be deferred, objected to, discussed, until major opposition disappears. Compromise is almost always a rational procedure, even when the compromise is between a good and a bad proposal.

Integrative decisions are more similar to political decisions in that they deal primarily with relations internal to the group or organization, though not only within its decision structure. But in other respects the two are quite different. In the integrative process ideological differences are progressively assimilated and resolved, or if this is not possible, excluded from the system entirely. For example, in conversation between people trying to relate socially, topics on which agreement cannot readily be reached are quickly dropped, so that discussion can exhibit as much agreement as possible. In the political process ideological differences are preserved within some basic unity; specific agreements on action are reached by mediation and compromise without destruction of differences. Integration, like technological and economic progress, is a cumulative process which continues indefinitely without any necessary limit, while increase of political rationality always involves a delicate balancing of opposites — unification and differentiation — which are never reconciled. The need of the center to maintain independence which is basic in political decisions is nonexistent in an integrative process.

So far I have described the two ways in which a group center can deal with the various pressures focused on him and maintain his independence. The two ways are to take a mediating role and thus shunt pressure off to other parts of the group, and to assert the validity of group beliefs against deviant proposals and special interests. By the first way the pressures are dodged and neither yielded to nor resisted; by the second way they are squarely resisted.

The effectiveness of these two procedures depends directly on the strength and composition of the pressures focused on the center. If a particular pressure is too strong, no amount of authority will be sufficient to resist it; and if all the strongest pressures come from one direction, they cannot effectively be balanced by the weaker pressures from the opposite direction. Thus a second, more long range, type of action is necessary. The center must so structure the group that the pressures on him are moderate and well balanced. Again, there are two ways of doing this. First, the center can increase his authority until it is strong enough to resist any particular pressure, and second, he can work to distribute power more evenly throughout the group so that no one power is too strong to be balanced off by any combination of weaker powers.

The authority of the center is strengthened by his clearer identification with shared values, but also by any increase in importance or strength of these values. Groups with few shared values cannot support any strong central authority, because there is little for him to represent. For instance, a loose group associated for temporary purposes, such as a student housing group, has little that a central authority can stand for. Any positive action that he tries to take on behalf of the group tends to be regarded as dictatorial and an arbitrary intrusion on members' privacy, and any resistance to individual suggestions and actions is similarly suspect. Groups composed of widely divergent, strongly opposed interests, such as the UN, also cannot support a strong central authority. The demands for action in such groups are all strongly partisan, and any action that the central person takes toward them tends to be interpreted as partisan by one or another subgroup.

When shared value bases for central authority are weak, it is advisable for the central person to attempt to strengthen them. Any increase of group unity, of shared values and beliefs, shared experiences and purposes, mutual understanding and trust, will strengthen his authority and widen his area of independence. In a loose housing group, for instance, group unity is increased by ceremonial activities such as parties and dances, by warfare with other groups, by developing traditions, rituals, symbols, creeds, idealized purposes. Until such bases of authority can be developed, the weak center must maintain his independence primarily by mediating activity rather than by direct action. Thus the house chairman must mediate between external demands on the group and the private wishes of members, and the UN secretary-general must mediate between pressure groups. This restricts their areas of action considerably.

The other way to structure the group is to work for a wider and more even distribution of power and respect. This is particularly necessary when there is only one source of strong pressure in a group. In such a group the center is always in danger of losing his independence and becoming a front for the pressure source because he has no way of resisting it. A suggestion coming from a strong power cannot be shunted off to someone else for comment and criticism if no one is available with ready and plausible ideas that can command respect. Nor can it be opposed on behalf of other parts of the group if the other parts do not care or have little authority. Suggestions for change or compromise are similarly useless if no one is strong enough to make a compromise necessary. So any suggestions coming from such a pressure group must either be accepted or openly resisted. If they are regularly accepted, the center becomes a figurehead; if they are regularly resisted, the center loses the trust and confidence of the subgroup and becomes merely a second, antagonistic power within the larger group. In this case a new, weak center will appear and will mediate between the two antagonistic powers.

To avoid this dilemma the central person must work for a wider distribution of power and respect and must particularly try to build up a second subgroup with which he can resist the first. He must be especially attentive and appreciative of any suggestions coming from weaker parts of the group, even to the point of actively soliciting them. Any such suggestions should be interpreted in the most favorable light to other parts of the group, and later improvements credited to the original suggestion. Whatever sources of power and opportunities to achieve respect are available to the center should be distributed as much as possible to the weaker parts of the group. If such devices succeed in building up the weaker parts of the group, the independence of the center will be increased. He will be able to use both mediating tactics and direct assertion of authority, instead of relying only on the latter.

The process of structuring the group in such a way as to balance power or to increase central authority is a long-run process which is never satisfactorily completed. The devices of mediation and of direct resistance, in contrast, are day-to-day devices which must be constantly used. Both together are the main ingredients of political action, and their judicious selection is the main task of political decision making.

External pressures are dealt with in much the same way as internal pressures. Suggestions, demands, threats coming from an external pressure source can either be conveyed to the group in a mediating process or they can be resisted with the force of the whole group. The main difference is that since authority based on respect ordinarily exists only within groups, resistance to external pressures usually has to be a matter of force. The success of such resistance depends on the relative power of the group, so there remains the long-run task of increasing the group's power relative to other groups.

If all the actions outlined up to here are successfully carried out, the result is a certain measure of independence for the central person. If he has built up sufficient external power and internal authority and has succeeded in distributing and moderating the pressures within the group, he will be able to either mediate or resist any given proposal as he chooses, or even accept it. In other words, he can concern himself with the intrinsic merits of the proposals coming to him, and can shift to some form of nonpolitical decision making.

This independence is, of course, only as secure as the structure on which it is based. Changes in the structure are bound to affect the position of the central person and may again threaten his independence. So one more task remains for the person who has achieved a short-run independence: he must prepare for future pressures resulting from changing conditions. Future pressures are dealt with in the same way as immediate pressures, either by preparing the means for direct resistance, or by locating opposing pressures that can be used for balancing. But the detailed ways of doing this vary endlessly. Centers of power deteriorate and must be rebuilt or replaced; new sources of power appear and must be incorporated and balanced; points of view become antiquated or lose adherents and new divisions of opinion develop; the tasks and commitments of the group change; and the central person himself must some day be replaced. If all of these contingencies can be foreseen and prepared for, the position of the central person is assured and the task of political decision making is completed. The decision structure can then deal with whatever nonpolitical problems it is faced with, unhampered by structural difficulties.

In summary, political decisions made by a person in a central role of a decision structure are based on three principles or imperatives: (1) *Maintain independence in the face of all pressures.* This can be done either by direct resistance or by a mediation in which the pressure is balanced by some opposing pressure. Mediation is advisable in structures with a weak center and strong subgroups; direct resistance is advisable in structures with a strong center and unbalanced subgroups, though neither tactic should be relied on exclusively. (2) *Act to so structure the group that pressures are moderate and balanced.* This can be done by (a) building up the authority of the center through increased group unity or increased central power, and (b) by building up the weaker parts of the group. (3) *Prepare for future pressures.*

The effect of adequate political decisions is to increase the functional rationality of the decision structure involved. Increase of rationality results especially from carrying out the second and third imperatives, which deal directly with the structuring of the group. The two kinds of activity produce the two characteristics of a rational structure, unification and differentiation. First, the usual way to increase the authority of the center is to increase the importance of group values and beliefs for which he stands. This can be done by interpretation of the various points of view to each other, so their adherents understand and trust each other more; it can be done through group activities, both ceremonial and purposive, which bring people closer together; it can be done in the socialization process by which new members are brought into participation in the group. These are all integrative processes, and they increase the integration of the group. But even apart from integration, any increase of central authority increases unification in the political sense of facilitating the reaching of final decisions. Second, the building up of the weaker parts of the group is a differentiation process. It involves the broadening and equalization of power and respect, broadening of participation, increased variety of points of view and of action proposals, all forms of differentiation. In both these ways, the central person must increase the rationality of the decision structure in the very process of stabilizing and securing his position in it.

The same point can be expressed in a different way by saying that the security of the center is dependent on the rationality of the structure, so that an increase of rationality brings increased security. In a relatively rational structure the pressures on the center are moderate and well distributed, so that they can safely be managed. The center has enough independence from immediate pressures so that he can look ahead and plan for future events with confidence. In a relatively irrational structure the center is always tied up with immediate pressures and demands; he can neither look ahead nor change the structure of the group; and his tenure is short and unsuccessful. One or another pressure pushes him out of his neutral position and he is replaced by some other aspirant.

POLITICAL DECISIONS IN LABOR ARBITRATION

While all political decisions made by a central person should follow the three general principles listed above, there is considerable variation in the way they are applicable in the various kinds of decision structures. Each kind of structure creates its own possibilities and makes its own requirements for success, resulting in its own characteristic kind of decision pattern. Therefore a more detailed account of political decisions in a particular kind of structure will bring out some phases of political decision making and obscure others. With this in mind, let us consider several examples of political decision patterns, beginning with labor arbitration.

The central person in arbitration is the arbitrator; he is responsible for reaching a final decision on the basis of materials, suggestions, and factual interpretations which come to him. He is the focus of pressures from two opposite directions, labor and management, and to a much lesser extent of pressures from government, public opinion, judges, and other arbitrators. The two main pressures take the form of factual interpretations, statements of general points of view, and suggestions or demands for a certain kind of decision. These pressures are backed by power, the power of either side to drop the arbitrator and to refuse further arbitration. Against this double veto the arbitrator has only his personal authority, the authority of his profession, and the vague unorganized power of public opinion, government, and law.

The immediate or short-run problem of the arbitrator is to maintain his independence of the two powerful pressures focused on him. If either side gets the impression that he has abandoned his neutrality and gone over to the other side, they will drop him from their list of acceptable arbitrators. In general, independence must be maintained primarily by mediating activity because of the relatively weak position of the arbitrator. It is not difficult to maintain independence during the hearings, because there the arbitrator is expected to stand aloof and withhold judgment. He is expected to take a mediating role, throwing the arguments of one side over to the other side for refutation and avoiding any personal commitment. The heart of the problem lies rather in the writing of the opinion and the award, because there it is necessary to take a definite stand.

In the written opinion the arbitrator must usually avoid a complete acceptance of the arguments of either side, since that would tend to identify him with the winning side. But neither can he completely reject any argument, for the same reason. He can accept or reject particular points in an argument and accept particular suggestions without danger; but if he unqualifiedly accepts or rejects a whole case, or even worse a series of cases, his neutrality will become suspect.

It is necessary therefore to qualify both acceptance and rejection in some way. He can, for example, accept all the contentions of one side, but give his own reasons for doing so. Or he can accept the premises and factual contentions of one side but come to a slightly different conclusion. In rejecting an argument he can give reasons which are different from those of the winning side; even if the reasons do not seem convincing to the loser they show at least that the arbitrator has an independent opinion. It is particularly necessary to avoid entanglement with the ideology of either side, because that would immediately identify him with that side. Therefore when an acceptable conclusion is buttressed by an ideological argument it is advisable to find a different argument to justify the same conclusion. Factual contentions, on the other hand, can be accepted without qualification, because facts are thought not to imply any particular ideology. Some facts do imply a particular ideology, and these must be treated with care. For example, union contentions that an employee was in fact discharged for union activity cannot often be accepted without qualification, even if an arbitrator has been convinced of the fact. "Discharged because of union activity" does not exist as a fact except from a union point of view, so acceptance of such a fact tends to imply acceptance of a union point of view.

The arbitrator's award must, in general, stay within the "limits of acceptability," that is, it must be at least tolerable to the loser. A series of unacceptable awards tends to sour a losing side on either the arbitrator or arbitration in general. The simplest way to stay within the limits of acceptability is to compromise and award something to both sides, but this has deficiencies which will be discussed later. A longer term type of compromise is to make sure that each side wins at least some cases over a period of time. But the best tactic is to relate the award to the relative importance of the case for each side. A case which is crucial to one side, in which a loss would be intolerable, should not be awarded against that side without exceptionally good reasons. In secondary or routine cases both sides can probably tolerate a loss, and here the award can be based on considerations other than immediate acceptability. Finally, there are sometimes cases which one side does not particularly want to win and is pushing only for appearances; here a win for that side would be intolerable to the loser and perhaps to both sides.

So far I have treated only the immediate, case-to-case tactics of the arbitrator. These may perhaps seem like deplorable, Machiavellian tactics which detract from the pure objectivity needed in arbitration; but they are necessary if the arbitrator's independence is to be maintained, given his own weak position and the incomplete, skeptical acceptance of arbitration by the contending sides.

The longer run problem of the arbitrator is to improve the structure of arbitration. In a structure dominated by two powerful hostile forces, the center has great difficulty in maintaining his independence, and must resort to continuous mediating activity to avoid being overcome. Consequently the primary type of improvement is to increase the authority of the center, so that the need for mediation can diminish.

The authority of the arbitrator derives from labor and management's picture of him as an impartial, wise evaluator of issues; consequently the best way to establish or increase authority is to fulfill these expectations. The arbitrator can do this by demonstrating in his opinions that his awards are based on careful reasoning and the application of cogent, consistent principles; the principles must, of course, be different from and in between those held by labor and management. Individual arbitrators can help each other in formulating principles and a style of reasoning by participating in organizations such as the National Academy of Arbitrators, which holds conventions and issues publications. By comparing notes, arbitrators can discover which specific principles have produced generally acceptable results, and have led to re-employment of the arbitrator in parallel cases, and which have not; presumably then the acceptable principles will be more widely adopted, and the others will drop out — or the arbitrators who insist on holding to them will drop out.

Gradually an ideology of arbitration will develop which arbitrators can draw on to show their thoughtfulness and adherence to principle.

Possession of an intermediate ideology also helps arbitrators to stabilize their intermediate, neutral position, and thus to achieve the good effects of compromise without the bad effects. The value of a compromise award is that it is likely to be acceptable to both parties; its weakness is that it is unprincipled and therefore destroys the authority of the arbitrator and eventually also his independence, since compromises are too easily predictable. But awards based on principles which are themselves a compromise can affirm the authority and independence of the arbitrator without sacrificing acceptability. Such awards achieve a general compromise effect without actually being a compromise in any particular instance. That is, a particular award need not fall between the contentions of the two sides at all, but may conform to one or the other side completely; but over a period of years both sides will win a substantial number of cases, particularly the ones embodying more moderate demands.

Another way to increase the authority of the individual arbitrator is to work for greater mutual tolerance and understanding between labor and management. As the two opponents come to perceive themselves as two different but necessary parts of the industrial system they develop some elements of a common outlook and common goals, and become working partners rather than antagonists. The arbitrator can help formulate this common outlook in his written opinions, by stating principles likely to be acceptable to both sides. The common outlook is authoritative over the private interests of the two parties, and if the arbitrator succeeds in becoming its spokesman his authority is increased. He can reject particular claims and support his decisions by reference to it without losing his impartiality.

Increase of mutual tolerance and understanding also has the effect of decreasing pressure on the arbitrator and increasing the area of acceptability. As each side comes to accept the other as a permanent partner in industry, the intensity of their demands in arbitration decreases. Neither is trying to annihilate the other, but both are content with small gains or clarification of existing relations. This makes it easier for the arbitrator simply to accept or reject particular claims without fear of provoking withdrawal from arbitration.

All the above improvements in the structure of arbitration increase the arbitrator's range of freedom. They strengthen his position and enable him to de-emphasize his case-to-case mediating tactics, and to speak out with confidence. Consequently he can attend more to the problems presented in the cases before him, and concern himself less with his own position. His procedures can be based on the nature of the problems placed before him, and will involve varying combinations of economic, integrative, and judicial principles. Political considerations will not disappear but will move into the background.

It was stated earlier that any example of political decisions will be unusual and misleading in some respect, since political decisions are relative to the structure in which they occur, and there is great variation in decision structures. Political decisions in arbitration are no exception to this rule. The political position of a labor arbitrator is uncharacteristic in three respects. First, practically all the pressures on him come from inside the structure; there are relatively few external pressures. Second, the structure requires an unusual degree of neutrality from him. All central persons must be neutral on some issues and to some degree, but centers of a judicial structure must be far more neutral than other types of centers, as I have indicated earlier. Third, the position of arbitrators is an unusually weak one; judges usually have much more authority. Nor is this kind of weakness similar to the permissiveness of a therapist or other integrative-expressive leader, which is actually based on inner security and strength.

Let us therefore briefly consider two other examples of political decision making which contrast with arbitration decisions in these respects, in order to establish a more balanced picture of political decision making. This will not be a detailed treatment of the two examples, but just enough of an account to show the contrast with arbitration.

Consider first an ordinary judge in a United States court, whose strong position contrasts with the unusually weak position of labor arbitrators. Judges do not always have a strong position, but in the United States they have achieved a position of unusual respectability and power. Their power lies in the enforceability of their decisions, which in turn is based on their unquestioned authority over police. Their respectability derives from the popular beliefs in the almost automatic impartiality of judges and the supremacy of Law. The difficulty of removal of judges is another element in judicial power, which in turn is based largely on the belief in the impartiality and supremacy of Law. If, for instance, Law were thought to be an expression of ruling-class ideology, judges would be less respected and there would be more pressure for easier removability.

Because of the great authority of the judge he has almost no short-run political task. The belief in his automatic impartiality is so strong that he can accept the contentions of one side almost indefinitely without shaking the belief. The limits of acceptability are so wide and vague that almost any decision will be accepted; and because of the judge's power, even unacceptable decisions — for instance, in segregation issues — will be enforceable for a time. In short, the judge's position makes mediation almost unnecessary as a means of maintaining independence.

Political considerations, particularly questions of acceptability, become important when well-organized groups face each other in court over a long period of time. If interest groups are well organized, their goals and standards of acceptability are relatively clear and specific, and they can evaluate court decisions with greater confidence. Also such groups are likely to be strong and permanent enough to take action against a court or system of courts whose decisions have become consistently unacceptable. Courts also face danger when new groups of uncertain power and limits of acceptability suddenly come into existence.

In the United States' judicial system these group pressures and conflicts usually, though not always, focus on the Supreme Court. Opposed interest groups ordinarily carry their struggle up to the Supreme Court, and new organizations usually, though not always, make their power felt most effectively at the national level. Consequently, the use of political reasoning — staying within the limits of acceptability, mediating, building up weaker groups, and binding opposed powers together in joint actions and under common principles and values — is most important in the Supreme Court, while lower courts can ordinarily omit political considerations. The contrast between the semipolitical problems of the highest court and the more purely legal and social problems of lower courts justifies a difference of decision structure — many judges instead of one — and a difference in the qualifications required of judges. Judges in the highest court need the political sensitivity and imaginativeness of good arbitrators, since their political problems are similar to those of arbitrators, while lower judges need primarily legal clarity and sensitivity.

Consider next the position of the leader of a political party or other action group. His position differs from that of an arbitrator in at least two respects: he is concerned mostly with the party's relation to external goals and pressures, and he need not be particularly neutral within the party, because the shared goals of the party unite it and give him considerable authority.

When an organization is concerned mainly with external matters, for instance, when it seeks to achieve definite goals against strong opposition, the main political problem is external. The leader must try to set up a decision structure which includes his party and the opposition, and which enables the party's goals to be reality tested, adjusted, compromised, and accepted by the opposition. This will be a decision structure with no central figure, or only a weak one, and the party leader will not be a central figure in it. Consequently he cannot follow the principles of political decision discussed above but must follow principles appropriate to noncentral roles, to be discussed in the next section. Prominent among these principles is the requirement of building up and marshaling the power of one's organization; this requires a kind of goal-oriented technical ability wholly unnecessary for an arbitrator.

If the party is strong enough and the opposition is weak it may be possible to simply override the opposition and push through the party's goals. In this case no external decision structure need be set up and no external political problem exists. The only danger here is that the loss of criticism and information which an opposition could have provided will allow the party's goals to become too rigid and unquestionable and prevent reality testing.

The short-run internal political task of the party leader with great authority is exactly the opposite of the labor arbitrator's political task. Arbitrators have little authority, so their main means of keeping independence is mediation; the political leader with great authority maintains independence against persistent internal pressures by asserting his authority rather than by mediating. That is, he can negate any suggestion from any of his followers on the ground that it will not help achieve the party's aim. Since the party's aim overrides any private interests, and since the party leader is responsible for achieving the common aim, his word will be respected — as long as he is successful. In other words, the party leader need not be neutral or impartial at all, because he stands for something definite and overriding, the party's aim. He can, for instance, be entirely identified with one wing of the party and can continually negate suggestions of the other wing without losing their loyalty, so long as they remain attached to the party's goals. Or he can, if he wishes, reject suggestions coming from his own wing.

On the other hand, the party leader must be neutral on any issue dealing entirely with internal party relations, unrelated to goal achievement. This might include such things as local issues, personal rivalry, selection of party officials. On these matters the leader has little or no authority, that is, his decision will not command respect, because they are unrelated to his source of authority, the party's goals. Therefore he must maintain his independence either by ignoring the issues or by remaining neutral and mediating the opposed sides if he is drawn into the quarrel. If he mistakenly tries to assert authority where he does not have it, other mediators will appear within the party to do what he should have done.

The chief long-run internal task of the party leader is to safeguard the party's goals, since these are the source of his authority. Goals can be threatened both internally and externally: internally by loss of the allegiance or enthusiasm of party members, externally by changing circumstances which make their achievement more difficult. The party leader must be able to balance these two considerations, shifting goals until they are both acceptable and realistic. Frequently this involves the task of shifting party loyalty from old goals which have become unrealistic (or have been achieved) to new, more realistic substitutes. Examples are the British Labor party with its highly prized goal of nationalization, and the Asian and African independence parties which have achieved independence. Sometimes a party leader can substitute personal charisma for abandoned or achieved goals, but this expedient can last only during the leader's lifetime. If both of these long-run ways of maintaining central authority fail, the leader is forced into short-run mediation to maintain independence while the search for unifying goals can continue.

The external and the internal problems of a party leader are related, and neither can be entirely solved without the other. Successful establishment of an external decision structure enables the party's goal to be realistically achieved, and this strengthens the leader's internal authority and simplifies his internal problems. Conversely, a secure internal position facilitates concentration on the external problem. Only a leader whose internal authority is temporarily secure can afford to concentrate on establishing good working relations with the opposition, because this involves making concessions or apparent concessions, flirting with alien ideologies, and appearing, temporarily, to neglect his own party's interests. In other words, a leader with a weak position must be a politician to survive, while the secure leader can afford to be a statesman.

The procedures I have discussed under the heading "political decisions" may perhaps be conceived as a special class of techniques appropriate for maintaining decision structures. If a person gets into a central position in a decision structure and wishes to do a good job there, he must use these techniques. But here again, as in the case of law, we are dealing with public "techniques." They are public because they serve a public goal, the rationality of a decision structure. This goal is public in the sense that it belongs to a structure rather than to an individual, and is rationally prior to the aims of group members. Unless the decision structure to which they belong is maintained, any joint decision and action on their own personal wishes becomes impossible. The proper selection and use of these "techniques" leads primarily to structural changes, not changes in the fortunes of private individuals. If an increase of central authority is called for and achieved, the results accrue to a role, not to a private person, and can only be used for personal ends to a very limited extent. Indeed, the neutrality and impartiality often required of a central person sometimes involve the giving up of private ends and even the giving up of a private point of view. The increase of an arbitrator's authority, for instance, does not enable him to use labor and management as he pleases; it merely enables him to preserve the structure and carry out impartial arbitration. When the party leader shifts party goals, he cannot consider what he personally wants, but only what is acceptable to the party and what is realistic.

I am not contending that these public techniques are always used, and that central persons in decision structures never pursue personal power and private interest. Sometimes people who have reached a central position do use it for personal ends, even to such an extent that the structure is wrecked, and with it their own power. More frequently central figures impose on their position just a little, to satisfy some special personal aim. But there also are people who identify themselves with their position and consistently use the public techniques I have described; and for others the distinction between what they personally want and what is required by the structure is difficult to make. Identification is facilitated, as I have indicated earlier, by the fact that the improvement of a decision structure ordinarily also makes its central position easier and more rewarding.

It may seem that political decisions are made by comparatively few people, since the number of people who occupy central positions in organized groups is relatively small. But when one considers individual decision structures it becomes apparent that everyone is at the center of his own individual decision structure and in this sense everyone makes political decisions.

Everyone is the center of a variety of demands for action: desires that press for satisfaction and environmental stimuli that entice desires into activity; forces both internal and external that disapprove and urge repudiation of particular desires; aspirations and expectations; resources and skills that suggest particular uses; commitments and obligations. All these demands, or habits as I have called them earlier, constitute pressures on the ego, and they must be dealt with in such a way as to maintain the independence of the ego. When habits are in balanced opposition to each other, independence can be maintained by mediating between them, working out suitable compromises and accommodations; when a habit is too overpowering, extreme, or otherwise disruptive, it must be opposed on behalf of the whole personality. The long-run task of the ego is to cut down the strength of the too insistent habits and build up the weak ones, to increase unity and integration when the personality is too divided and to develop new outlooks when it is too settled in a single pattern. These points can be worked out in detail by referring to recent works on ego psychology, perception, and cognitive processes.

If the ego is successful in its task of preserving independence, the result is a movement toward a more rational personality. A rational personal structure would be one in which habits are strong enough to make suggestions and strong enough to counter or oppose the suggestions of other habits, but not strong enough to override or shut out (repress) opposing habits; in which there is enough mutual

tolerance and trust among habits so that each can accept modification of its suggestions by others, but in which habits are not so
tightly integrated as to prevent the development of novel habits
and the acceptance of novelty.

NONCENTRAL POLITICAL DECISIONS: LABOR CONTRACT NEGOTIATIONS

Political decisions must be made by persons not in a central role
when two or more organizations find it necessary to work together for
an extended period. The necessity of working together brings with
it the necessity of joint decisions, and the rationality of these decisions
will depend on the rationality of the joint decision structure that is
created. Consequently it is necessary for the representatives of the
organization to set up and maintain a decision structure, that is, to
"establish working relations." In fact this is their first, basic, and
permanent task, since without adequate working relations no successful joint activity is possible.

The decision structure thus created will have no central position,
since the only participants will be partisan representatives of the two
organizations. To be sure, if they foresee the necessity of working
together permanently, they may set up some central position, some
secretary general or high commissioner, and they may also call in
temporary central figures, mediators and conciliators, in times of
difficulty. But apart from such occasional weak central figures, the
main participants will be noncentral and nonneutral, and the task
of setting up discussion relations will fall almost entirely on them.

The setting up of relations is no problem when the organizations
already possess highly similar ideologies, as in the case of businesses
desiring to trade with one another. Such organizations will immediately understand each other's purposes, procedures, and principles,
and their representatives need only establish a minimum personal
rapport in order to enter into fruitful negotiation. A problem exists
only when the organizations have extremely different ideologies, as
in the case of most unions and managements or capitalist and communist countries. Here the possibility of misunderstanding, mistrust,
and breakdown of joint efforts is great, and the task of setting up
discussion relations is correspondingly important. Similarly, in both
industrial and international relations the degree of difficulty in
working together will depend on the degree of ideological diver-

gence. Unions and managements which are job- and profit-oriented and are therefore similar in outlook will have easier dealings than organizations which have elaborate and divergent politico-economic ideologies.

Let us take as an example the problem facing union and management negotiators when there is a new union and considerable distrust between the two sides. Good relations are not built only in negotiation sessions, but the problems facing negotiators are typical of those facing any pair of union-management representatives who meet together regularly. There are four principles which are basic to the establishment of good working relations among negotiators.[1]

1. *Maintain at least a minimum of power.* Good relations are not necessary when one side has an overwhelming and permanent superiority of power. In such cases the strong power takes what it wants and the weak one must be satisfied with what it can get. Indeed, one can hardly say that a relationship exists when one side makes decisions unilaterally. But when each side is powerful enough to inflict considerable damage on the other, unilateral dictation is no longer profitable and bargaining becomes necessary. Consequently the first step in establishing a relationship is to organize enough power to prevent dictation by one's opponent.

Any increase of power beyond the necessary minimum increases one's voice in the joint decision structure, but does not improve the structure. It may even weaken it. The danger of any power increase is that it may be perceived as a threat by one's opponent, to be answered by the development of deterrent power. If this happens the energies of the two sides are likely to be absorbed in a spiraling power race, and the resulting hostility and suspicion will make the development of relations more and more difficult.

To avoid this result power must be built up in such a way as to minimize threat to one's opponent. Although there is no sure formula for doing this, threat can usually be reduced by putting recognizable limits on one's own power. Thus a slow, short-term build-up with definite, moderate objectives and definite moral limits is less threatening than a fast, general, unscrupulous, and apparently unlimited build-up. A power that is accepted as legitimate by the other side is also less threatening than one that is regarded as illegitimate and

---

[1] These principles are illustrated more extensively elsewhere (Diesing, 1961).

therefore wild and unlimited. The reduction of misunderstanding and suspicion and the building up of mutual confidence by other means also decreases the threatening effect of one's power. Since the three following principles deal with the problem of developing confidence and understanding, their application will help reduce the danger of threat and retaliation.

This principle corresponds to the principle that obliges a central person to so structure the group that the pressures on him are moderate and balanced. A central person achieves balance by supporting and building up the weaker parts of a group against the stronger; when there is no center the weaker powers must build themselves up.

2. *Respect the central power position of the other side.* It is to be expected that each side, in working toward what it conceives to be a balance of power, will try to weaken the power of the other side; but this struggle should always have limits. Neither side should try to penetrate and destroy the basic power resources of the other side. Any such attempt will threaten the extermination of the other side, and will consequently provoke a desperate struggle for survival. Conversely, a demonstrated respect for the vital power resources of the other side signals acceptance of it as a permanent partner, and this creates the security that enables both sides to begin working together.

The central power of the union lies in the loyalty of its members and the jobs of union leaders. Any attempt by management to communicate directly with union members so as to wean them away from the union, attempts to undercut union leaders by wage offers which bypass the negotiation structure, and preferential treatment of non-union members are all three a threat to the union's existence. Even a refusal to accept union security clauses such as maintenance of membership signals that management still hopes for the disappearance of the union, and makes union good will toward management impossible. The central power position of management is its profit balance, and if a union demonstrates that it has no respect for at least minimum profits, even well-established relations can be quickly destroyed.

Note that this principle requires a voluntary self-restraint on both sides; it cannot be forced or induced by one side only. The union may force management to accept all kinds of union security clauses, but if management clearly indicates that its acceptance is involuntary and that it will evade or overthrow these clauses on first opportunity, working relations cannot be established. Nor can management automatically induce a union to abandon militancy by offering security clauses and other signs of acceptance, since the union leaders' suspicions and beliefs may be too strong to be immediately overcome. This is especially true if the suspicion has an ideological basis. But without strong evidence of voluntary management acceptance, union suspicions can never be overcome.

3. *Find principles and goals which can be shared.* Shared principles and goals provide the premises, standards, and objectives that enable joint discussion to proceed. Procedural principles specify the proper steps to be taken in discussion as well as the proper responses, and thus enable action to proceed without confusion and misunderstanding. Substantive principles and goals provide the arguments by which proposals can be validly defended and criticized.

For example, procedural principles in a strike clarify the meaning of such activities as picketing, banking the fires, admitting supervisory personnel. These activities become normal routines requiring normal responses, with no mysterious overtones and no power to produce anxiety or unnecessary hostility. The shared goal of settling the strike soon so the strikers can return to their former jobs provides the general objective which orders the activities of each side and makes them intelligible. Other procedural principles specify the detailed steps to be taken by each side in reaching a settlement — such as, calling a conciliator — and substantive principles, such as the principle that the prevailing wage for the area (or the industry, or the union, or the wage leader) should be paid, set the terms and limits within which negotiations proceed.

Each local union-management pair must work out its own set of shared principles and goals, either by adapting nationally accepted principles or by devising principles appropriate to local circumstances. When there is a central person in a decision structure one of his tasks is to encourage the development of shared principles and goals; but in the absence of a central person this task falls to the two participating sides. The task is identical in function to what March and Simon (1958:129) call "persuasion," though as we shall see persuasion is a very misleading term for what should occur.

Ordinarily each side tries to carry out this task by urging its own ideology on the other side. Each side supposes that its own principles are entirely sound and adequate for all purposes, and that the only obstacle to co-operation is the failure of the other side to recognize this obvious truth. Consequently negotiation sessions turn into persuasion contests, and disappointment at the obstinacy of one's opponent soon turns into suspicion of his intentions.

This approach is mistaken. The beliefs of either side are, as a rule, not suitable for sharing because they are too clearly bound up with the partisan interests of that side. Acceptance by the other side would normally involve a heavy sacrifice of its claims and interests and thus would be a defeat.

For example, management frequently argues for the acceptance of a "management responsibility" theory during negotiations. This theory states that management has the legal responsibility, and the ability, and the experience, and the information necessary for making all major financial and administrative decisions. These decisions are not arbitrary; they are made according to well-established principles and procedures, which normally insure that the results are beneficial to all. The proper task of the union is to check on management's application of these principles and procedures, call attention to errors, misinformation, arbitrary action, and thus insure the correctness of decisions. Another check is provided by competition, which penalizes inefficiency and corrects inequitable distribution of resources, such as overly low wages, by creating shortages which force an equitable distribution.

The application of this theory to collective bargaining produces the conclusion that wage levels as determined by management are adequate unless the union can show that management's facts or predictions of business trends are mistaken. Any increase of wages above their proper level will damage the competitive position of the firm, and this will cause hardship for everyone, particularly the workers.

The truth or falsity of this theory is not in question here. What is relevant is that its acceptance would nullify most union wage claims. In addition, a parallel application of the theory would nullify most claims to job security based on seniority, as well as many claims for improved working conditions with regard to job scheduling and assignment. Any union that accepted this theory without qualification would be imposing a heavy, continuous, and unilateral sacrifice on itself. Union refusals to accept the theory are not based on stubbornness, irrationality, or malevolence, but on a recognition of its practical consequences.

A similar result would follow from management acceptance of the union "living wage" theory. This theory states that, in the richest country on earth, workers are entitled to a decent standard of living. The exact definition of "decent" varies, sometimes even in a single negotiation session. Sometimes the figures of the Bureau of Labor Statistics on adequate living standards are cited, sometimes rises in living costs or abnormally high local prices are referred to, or more frequently comparison is made with some other group of people who are better off. Management acceptance of this theory would entail rapid and continuous wage rises, particularly when the criterion of decency is vague enough to shift occasionally. Similar results follow from labor's "anti-depression purchasing power" theory, management's goal of efficiency, and management's "welfare of the consumer" theory.

The adoption of the beliefs of one side would usually also have the effect of minimizing the participation of the other side in decision making. For example, the "management responsibility" theory assigns the entire positive decision-making process to management, with the union limited to criticism and appeal. The "decent living standard" theory, because of the multiple criteria of decency, assigns unions almost the entire burden of deciding which criterion is relevant and what level of wages is decent. The efficiency goal and the consumer welfare principle usually are thought to leave decision making primarily to management.

Consequently, when one side argues the validity of its principles and goals, it is in effect trying to get a larger place for itself in the joint scheme of things, both in the distribution of rewards and in decision-making authority. The other side is naturally well advised to be suspicious of such arguments, and to look behind lofty ideological pronouncements for the one-sided advantages they imply. But when this happens, discussion between the two sides ceases entirely, and they are actually addressing the bystanders, government and the public, trying to win supporters for a power struggle.

What sort of principles and goals are suitable for sharing? Only those which imply a clear and definite limitation on the interests of both sides, *especially* on the side proposing the principle. Suspicions of ulterior motive can be overcome only when the proponent of a principle is clearly limiting himself and sacrificing short-run advantages.

For example, the "decent living standard" theory can be shared when decency is defined by a single unambiguous criterion, such as cost-of-living index, and when this index goes *down* as well as up. Tying the theory down to a single neutral criterion removes the union's unilateral ability to decide the adequacy of wage standards, and acceptance of an index that goes down as well as up shows that the union is really holding to an objective criterion, and is not merely rationalizing a limitless desire for more. Even here, if the "downs" of the index are rare and the "ups" are frequent, the index is likely to generate suspicion that it is a cleverly disguised trick. Management's goal of efficiency can be shared if *most* of the rewards of increased efficiency go to union members in a clear, unambiguous way, and if decisions on how to increase efficiency are jointly made. This means that gains due to efficiency should be distributed as a separate bonus, not merely as an improvement in the firm's position which "benefits everybody."

It is possible to achieve a sharing of principles even if the proposing side gains most of the short-run benefits, but these cases represent a gift and an act of trust by the accepting side, which must be reciprocated if the sharing is to continue. If the proposing side, like Jack Horner, views them as a personal triumph resulting from shrewd strategy, the trust will disappear and relations deteriorate. And, on the other hand, even eminently shareable principles are not shared whenever one side refuses to accept the self-limitation involved.

4. *Be honest to the proper degree.* Honesty is sometimes called "good faith" in labor negotiations (Peters, 1955, chap. 13), but this term has become a legal term and undergone the effects of legalism, so it cannot be used here. Honesty is a prerequisite of communication, and without some communication no negotiations are possible. The automatic penalty for dishonesty is a breakdown of communication channels in the immediate area involved. As soon as one's words are discovered to be deceitful, all future words on that subject begin to lose their trustworthiness, and one's power to communicate is narrowed. Dishonesty is useful when one wishes to break up established communication channels, as when children wish to overthrow the constant supervision of their elders. But the task in labor negotiations is the opposite one of establishing new communication channels, so here honesty is quite essential.

Since honesty is prerequisite to communication, the exact degree of honesty required depends on the kind of communication channels that are found to be necessary for negotiation. When bargaining is primarily based on power and agreements reflect the relative power position of each side, the crucial kind of communication consists of statements about one's own power and one's readiness to use power. A certain amount of bluffing is possible without destroying negotiations, if it is expected by both sides and limited in some way. But it is always necessary to reserve some communication channels, some form of words or some special intermediary, for urgent honest statements. If all channels have been destroyed by constant bluffing so that communication is impossible, bargaining is in serious danger of breaking down completely. The same point holds for bargaining between parents and children, when parents threaten punishment and fail to carry out their threat on schedule. As soon as the child discovers the bluffing, the parent's ability to exact obedience by threatening punishment disappears, since the threats are simply ignored. Punishment becomes an outlet for parental frustration and an unexpected, meaningless calamity to the child.

When bargaining is a matter of give and take, each side making concessions in return for counter-concessions, the crucial kind of communication is an offered concession or a promise to make a counter-concession. If the offers or promises prove to be spurious, no further mutual concessions can be arranged and negotiations break down. When bargaining involves a search for an agreement which is of maximum benefit to both sides at minimum cost, it is necessary for both sides to understand each other's real aims and real resources. In this case it is necessary to be honest about the real, underlying reasons for one's requests and refusals, and about one's ultimate aims and discontents. If communication in this area breaks down the aim at mutual benefit becomes impossible, and each side is forced to look out for itself, as in the other forms of bargaining.

In the deeper personal relationships, which exceed anything that would be appropriate for political relations, a still greater degree of honesty is required. Friends must be honest about their deeper feelings as well as their real aims and their frustrations.

If union-management negotiators follow these four principles, they will develop a discussion structure which will enable them to work toward both joint and separate goals with maximum mutual assistance or minimum hindrance. They will also move themselves into the central position of a larger decision structure including the rest of the workers and the rest of management. As central persons, they will have the primary concern for the success of joint activities and the preservation of the decision structure. To that end they will try to mediate between the extremists on both sides and cut down on the extremists' power; also they will try to strengthen the authority of shared principles, with which they themselves become identified. In short, as centers of a larger decision structure, they will have to follow the principles of political decision making appropriate to central persons.

The main limitations on the foregoing principles come from pressures which limit the freedom of the negotiating sides. The union may be a local of a larger union with larger aims which override local considerations, and management may be a branch of a large corporation or industrial association. Opposing union or management factions ready to take advantage of errors may induce the negotiating parties to take a "firm" line and thus avoid the risks involved in improving relations. Difficult economic conditions may make the negotiators desperate and disinclined to have patience with each other. In general, union-management relations never form an entirely closed system, so the problem of developing good relations is always involved with the larger problem of maintaining or improving other relations.

SCOPE OF POLITICAL DECISIONS

Political decisions are necessary whenever an organization, or society, or person is faced with a political problem; that is, whenever there is a deficiency in its decision structure. The deficiency may be some form of narrowness, in that the structure is not receptive to an adequate range of facts, or that it is not able to break away from well-known formulas in its estimates of problems and suggestions for action, or that it is insufficiently self-critical and slow to admit error, or that its procedures are excessively rigid and thus shut out novelty. The deficiency may be some form of indecisiveness or internal conflict, in that decisions are excessively difficult to achieve, or that they are nullified or changed by concealed internal opposition, or that the system "changes its mind" too readily after reaching a decision.

The symptom of a political deficiency is the existence of numerous and increasing nonpolitical problems for the organization. Since the function of a decision structure is to deal with problems, any deficiency in functioning leads to an accumulation of unsolved problems. Also the way in which the problems accumulate points to the specific kind of deficiency. If the accumulating problems are apparent to an outsider but not to the decision structure, the deficiency exists in the information receptors; if the problems are recognized but solutions are late and erratic in appearing, the difficulty is one of indecisiveness; if solutions consistently fail, the deficiency is one of inventiveness; if erroneous courses of action are not readily changed, the deficiency is one of self-criticism; and so on. Sometimes political deficiencies can be discovered directly, by studying the internal workings of the structure and comparing it with similar structures, but the easiest way to locate deficiencies is to work back from the results.

Though a political problem is always accompanied by numerous nonpolitical problems, the political problem is always basic and prior to all the others. Sometimes one of the other problems has a temporal priority in the sense that if something is not done about it within two weeks the organization will go out of existence. This may be the case with threatened bankruptcy, or with a violent internal dispute which is about to force crucial members out of the organization. These are emergencies, to be settled by whatever temporary expedient will succeed. But nothing is basically solved until the political problems of an organization are solved. The reason is that without a well-functioning control system the organization, or society or person, is unable to deal with its other problems in a continuing fashion. They may be temporarily solved by outside help or some emergency action, but they are sure to reappear and get worse unless the organization is politically sound. Conversely, once the decision structure has been put into working order, the organization can be expected to take care of its other problems as they come up.

This means that any suggested course of action must be evaluated first by its effects on the political structure. A course of action which corrects economic or social deficiencies but increases political difficulties must be rejected, while an action which contributes to political improvement is desirable even if it is not entirely sound from an economic or social standpoint. It sometimes happens that political and nonpolitical problems can be solved together, but if this is not possible, the political problem must receive primary attention.

Further, a person who is dealing with a nonpolitical problem must always be ready to ask whether his problem is a symptom of some political deficiency. This is especially necessary if his problem is a persistent one, if it keeps reappearing in various forms. Isolated, unusual problems are likely to be the result of environmental circumstances, but a persistent problem is likely to be the result of some political inability to deal with that kind of problem. If it does appear that a political deficiency exists, attention should be turned away from the original problem to the political problem. Unless this is done, attempts to solve the original problem are likely to be futile, as the political deficiency will cause the same problem to reappear in another form.

For example, experts have recently been concerned with problems of technological development in the Middle East, Latin America, and other areas. In many cases they have defined a primary technoeconomic problem whose salient characteristics are a stationary economy in contact with a continually developing Western economy and an expanding population. Inaction would convert the stationary economy into a declining one because of population increase, and the contrast between declining local standards of living and rising Western standards would increase dissatisfaction even more. In general, the experts have devised technical-economic solutions which consist of (1) calculating the efficiency of existing productive practices, (2) substituting more efficient practices, and (3) injecting as much capital into the system as it can absorb, to pay for the capital costs of increased efficiency. By this solution they have hoped to force a radical, discontinuous jump into a pattern of sustained economic growth. Sometimes a social dimension of the problem has also been recognized, in that the existing economy is integrated into a social system and culture which resists certain kinds of change. This recognition has led to more complex solutions, involving in addition to (1) and (3) above, (4) (in contrast with (2) above), introducing practices which are both more efficient and acceptable to the social system, (5) attempting to resolve pressing social problems in order to release social energy for adjustment to technological change, and (6) introducing sociocultural changes that will make needed increases in efficiency acceptable.

However, the political deficiency that in some cases accompanies this socioeconomic problem has unfortunately too often been neglected. Particularly in some Middle Eastern countries the governmental structure is unable to deal with the continuing problems accompanying rapid technological change. Governments are dominated by upper-class landlords and chieftains, with the landless peasants excluded from participation. Consequently government decisions tend to be biased by the beliefs and interests of the landlord class, including their desire to prevent socioeconomic changes which would weaken their social status. The excluded classes are prevented from counteracting this bias; also it is difficult for them to understand and accept changes made without their participation, and the development programs come to be seen as further machinations of their distant overlords. Thus where the governmental structure remains unchanged its conservatism tends to cause development programs to stagnate; where the structure is overthrown by revolution the development program is also overthrown. The most obvious example of this sort of failure is Iraq.

Consider in contrast the situation in Mexico, where the political structure was corrected first, by a social-political revolution, land reform, expropriation, and other measures. These measures integrated the Indians and mestizos into the society and government and enabled them to accept governmental programs as their own. Consequently several decades later when programs of sustained technological development began to take effect, the changes could be contributed to and accepted by all classes of society, and they were not distorted by the influence of those fearing loss of status. Specifically, the land reform program was undesirable technologically because it probably decreased efficiency and diminished the scope of the market economy; but it contributed to a solution of the political problem and thus made possible the successful prosecution of development programs decades later. If the reverse order had been followed and technological development had been undertaken on an unsound political basis it would have been in danger of the same fate as the Iraq program.

So far I have argued that whenever political and nonpolitical problems occur together, the political problem must be solved before one can hope to achieve a lasting solution of the nonpolitical problems. But the primacy of politics extends beyond this. Even when no marked political deficiency exists, a person dealing with nonpolitical problems should make sure that his solutions do not produce a political deficiency, as this is likely eventually to undo any nonpolitical improvements he can make. This point is not so important in dealing with small, isolated problems, as changes here are not likely to affect the political structure markedly. But it is important when one is initiating large-scale long-term changes which are likely to alter the whole organization or society considerably.

For instance, strategists planning a national technological development program should consider the long-term political effects of the changes they are initiating. What will be the optimum-size producing unit with the new technology? If it is small, will this decentralize economic power to a new small-holding class, and can the political system absorb the resulting increased participation? If it is large, will this unduly centralize power and promote a narrow oligarchical political system? Can the economic power of large-scale units be diffused through co-operative ownership or other forms of mixed control? What effects will expected population shifts have on kinship, status systems, life patterns, and what effects will these changes have on levels of personal security and political toleration? What effects will new patterns of experience have on belief systems and on political ideologies? These are difficult questions and in many cases it is not yet possible to answer them, but if any answers which are possible disclose a likelihood of producing political deficiencies, the development program should be modified. Usually there is enough indeterminacy in the requirements of technological development to make modifications possible, and the planner sensitive to political effects will find these modifications as he proceeds.

Political decisions, then, are relevant whenever a political problem exists, and political considerations can be raised whenever a political problem is likely to be produced by planned secular changes. But this means that politics is almost always relevant, because there rarely, if ever, has been a decision structure which was both perfectly adequate for all its tasks and immune to long-term change. And wherever political considerations are raised, they have priority over other considerations. Political rationality is the fundamental kind of reason, because it deals with the preservation and improvement of decision structures, and decision structures are the source of all decisions. Unless a decision structure exists, no reasoning and no decisions are possible; and the more rational a decision structure is, the more rational are the decisions it produces. There can be no conflict between political rationality and any other kind of rationality, because the solution of political problems makes possible an attack on any other problem, while a serious political deficiency can prevent or undo all other problem solving.

POLITICAL VALUE

The whole value of decision structures lies in the decisions they make possible, but it is not immediately clear whether any special kind of value is involved in this. Decisions are useful for the achievement of all kinds of goodness, but do not thereby take on any unique value of their own. To see whether and in what sense a special value is produced by decision structures, let us consider once again just how they make decisions possible. This will come out most clearly by contrasting an irrational decision structure with a rational one.

The psychiatric literature provides endless case histories of people who are unable in one way or another to make adequate decisions. These people display in exaggerated form the irrational tendencies we all experience, and which are also present in group decision structures. The classical cases are those dealing with a deadlocked conflict between id and superego; one part of the person disapproves what another part wants, and the two are unable to come to terms. This is a simple form of indecisiveness. It may express itself directly in irresoluteness or inhibition, or more indirectly in self-defeating behavior, or in self-punishment, or in other ways. In all of these cases of internal warfare satisfaction is not achieved, and the warring elements are rendered incapable of growth, and retain their infantile form.

Sometimes one side wins out and thereafter dictates action. This kind of personality is characterized by rigidity and compulsiveness; the ruling element is always pushing in the same direction, and it cannot relax or change for fear of giving an opening to the elements it has submerged. Whenever any one component rules by force it also carries a large measure of anxiety with it, based on fear of the unknown submerged elements.

Internal conflicts also bring with them a deficiency of contact with external events. One function of personality components is to structure the perceived environment, and any internal disorder reflects itself in a disordered perception. A person ruled by some master desire, for instance, tends to see everything as either helping or hindering that desire, even at the cost of considerable distortion.

To avoid needless repetition of familiar matters, let us sum up by saying that irrationality — neurosis and psychosis — involves such things as conflicts and indecisiveness, repressions, anxiety, compulsions; externally, delusions and obsessions, rigidity, narrowness, withdrawal from reality. The rational man has self-mastery; he can be open, decisive, flexible, perceptive, and realistic in his dealings. Negatively a rational decision structure removes internal obstacles to decision, such as conflict, rigidity, and disproportionate influence. Positively, a decision structure so organizes a person's or group's perceptive, creative, and communicative faculties as to enable him to reach effective decisions.

The good produced by this sort of rationality might be called freedom, in one sense of that much used term. The characteristics referred to above correspond to Wertheimer's description of a free man (1940), and others such as Plato (*Republic*, IX), Fromm (1941), and Bay (1958, chap. 4) have given similar accounts. Bay in particular has provided both a detailed description of freedom and an illuminating contrast between freedom and the closely related value of mental health, which is a product of integration. He notes that both involve a high degree of integration and low level of anxiety, and both can be produced by psychotherapy. But the emphasis in mental health is on the relative absence of conflict, frustration, and anxiety, while the emphasis in freedom is on the cognitive ability to understand and deal with problems as they come up. Mental health is compatible with a low level of self-awareness, particularly when it is produced by a highly integrated society. For freedom, on the other hand, some degree of conscious understanding is essential, even if this implies the necessity of some disharmony, anxiety, and suspicion. "Mental health is measured by the individual's capacity to maintain anxiety-reducing social relationships. Psychological freedom is measured by his capacity to accept and act upon a realistic image of his self and of other people. . . . Psychological freedom means acceptance of and capacity to cope with all the anxieties to which man in modern society may be exposed" (Bay, 1958:187–188). Mental health is the health of the unconscious integrative process; freedom is the ability to make effective conscious decisions of all sorts.

To be sure, the other types of rationality might also be said to produce freedom, so vague has that term become. Technical and economic rationality produce freedom in the external sense of power over resources. Social rationality produces freedom in the internal sense of the ability to act without internal hindrance. Legal rationality produces freedom in the sense of dependable noninterference with one's rights. Then there is the political freedom of participation in the decisions which govern one's life, whether or not those decisions are rational. In view of the many meanings of the term it is doubtful whether one can say that decision structures produce freedom in any unique or special way.

Another term that might be used to describe the political good is practical intelligence, or intelligence in Dewey's sense. This term has the advantage of having important social connotations, since Dewey insists that intelligence is primarily a product of social organization and only derivatively an individual attribute. Freedom, on the other hand, is usually thought to inhere primarily in individuals and derivatively in societies, while the political good I wish to name appears in any kind of decision structure, both individual and social. The disadvantage of the term "intelligence" is that it often is conceived in terms of "I.Q.," an intellectual ability to deal with mathematical and linguistic abstractions. Intelligence in Dewey's sense is the ability of the whole society or personality to effectively solve the problems confronting it, and this is the sense intended here.

In the hierarchy of values, intelligence (or freedom) is the supreme value. It is supreme, even absolute, because it is instrumental to all other values. The other values — such as utility, shared experience, justice, beauty, and play — are intrinsic and therefore conditional and relative. An excessive pursuit of any of them can be destructive to other values and even self-destructive, so they are valid only to a limited extent. Excessive reliance on calculation in the pursuit of utility alienates people from each other and from themselves and so destroys the integrity and the community of value which makes both calculation and bargaining possible. Excessive integration reduces the neutrality of resources which makes calculation possible, and eliminates the difference and novelty that are necessary to deal with rapidly changing conditions. Excessive reliance on judicial reasoning legalizes a structure and makes it insensitive to nonlegal problems. But no excessive pursuit of intelligence is possible, because intelligence makes all other values achievable. If history does move toward a goal, that goal can only be intelligence (or freedom), because intelligence is the only unconditional value.

Chapter **6**

What Is Reason?

The basic plan of this work as stated in chapter 1 has been to treat technical rationality as a starting point in a discussion of other kinds of rationality analogous to but not identical with it. As part of this plan, the technical definition of reason as efficiency was replaced by the somewhat broader definition of reason as effectiveness, with efficiency as a special case. The concept of effectiveness was purposely left vague and empty. Too explicit an initial definition would have closed off the inquiry prematurely and reduced it to a working out of initial assumptions. Instead, attention was focused on a method which would uncover other kinds of reason, and the method was illustrated by application to technical rationality.

Now that we have worked through several kinds of rationality it is time to turn again to the question of what reason is in general. Our definition will be a generalization from the conclusions of the previous chapters, dependent on them for its validity. As such, it will not introduce any new material but will only bring together material already presented — or, perhaps, bring out the assumptions hidden in the method used. In any case, it would be a mistake to separate this chapter from earlier chapters and treat it as an independent statement. To do so would rob it both of detailed meaning and of supporting evidence, and reduce it to vague speculation.

We have been distinguishing two phases of reason all along, the rationality of organizations and the rationality of decisions. Consequently a general definition of reason should also have two parts. With regard to functional rationality, the simplest generalization is that reason is order or negative entropy, and rational norms are principles of order. When the relations of which all societies are composed are ordered according to some principle, the society is rational in some sense.

This generalization easily fits all the cases we have considered. First, the efficiency of which Mannheim wrote is an order of production. Raw materials enter the system, more along channels in which they are processed, and leave the system as products. The parts of the system are specialized, each one performing one task in the series of receiving, storing, moving, processing, and exporting. The operations are designed to avoid waste, that is, to achieve a maximum transformation of materials and operating parts into product. This is an impersonal sort of order which can occur both in human and nonhuman materials. It occurs in machines, factories, hospitals, schools, one's daily schedule, living quarters, planned cities, entertainment, religious exercises.

Then there is economic order, an order of measurement and comparison of values. It includes media of measurement — money, time, calories — and values or commodities which are measured by them. Each commodity has a number assigned to it which states its exchange or comparative value and gives it a rank in an order of values. Individuals can construct their own rankings, using the common media of measurement; and the discrepancy among individual rankings leads to exchange.

The order of production is an abstraction which cannot exist apart from the order of value measurement. Its objective is to transform available resources into maximum product; but "maximum" here means not maximum quantity but maximum value, and maximum value is indeterminate apart from some way of measuring value. Only after the economic problems of pricing and valuation have been in principle solved does it make sense to talk about a problem of production.

Social rationality is an order of interdependence or solidarity. It exists when people engage in joint action, when they share experiences and understand one another. People who constantly share action and experience are interdependent in the sense that a change in one produces an answering change in others; they are constantly

adjusting to one another, constantly changing. The parts of an interdependent system fit together and complete each other. Conflict and
disjunction are both absent since each would destroy mutuality. In
addition the people involved in such a system must each have the
same cognitive map of the system, since divergences in maps would
lead to conflict or separation in action. Because of the identity of
the cognitive map, each action by a part of the system is understood
and appreciated by the other parts; it is accepted, supported, and
carried to completion. The persons participating in shared action
develop both trust and self-assurance because of their mutual support.

An order of interdependence develops through the mutual adjustment of parts; it is not focused on any external product, as is a productive order. Its parts are internally related in contrast to the
external ranking relations occurring in an economic order. But
the fact that abstract distinctions can be made among the kinds of
order does not imply that they are mutually exclusive in reality. A
concrete system can exhibit an order both of production and of interdependence, if the parts are adjusted both to each other's expectations and to the requirements of a productive process. It may be
difficult to satisfy both requirements together since they frequently
conflict, but it is certainly possible in principle.

The legal order is an order of availability. It determines what
resources are available to each legal person, what persons each can
count on to perform which actions, what actions each person must
perform. Orderliness here consists of a clear and exact assignment
of each resource and action to some specific person or persons, and of
an exact match between the acts one person expects and the acts
other persons are required to perform. When there is no confusion
about what each person can do and what he must do, there is legal
order.

Finally, there is an order of discussion and decision. Information
of various sorts enters the system; it is interpreted, both for its
factual implications and for normative connotations; the interpretations give rise to suggestions for action; these suggestions are modified, combined, tested, and narrowed to two or three alternatives;
and there is a final choice or compromise. In addition to this more or
less temporal sequence, there are provisions for checking and correct-
ing at all stages. Factual reports are checked against observations
from different standpoints; inferences are checked against new ob-

servations and against counterinferences; action suggestions are modified by countersuggestions. The system is rational if there is adequate provision for gathering and checking information, adequate provision for inventing and checking suggestions, and adequate procedures for combining suggestions into a decision. "Adequacy" here means effectiveness in dealing with the problems facing the system.

Two of these orders, the legal and the economic, are nontemporal, while the others include a temporal dimension. The nontemporal orders are valuational, consisting either of a rank ordering of values or a distribution pattern of norms. The temporal orders deal with action; they make action either productive, or expressive and evocative, or governing.

Presumably there are also various other kinds of order not mentioned in these pages. There is artistic and ceremonial order, very similar to social order and productive, like social order, of experience or shared experience; there is an order in the development of science, an order in communications systems, in sports perhaps, and maybe other kinds as well.

Order exists insofar as the parts of a system are arranged according to some principle. In the nontemporal, valuational orders it is the *position* of the elements which is determined by principle, so that each element belongs just where it is and no place else. In the temporal action systems the *function* of each part is determined by principle, so that all the parts work together in some characteristic way. Once the principle governing a system has been discovered, the system becomes intelligible. That is, it becomes possible to understand why each part is where it is and does what it does, and to predict what changes will occur in it. Further, the system can then be explained and justified, to someone questioning it. Finally, since no actual system is completely rational, knowledge of the governing principles of a system enables one to discover malfunctions and to make improvements.

The opposite of order is randomness or arbitrariness, the absence of principle. Complete randomness is just as ideal as complete order and does not exist outside of pure mathematics, but approximations can easily be discovered, for instance, in the arrangement of people in a crowd. Here society is at a minimum, and the order one can find is of a subsocial kind. The term "order" is sometimes used more broadly to refer to any arrangement whatever, whether random or not. In this broader use of the term, rationality is a special kind of order, that which is intelligible due to the presence of a governing principle.

Any actual society, or organization, or personality, exemplifies all, or nearly all, the kinds of order discussed in this book. One or two kinds of order may dominate a given organization, but the other kinds will also be present for the trained observer. Formal organizations, for instance, are primarily productive systems and are dominated by productive and economic order. The organization is created to achieve a definite goal or goals, it stays in existence by maintaining an economy of incentives for its members (based on economic order), and it maintains the resource level needed to do this by efficient transformation of input into output (productive order). But any organization composed of people will also develop a system of social relations — usually called "informal organization" — among its members. The informal organization will be celebrated or expressed by and to its members in rudimentary ceremonies — strikes, drinking bouts, "binging" (Homans, 1950, chap. 3), Christmas parties. If the organization is large it will also develop a status system or bureaucracy among its members, and a set of rules by which disputes are settled or prevented (legal order). Finally, the need to maintain production and the economy of incentives will lead to the development of a decision structure, or control system, or government, which may or may not coincide with the formal executive chart of the organization.

Kinship groups and families exhibit primarily social order, supported by a set of well-developed ceremonies. But here also a status system can always be found underlying the particular kin relations, and a government to control joint activity. Also the joint actions of which kinship relations consist always involve exchanges of some sort, and these can be analyzed in terms of the pattern of valuations revealed (economic order) or in terms of the division of labor and transformation of resources involved (productive order).

These forms of order will always appear because they all represent functional necessities. A society or organization can continue in existence only by appropriating materials from its environment. In order to get these needed materials it must produce other materials for use in dealing with its environment, whether the dealing consists of exchange or of theft. It must evaluate its input-output balance to see whether the values produced are satisfactory in terms of individual desires and organizational survival. If its members are human beings they will develop expectations toward one another, and these must be co-ordinated in order to maintain the required level of group action. Failures of co-ordination will lead to disputes, and these must be settled according to some predictable, equitable pattern. Finally, all of these necessities call for the making of group decisions, for communicating information and decisions, for checking and evaluating, and this too requires a structure which must be maintained.

The subject of functional necessities or functional requisites is a large one which is not of direct concern here. I have touched on it only because it provides the connecting link between reason and existence. Existing societies are reasonable because they must be in order to survive. Reasonableness occurs because it is rewarded by continued existence, and beyond that by increase of power, security, adaptability. Unreasonableness is punished by bankruptcy, loss of membership, internal paralysis and strife, indecisiveness.

This fact also provides a justification for the method used here to discover the characteristics of the kinds of rationality. Reason can be discovered and studied in society because completely unreasonable societies and organizations do not exist, and because any achievement of rationality tends to persist, expand, accumulate, due to the rewards it brings.

I do not mean to assert that all functional requisites are connected to some sort of reasonableness. Presumably there are a number of more specific, detailed requisites which are not directly related to any unique kind of rationality. Only those requisites which must be met by the establishment of some order throughout the society or organization are directly connected to rationality and are of concern here.

If functional rationality is order, substantial rationality can most simply be conceived as the making of order, or creativity. Every decision is a creative act; it brings together observations, judgments, values, and norms into a new particular concept. More important, every rational decision contributes to the building up of some kind of order. This point holds for each of the kinds of rationality, though in varying ways.

It applies most directly in the case of social and political rationality because social and political decisions deal entirely with the organizing of structures rather than with external products. A social decision involves the discovery of an act or feeling that will integrate conflicting vectors where this is possible, distinguish them if integration is not possible, reduce strains where necessary, and prepare for future strains where possible; but these are all changes in the structure of interpersonal relations. For instance, suppose that A, an adult, is treating B as a father figure in certain contexts, and the two of them subconsciously discover ways of acting that will relate them as equals; this is an integrative decision, which discovers or creates a new relationship that fits better into an existing pattern of expectations and thus reduces strain or anxiety. Political decisions are concerned with the reduction, building up, or redirection of pressures, or with the building up of authority and power, and these are also all structural changes.

In the case of economic and legal decisions order is an indirect result of a process which is primarily focused on something else. Each individual decision contributes a little bit to the building up of an order, so that a developed economic or legal system is a product of countless decisions.

Economic order emerges out of the continual measurement and comparison of values that occur as individuals search for the most desirable alternative to choose. Each act of measurement and comparison, however crude, helps to put the individual's values into a rank order, and further comparison within the order serves to increase its clarity and precision. Discrepancies between the orderings of different individuals leads to exchange and creates a market, in which a standard exchange price tends to get assigned to values. The existence of a market and of exchange prices makes it easier for more individuals to establish their own rankings. Also as values enter a market they become standardized; their measurable aspects are measured more and more accurately, and their nonmeasurable, incomparable aspects get rubbed off and forgotten. So they become commodities.

A legal order develops, in favorable circumstances, out of the continual application of rules to cases. The decision maker may be interested only in resolving an immediate dispute or clarifying an immediate confusion over rights; but in the process the rules he expresses and uses as instruments undergo the characteristic legalistic transformation into rules of law. Initially the rules may have been derived from vague, unexpressed expectations of the social system, but when they are used in disputes they become more and more precisely formulated, the limits of their applicability are clarified, and their hierarchical relations to other rules established. They leave the fluid, inexplicit, living context of social relations and enter the world of legal precedent, the world of exact terms and technical meanings. Through an accumulation of such rules, a legal system is built up.

The creative effect of decisions is obscured by too exclusive a concern with the individual. When one is concerned only with the reasoning of individuals, there is a tendency to think of the individual as operating in a field of values that is all settled and complete, to which his decisions and actions contribute nothing. Statistical decision theory, for instance, assumes that the deciding individual's order of preferences is already established and that values are already comparable. Such a theory is important within its chosen limits, but it should be supplemented by other theories which allow for the effect of calculation on the comparability and ranking of values. Similarly, ethical theories which deal only with the moral judgments of individuals tend to treat moral rules as settled and codified, ignoring the structural changes that occur in a body of rules through continued application. Students of law have learned to recognize the tentacles of legalism slowly growing in countless legalistic decisions, but students of morals have yet to make this discovery because of a too exclusive concern with the individual.

The conception of reasoning as creativity agrees closely in some respects with Plato's account of reason. In the *Timaeus* Plato identifies reason with creativity, the bringing of the world into existence. He says,

For the generation of this universe was a mixed result of the combination of Necessity and Reason. Reason overruled Necessity by persuading her to guide the greatest part of the things that become towards what is best; in that way and on that principle this universe was fashioned in the beginning by the victory of reasonable persuasion over Necessity (Plato, 1957:48A, Cornford tr.).

These words suggest a contrast between reason, the guiding and controlling activity, and necessity, the blind compulsive forces that erupt and knock each other around. Reason achieves its creative effect through persuasion, that is, it works with natural forces rather than against or apart from them. It encourages some, redirects others, combines, balances, suggests changes, but never opposes directly. So it gradually brings some order out of chaos. The forces of necessity pushing about aimlessly and at random are organized into enduring structures. These structures are never entirely completed and are always breaking down, so the work of reason is never finished; there is always repair work, correction, adjustment left to do.

Plato's theory is deficient in that it gives no account of the growth of reason itself, as apart from the growth of its products. Reason is treated as an already completed entity, without any history of its own. Nor is it easy to see how such a history could even be possible in Plato's theory. Reason is not affected by its own activity or by its products, nor can it be brought into existence by some other force. It can have no history; it is unchanging and unchangeable.

Our present theory, in contrast, states that reason is in a sense itself a creature of the order it creates. There is a circular relation between reason as order and reason as creativity, each producing the other. In saying this, I do not mean to impute "causal efficacy" to patterns of order. Presumably causal efficacy can be attributed only to individuals in roles, and not to patterns of any sort. But individual creativity is not a transcendent, self-contained substance; it is strictly limited by and dependent on the order in which it occurs, and in this indirect sense one can say that creativity is a product of order.

There are two ways in which this is true. First, reason as order provides the shaped materials out of which decisions are made. The more highly structured these materials are, the greater the range of subtlety and complexity that is possible in decisions. For example, the complex marginal utility decisions that occur in modern industry are made possible by the detailed substitutability of both raw materials and products that in turn is made possible by a highly developed market (cf. chap. 2). The subtlety of distinctions and inferences that characterizes modern legal decisions is made possible by the vast body of clear and detailed rulings available to the judge; by comparing similar rulings the judge can discover distinctions and find inferences that he can then embody in his own decision.

Second, the order in decision-making structures provides a structure for the creative process itself. The more complex a decision structure is, the more complex are the decisions that can occur in it. Decision structures determine what kinds of information will go into a decision, what kinds of proposals can be devised, and what kinds of changes can be made in initial suggestions.

The circular relation between order and creativity means that reason itself is its own chief product. By gradually building the medium in which it must work and by fashioning its own materials, reason makes itself into an effective force in the world. It does not descend all ready-made from some transcendent home, but emerges bit by bit from the disorderly matrix of necessity. The transformation of necessity into order is simultaneously the growth of creative ability.

Nor is this growth merely a coming into self-consciousness of something that was implicitly there all the time, as Hegel seems to have asserted. Self-consciousness is an increasingly important characteristic of reason as it develops, and becomes even essential to higher development, but it is not merely a recognition of what was there all the time. When reason becomes self-conscious it changes into something it never was before. It becomes capable of studying its own working, as this occurs in decision structures, and of improving this working by changing the structures. Thus it can begin consciously to correct itself in some degree, whereas previously self-improvement was an accidental result of activities concerned with other problems. So self-consciousness represents a real increase of power, a genuine novelty, and not just a passive, useless contemplation, as Hegel seemed to believe.

The conception of reason as creativity is one of the three major conceptions of practical reason in the history of philosophy. The other two are the conception of reason as the discovery and application of rules to cases, and the conception of reason as calculating, literally adding and subtracting. Reason appears as creativity in some of the works of Plato, Hegel, and Whitehead, among others; it appears as the application of rules in the natural law theorists, such as Aquinas, Locke, and Kant; and it appears as calculation in Hobbes, Bentham, and the utilitarians. Each conception agrees closely with one of the kinds of reason discussed in this book, and each can be extended to the other kinds as well, though with varying degrees of difficulty.

In the natural law tradition, man is distinguished from the animals by his rationality, and this consists of the ability to apprehend general principles and freely act on them. Animals, in contrast, were thought to perceive only particulars and therefore not to have any free will. The general principles man apprehends are part of the nature of things; they are eternal and universal. Kant put the theory very succinctly in one of his dogmatic moments: "Everything in nature works according to laws. Rational beings alone have the faculty of acting according *to the conception* of laws, that is according to principles . . . the deduction of actions from principles requires *reason* . . . " (1949:32).

This kind of rationality is what I have called legal-moral reasoning, which in the natural law tradition constituted nearly the whole of practical reason. There was no place for political rationality in the theory because reason was conceived to be a faculty of individuals which matures of itself, through practice, and thus is essentially independent of social conditions. Particular decisions might be influenced by social conditions or individual passions, but this was thought to be a deplorable shortcoming which negated the rationality of the decision. Hegel's insight that man makes himself by gradually, unconsciously building up the culture which makes rational action and thought possible, that reason is a product of society as well as its creator, is missing in the natural law tradition. Nor was there any place for social rationality, because individuals were conceived to be self-contained substances which matured through their own inner action, rather than through the transactional learning-creating of a series of roles and relationships. Social relations were conceived as contracts or voluntary actions which proceeded from the individual but did not constitute the essence of his personality. Society itself in its rational part was conceived to be a system of laws, external to the individual and derived by imitation from the laws of nature. Techniques were rules too, though of a less important sort, since they obliged conditionally rather than absolutely. Sometimes the existence of calculation was also affirmed, but its use was thought to be limited to the achievement of selfish, unimportant ends.

Though the traditional natural law theory of practical reason is thoroughly inadequate, it can be greatly improved by being related to an adequate theory of man and society. A well-grounded social theory would not attempt to reduce all social relations to rights and duties, but would distinguish a variety of relations and a variety of modes of organization. Each of these would call for its own kind of treatment, and each kind of treatment could be systematized as rules or principles of procedure. These rules could even be called natural laws because they derive from the nature of society. Rationality then would consist of the successful application of the appropriate principles of transformation to cases. This conception is not in conflict with the conception of reason as creativity, since the application of general principles inevitably involves some degree of discretion, and creativity in turn must proceed in some regular fashion.

The conception of reason as calculation appears most clearly in Hobbes: "When a man *reasoneth*, he does nothing else but conceive a sum total, from *addition* of parcels; or conceive a remainder, from *subtraction* of one sum from another . . . reason, in this sense, is nothing but *reckoning*, that is adding and subtracting . . ." (*Leviathan*, 1939:143). It also is basic to the theory underlying the construction of decision-making machines, since these machines operate by addition, subtraction, and simple comparison.

Calculation is what I have called technical and economic rationality. In the classical utilitarian theory there was no place for any other kind of reasoning. The problem of individual integration was avoided by the assumption that people know what they want and that their wants are integrated enough to make comparisons possible. The problem of political structure was avoided by assuming that people are internally free and therefore capable of making sound decisions if they are careful. Reason was held to be the slave of desire only in the sense that desires provide goals for calculation, but it was supposed that desires normally did not interfere with the actual calculation process. Problems of social integration were avoided by treating society as an economy in which people entered into exchange relations but had no other relations with one another. Even laws were thought of as hypothetical bargains which, like real bargains, could be evaluated in terms of the satisfactions they gave people. Judicial reasoning was recognized but given a subordinate place, since judges were only making sure that the hypothetical bargains were all being properly carried out.

When these various assumptions were shown to be false, the utilitarian response was to narrow the area in which rationality was held to operate. It was said to operate in the long run, or statistically in large numbers, or in the calculations of city men only; and the rest of the world was abandoned to irrationality. The proper response should have been the opposite one of broadening the conception of rationality to fit the broadened conception of society which was developing. The aim should have been to locate and describe new types of calculation, or quasi-calculation, appropriate to social, political, and legal problems.

For instance, this might be done by broadening the conception of a goal and defining appropriate noneconomic "goals": maintaining optimal tension levels for social rationality, resolving and preventing conflicts for legal rationality, staying in power and preserving communication lines, and so on, for political rationality. The appropriate techniques for each "goal" could then be described, in such a way that they are comparable both for costs and for results. Finally, less exact methods of summation and comparison would have to be devised, since it is impossible to achieve the precision of statistical decision theory in social and political rationality. Most and perhaps all of this program remains an aspiration rather than an achievement, and it seems unlikely that such a program can ever be completed, because of the difficulty of adequately describing social and political rationality in terms of goals and techniques. However, even though complete success may be impossible, any partial achievements would be interesting as throwing new light on reasoning processes.

The three conceptions of rationality are not basically incompatible, but differ primarily in emphasis. Each approach must eventually include the others within itself in some fashion. In the present approach, it is important to realize that creativity is not formless and indescribable, but proceeds according to principles, even in social relations. Also economic and legal reasoning are more directly and specifically describable as calculation and the application of rules. They are creative only in the indirect sense that calculation gradually creates commodities and a whole mode of social organization, while the continuous use of rules gradually transforms them into laws; and they are creative in the general sense that every decision involves some novelty.

The principal advantage in treating reason as creativity is that it facilitates the study of social and political rationality, which are more difficult to characterize in terms of the other conceptions of reason. Social and political rationality are the most neglected of the forms of rationality today and their study is the most important, both in theoretical terms and in relation to the principal world problems of today.

BIBLIOGRAPHY

AUSTIN, JOHN
  1954. *Province of Jurisprudence Determined*. London: Widenfeld and Nicolson.
AYRES, C. E.
  1942. Economic Value and Scientific Synthesis. *American Journal of Economics and Sociology*, Vol. I, No. 4, 343–360.
  1944. *The Theory of Economic Progress*. Chapel Hill: University of North Carolina Press.
BAKER, HELEN
  1948. *Management Procedures in the Determination of Industrial Relations Policies*. Princeton: Industrial Relations Section, Princeton University.
BALES, ROBERT F.
  1955. Role Differentiation in Small Decision-Making Groups. In Parsons and Bales, *Family, Socialization and Interaction Process*.
BARBER, BERNARD
  1957. *Social Stratification*. New York: Harcourt, Brace.
BARNARD, CHESTER
  1938. *The Functions of the Executive*. Cambridge, Mass.: Harvard University Press.
BARTON, ROY
  1949. *The Kalingas*. Chicago: University of Chicago Press.
BAY, CHRISTIAN
  1958. *The Structure of Freedom*. Stanford, Calif.: Stanford University Press.
BELSHAW, C. S.
  1955. *In Search of Wealth*. American Anthropological Association. Memoir No. 80.

BENNETT, JOHN W., and ROBERT K. McKNIGHT
   1956. Misunderstandings in Communication Between Japanese Students
      and Americans. *Social Problems*, Vol. 3, 243–256.
BENTHAM, JEREMY
   1939. *Principles of Morals and Legislation.* In *The English Philosophers
      from Bacon to Mill,* ed. E. A. Burtt. New York: Random House.
BERMAN, H. J.
   1958. *The Nature and Functions of Law.* Brooklyn, N.Y.: The Founda-
      tion Press.
BLAU, PETER M.
   1956. *Bureaucracy in Modern Society.* New York: Random House.
BOHANNAN, PAUL
   1957. *Justice and Judgment Among the Tiv.* London: Oxford.
BOSANQUET, BERNARD
   1930. *Philosophical Theory of the State.* London: MacMillan.
BRADLEY, F. H.
   1951. *Ethical Studies.* New York: Liberal Arts Press.
BRAUN, K.
   1955. *Labor Disputes and Their Settlement.* Baltimore, Md.: Johns
      Hopkins University Press.
BROWNELL, BAKER
   1950. *The Human Community.* New York: Harper.
CARDOZO, BENJAMIN
   1921. *The Nature of the Judicial Process.* New Haven, Conn.: Yale
      University Press.
CARR, E.H.
   1948. *The Twenty Years' Crisis.* London: MacMillan.
CHANDLER, MARGARET
   MS.   Decision Making in Labor Arbitration.
COSER, LOUIS
   1956. *The Functions of Social Conflict.* Glencoe, Ill.: Free Press.
DAVEY, HAROLD W.
   1955. Labor Arbitration: A Current Appraisal. *Industrial and Labor
      Relations Review,* Vol. IX, 85–94.
DEWEY, JOHN
   1930. *Human Nature and Conduct.* New York: Random House.
DEWEY, JOHN, and A. F. BENTLEY
   1949. *Knowing and the Known.* Boston: Beacon Press.
DIESING, P.
   1955. Noneconomic Decision-Making. *Ethics,* Vol. LXVI, No. 1, 18–35.
   1958. Socioeconomic Decisions. *Ethics,* Vol. LXIX, No. 1, 1–18.
   1961. Bargaining Strategy and Union-Management Relations. *Journal
      of Conflict Resolution,* Vol. 5, No. 4, 369–378.

DOMKE, MARTIN
 1958. Creeping Legalism in Labor Arbitration: An Editorial. *Arbitration Journal*, Vol. XIII, 129–132, 161.

DUNLOP, JOHN T.
 1949. *Collective Bargaining: Principles and Cases.* Chicago: Irwin.

DURKHEIM, EMILE
 1947. *Elementary Forms of the Religious Life*, tr. Swain. Glencoe, Ill.: Free Press.

EHRLICH, EUGEN
 1936. *Fundamental Principles of the Sociology of Law*, tr. Moll. Cambridge, Mass.: Harvard University Press.

FIRTH, RAYMOND
 1939. *Primitive Polynesian Economy.* London: Routledge.

FROMM, ERICH
 1941. *Escape from Freedom.* New York: Rinehart.
 1947. *Man for Himself.* New York: Rinehart.
 1949. Psychoanalytic Characterology and Its Application to the Understanding of Culture. In *Culture and Personality*, eds. Sargent and Smith. New York: Viking.
 1955. *The Sane Society.* New York: Rinehart.

GARLAN, E. N.
 1941. *Legal Realism and Justice.* New York: Columbia University Press.

GEARING, FRED
 1958. The Structural Poses of Eighteenth-Century Cherokee Villages. *American Anthropologist*, Vol. LX, No. 6, 1148–57.

GEERTZ, C.
 1956. Economic Behavior in a Central Javanese Town: Some Preliminary Considerations. *Economic Development and Cultural Change*, Vol. IV, No. 2, 134–158.

GLUCKMAN, MAX
 1955. *The Judicial Process Among the Barotse of Northern Rhodesia.* Glencoe, Ill.: Free Press.

GOFFMAN, ERVING
 1956. *The Presentation of Self in Everyday Life.* Edinburgh, Scotland: University of Edinburgh.

GOLDEN, CLINTON, ed.
 1955. *Causes of Industrial Peace.* New York: Harper.

GOULDNER, A. W.
 1952. Red Tape as a Social Problem. In *Reader in Bureaucracy*, ed. Merton. Glencoe, Ill.: Free Press.
 1954. *Patterns of Industrial Bureaucracy.* Glencoe, Ill.: Free Press.
 1959. Reciprocity and Autonomy in Functional Theory. In *Symposium on Sociological Theory*, ed. L. Gross. Evanston, Ill.: Row, Peterson.
 1960. The Norm of Reciprocity: A Preliminary Statement. *American Sociological Review*, Vol. XXV, No. 2, 161–178.

GRAY, JOHN C.
1909. *The Nature and Sources of Law.* New York: Columbia University Press.

GREEN, T. H.
1883. *Prolegomena to Ethics.* Oxford: Clarendon Press.

HARBISON, FRED, and R. DUBIN
1947. *Patterns of Labor-Management Relations.* Chicago: Science Research Associates.

HEGEL, G. W. FRIEDRICH
1942. *Philosophy of Right,* tr. Knox. Oxford: Oxford University Press.

HICKS, J. R.
1939. *Value and Capital.* Oxford: Clarendon Press.

HOBBES, THOMAS
1939. *The Leviathan.* In *The English Philosophers from Bacon to Mill,* ed. E. A. Burtt. New York: Random House.

HOEBEL, E. A.
1954. *The Law of Primitive Man.* Cambridge, Mass.: Harvard University Press.

HOMANS, G. C.
1950. *The Human Group.* New York: Harcourt, Brace.

HUME, DAVID
1888. *Treatise of Human Nature.* Oxford: Clarendon.

ISHINO, I., and JOHN BENNETT
1952. *The Japanese Labor Boss System.* Columbus: Ohio State University Press.

JENSEN, O. C.
1957. *The Nature of Legal Argument.* Oxford: Blackwell.

JORDAN, E.
1952. *Business Be Damned.* New York: Schuman.

KANT, I.
1949. *Fundamental Principles of the Metaphysics of Morals,* tr. Abbott. Chicago: Regnery.

KARDINER, ABRAM
1945. *The Psychological Frontiers of Society.* New York: Columbia University Press.

KATONA, GEORGE
1951. *Psychological Analysis of Economic Behavior.* New York: McGraw-Hill.

KILLINGSWORTH, C. C.
1953. Arbitration as an Industrial Relations Technique. *Proceedings of the IRRA,* Vol. VI.

LADD, JOHN
1957. *The Structure of a Moral Code.* Cambridge, Mass.: Harvard University Press.

LAMONT, W. D.
   1955. *The Value Judgment*. New York: Philosophical Library.
LEVI, EDWARD H.
   1949. *Introduction to Legal Reasoning*. Chicago: University of Chicago Press.
LEVINE, SOLOMON
   1958. *Industrial Relations in Postwar Japan*. Urbana: University of Illinois Press.
LEWIS, C. I.
   1946. *Analysis of Knowledge and Valuation*. La Salle, Ill.: Open Court.
LINTON, RALPH
   1949. Problems of Status Personality. In *Culture and Personality*, eds. Sargent and Smith. New York: Viking Fund.
LLEWELLYN, K. N.
   1940. The Normative, the Legal, and the Law-Jobs. *Yale Law Journal*, Vol. XLIX, 1355–1400.
LLEWELLYN, K. N., and E. A. HOEBEL
   1941. *The Cheyenne Way*. Norman: University of Oklahoma Press.
MacPHERSON, WILLIAM
   1949. Should Labor Arbitrators Play Follow the Leader? *Arbitration Journal*, Vol. IV, No. 3.
MALINOWSKI, B.
   1926. *Crime and Custom in Savage Society*. London: Routledge.
MANNHEIM, KARL.
   1940. *Man and Society in an Age of Reconstruction*. London: Kegan Paul.
MARCH, J., and H. SIMON
   1958. *Organizations*. New York: Wiley.
MARX, K.
   1932. *Capital*, ed. Eastman. New York: Random House.
MEAD, G. H.
   1934. *Mind, Self, and Society*. Chicago: University of Chicago Press.
MEAD, MARGARET, ed.
   1954. *Cultural Patterns and Technical Change*. New York: Mentor.
MILL, J. S.
   1910. *Utilitarianism*. London: Everyman edition.
MISES, LUDWIG VON
   1960. *Epistemological Problems of Economics*. Princeton, N.J.: Van Nostrand.
MURPHY, GARDNER
   1953. *In the Minds of Men*. New York: Basic Books.
NASH, MANNING
   1958. *Machine Age Maya*. American Anthropological Association. Memoir No. 87.

NORTHROP, F. S. C.
  1960. A Comparative Philosophy of Comparative Law. *Cornell Law Quarterly*, Vol. 45, pp. 617–658.
PARSONS, TALCOTT
  1937. *The Structure of Social Action.* New York: McGraw-Hill.
  1949. *Essays in Sociological Theory.* Glencoe, Ill.: Free Press.
  1951. *The Social System.* Glencoe, Ill.: Free Press.
  1960. *Structure and Process in Modern Societies.* Glencoe, Ill.: Free Press.
PARSONS, T., and R. BALES
  1955. *Family, Socialization and Interaction Process.* Glencoe, Ill.: Free Press.
PARSONS, T., and E. A. SHILS
  1951. *Toward a General Theory of Action.* Cambridge, Mass.: Harvard University Press.
PEPPER, S. C.
  1958. *The Sources of Value.* Berkeley: University of California.
PETERS, EDWARD
  1955. *Strategy and Tactics in Labor Negotiations.* New London, Conn.: National Foremen's Institute.
PETRAZYCKI, LEON
  1955. *Law and Morality*, tr. H. Babb. Cambridge, Mass.: Harvard University Press.
PLATO
  1957. *Timaeus.* In Cornford, F. M., *Plato's Cosmology.* New York: Liberal Arts Press.
POPPER, KARL
  1950. *The Open Society and Its Enemies.* Princeton: Princeton University Press.   .
READ, K. E.
  1959. *Leadership and Consensus in a New Guinea Society. American Anthropologist*, Vol. LXI, No. 3, 425–436.
ROSS, ALF
  1959. *On Law and Justice.* Berkeley: University of California Press.
ROSS, ARTHUR M.
  1948. *Trade Union Wage Policy.* Berkeley: University of California Press.
SEMBOWER, JOHN
  1957. Halting the Trend Toward Technicalities in Arbitration. In *Critical Issues in Labor Arbitration*, ed. Jean McKelvey, pp. 98–111. Washington: BNA, Inc.
SEWARD, RALPH T.   .
  1957. The Next Decade. In *Critical Issues in Labor Arbitration*, ed. Jean McKelvey, pp. 144–150. Washington: BNA, Inc.

SILONE, I.
   1950. Chapter in *The God That Failed,* ed. Crossman. New York: Harper.
STONE, JULIUS
   1946. *The Province and Function of Law.* Sydney, Australia: Associated General Publications Pty., Ltd.
SULLIVAN, H. S.
   1949. Multidisciplined Coordination of Interpersonal Data. In *Culture and Personality,* eds. Sargent and Smith. New York: Viking Fund.
TRUMAN, DAVID B.
   1951. *The Governmental Process.* New York: Knopf.
UPDEGRAFF, C. M., and W. P. McCOY
   1946. *Arbitration of Labor Disputes.* New York, Chicago, etc.: Commerce Clearing House.
VEBLEN, THORSTEIN
   1934. *Theory of the Leisure Class.* New York: Random House.
WEBER, MAX
   1954. *Max Weber on Law,* tr. Shils and Rheinstein. Cambridge, Mass.: Harvard University Press.
WERTHEIMER, MAX
   1940. A Story of Three Days. In *Freedom, Its Meaning,* ed. Anshen. New York: Harcourt, Brace.
WESTERMARCK, E.
   1932. *Ethical Relativity.* New York: Harcourt, Brace.
WHEELER, HARVEY
   1957. The Political Limitations of Game Theory. *Western Political Quarterly.* Vol. X, No. 3, 669–674.
WHYTE, W. F.
   1951. *Pattern for Industrial Peace.* New York: Harper.
ZELDITCH, MORRIS
   1955. Role Differentiation in the Nuclear Family: A Comparative Study. In Parsons and Bales, *Family, Socialization and Interaction Process.*

INDEX